Memory Activism

Memory Activism

Reimagining the Past
for the Future
in Israel-Palestine

Yifat Gutman

Vanderbilt University Press

Nashville

© 2017 by Vanderbilt University Press
Nashville, Tennessee 37235
All rights reserved
First printing 2017

This book is printed on acid-free paper.

Library of Congress Cataloging-in-Publication Data on file
LC control number 2016030967
LC classification number DS119.76 .G889 2016
Dewey classification number 956.9405/4—dc23
LC record available at *lccn.loc.gov/2016030967*

ISBN 978-0-8265-2133-0 (hardcover)
ISBN 978-0-8265-2134-7 (paperback)
ISBN 978-0-8265-2135-4 (ebook)

Parts of Chapter 5 have appeared in the article "Transcultural
Memory in Conflict" (*Parallax* 17 [4]: 61–74, 2011); which was
reprinted in Rick Crownshaw (ed.) *Transcultural Memory*
(New York: Routledge, 2014).

To my parents and their generation,
and to my son and his generation.

Contents

Acknowledgments

My interest in memory and political activism was cultivated in ten years of learning, teaching, conducting fieldwork, and conceptualization. The empirical analysis of memory activism and the theoretical arguments that I present in this book have developed over these years through the exchange of ideas with many colleagues, advisors, and friends I have been blessed to have. I am deeply grateful to Jeffrey Goldfarb, my advisor, mentor, and friend, not only for guiding me through the long process that culminated in this book, but also for the intellectual dialogue on political culture and publics in the contemporary world that we developed via long and short conversations, seminars, research projects, and collaborative publications. Vera Zolberg has been an inspiration during my years at the New School for Social Research and after I graduated. Her scholarly work and teaching on memory politics and museums shaped my understanding of culture and memory. Elzbieta Matynia opened a window to the drama of political life, and Oz Frankel turned my attention to the subtle or explicit ironies and contradictions of memory and history in Israel-Palestine.

The intellectual community that surrounded me during my studies at the New School supplied academic freedom and encouraged me to take risks and be interdisciplinary in my inquiry. I am grateful to Monica Brannon, Marisol Lopez Menendez, Iysel Madra, Richie Savage, Dan Sherwood, Sam Tobin, Hector Vera, and Jeff Zimmerman, as well as to Roy Ben-Shai, Yoav Mehozay, Lorena Rivera-Orraca, Rafael Narvaez, Maija Andersone, and Karen Coleman for their intellectual and mental support.

Within the intellectual community, the New School Memory Studies Group, formed with fellow students and faculty in 2007, was a fruitful arena for my exploration of the relationships between collective memory and political change. I thank my fellow organizers, especially Lindsey Freeman, Amy Sodaro, Adam Brown, Alin Colman, Kimberly Spring, Rachel Daniell, Ben Nienass, Naomi Angel (who will always be remembered), Daniel Kressel, and Laliv Melamed. Special thanks go to Irit Dekel and Nahed Habiballah, with whom I have had meaningful dialogues, both on collective memory and on the Israeli-Palestinian conflict. The group became much more than we could have imagined it would when we first started. This interdisciplinary forum was established at a pivotal moment: when memory studies were gradually becoming institutionalized as a field yet were still flexible and open to questions. As junior scholars we had the nerve to direct these questions to senior scholars of memory from various disciplines, whom we invited to participate in conferences and publications. We also had revisions and answers: we argued, for example, that the future has been neglected in memory studies despite its influence on shaping our view of the past, and vice versa. Through these debates I came to know and converse with many of the leading memory scholars of our time; in addition to Zolberg, they are Jeffrey Olick, Marianne Hirsch, Andreas Huyssen, Daniel Levy, William Hirst, Robin Wagner-Pacifici, Eviatar Zerubavel, Yael Zerubavel, Barbie Zelizer, Selma Leydesdorff, Dori Laub, Leo Spitser, John Torpey, Elazar Barkan, Jonathan Bach, Ross Poole, and Vered Vinitzky-Seroussi, among others. I was also inspired by Ann Laura Stoler, James Jasper, and Gregory Maney. With many of these intellectuals I have crossed paths and collaborated in the following years.

Among scholars of Israel-Palestine, my analysis was inspired and enriched by conversations with scholars who see the complexities, ironies, contradictions, and constraints that the conflict situation reproduces every day, as well as the possibilities for change that emerge through the cracks. Among them are Tamar Katriel, Hanna Herzog, Uri Ram, Orly Lubin, Salim Tamari, Nadia Abu el-Haj, Rhoda Kanaaneh, Thomas Hill, Benoit Challand, Yehouda Shenhav, Nissim Mizrachi, Nachman Ben-Yehuda, Yfaat Weiss, Eitan Alimi, Louise Bethlehem, Edna Lomsky-Feder, and Yoav Peled. I also thank Merav Amir, Sagi Schaefer, Regev Nathansohn, Anat Rozenthal, Inna Lykin, Tom Pessah, Erica Weiss, Orli Fridman, Sigall Horovitz, Michael Shapira, Tamar Novik, Tamar Hostovsky Brandes, Dan Tzahor, and Uri Shwed for meaningful dialogues and feedback during my postdoctoral stage.

I have presented parts of the study in workshops and conferences over the years and was generously supported by many institutions and foundations: a New School for Social Research travel grant and fellowships; a Lady Davis Postdoctoral Fellowship; a research fellowship as part of a German-Israeli Foundation grant at the Minerva-Rozensveig Center of Hebrew University; a Rabin Fellowship at the Truman Institute for the Advancement of Peace of Hebrew University; a joint post-doctoral fellowship at the Truman Institute and the Davis Institute for International Relations; and a Shapira Postdoctoral Fellowship at the Department of Sociology and Anthropology at Tel Aviv University.

I am very thankful to Michael Ames at Vanderbilt University Press, with whom I found a common ground and mutual understanding from the start. He saw the potential of this book and of what it proposes for the future of Israel and Palestine, and I enjoyed my conversations with him not only about the book but also about current events in the Middle East. I am also grateful to my editors who have read versions of the book chapters over the years and especially to Siân Gibby, whose comments and suggestions have helped improve this final text significantly. Additionally, Galia Fischer, Rotem Ruff, Itay Katz, and Roy Eventov have greatly contributed both to the content and the appearance and form of this book.

Most important, this book is based on long-term fieldwork and owes a great deal to the Jewish Israeli and Arab Palestinian activists who let me enter their organizations and activities and shared their thoughts, goals, and hopes for the future with me through some of the most interesting conversations on memory I have ever had. While most of them are not listed by their real names because their work is still contested in their state and society, this book is one of the ways in which I would like to give back to these memory activists by sharing with them some of what I have learned.

Memory Activism

Introduction

The Logic and Practice of Memory Activism

In 2006 I heard for the first time of a small group of primarily Jewish Israeli activists who had been organizing tours of destroyed Palestinian villages to which they invite former Palestinian residents of the sites, today refugees. The refugees describe to mostly Jewish Israeli tour participants what their prestate life was like on-site and their fate in the 1948 war, which resulted in displacement within or outside the newly founded State of Israel. The massive displacement of Palestinians in the 1948 war is mourned as *al-Nakba*, "the catastrophe" in Arabic. The name of the group was Zochrot, which in Hebrew means "we remember" in female plural form.

These activities, I later learned, were an attempt to cross the idiosyncrasies of the national narrative of each of the conflict's sides by disseminating Palestinian memories, which have been excluded from the dominant collective memory of Israel within the Jewish-majority-dominated public debate.[1] What was most surprising to me was that these long-silenced Palestinian memories were aired and documented by Jewish Israeli activists in one of the most discouraging decades in the history of the Israeli-Palestinian conflict. Openness to memories of the other in ethnonational conflicts in general, and the Israeli-Palestinian conflict in particular, is usually attributed to periods of reconciliation (Bar-Tal 2000), but the first decade of the 2000s saw an escalation in violence and nationalist sentiment.

Another surprise was that despite their unusual destination and theme, the format of these tours of Palestinian ruins resembled the one cultivating knowledge, love, and ownership of the land among the Jewish majority, a tour that was granted hegemonic status in Israeli culture. In fact, both the tour and survivor testimony were deployed by the state and prestate Zionist organizations for the same national education that marginalized Palestinian citizens. These practices were now being appropriated and redeployed by these activists for the inclusion of Palestinian citizens in the dominant collective memory. I call these activities "memory activism," the strategic commemoration of a

1

contested past outside state channels to influence public debate and policy. Memory activists use memory practices and cultural repertoires as means for political ends, often (but not always) in the service of reconciliation and democratic politics.

At the New School for Social Research in New York, where I was studying at the time, I was already intrigued by the potential of cultivating countermemory of the past in local spaces. During a summer semester in Krakow, Poland, I became aware of some local initiatives to remember the shared past differently than how it is portrayed by the state. I began to conceptualize how collective memory, so powerful in cultivating national remembrance among state citizens, can also be utilized to change people's understanding of their shared past beyond the dominant national frame. Such countermemory, I thought, could even be cultivated using the same cultural memory practices that the state uses. Upon learning of the activities to produce countermemory in my own troubled home region of Israel and Palestine, I felt the urgent need to turn to these activities as my case study.

I joined Zochrot's tours, interviewed its founders and members, and soon found two other groups of activists in Israel who organized similar tours of pre-1948 Palestinian localities and collected testimonies from their former residents. In addition to the Tel Aviv–based Zochrot, the largest of the groups that operate throughout the country,[2] I started following the Jewish Palestinian artists' group in Jaffa called Autobiography of a City as well as the all-Palestinian youth association Baladna, which was formed in Haifa. The founders of these three NGOs are peace activists who were previously active in the binational "coexistence" meetings that swept civil society organizations on the left during the period of the Oslo Peace Accords in the first half of the 1990s. In 2001–2002, as hopes for peace were fading away, they began documenting and disseminating Palestinian memories as a new path for peace and reconciliation. Their tours and testimony collection were conducted in slightly different manners.

During Zochrot's tours of destroyed Palestinian villages, participants not only listen to refugee testimony on life in the village before and during the 1948 war but also post signs with the village's name in Arabic and Hebrew on the unmarked land.[3] A booklet is prepared for each tour containing information on the pre-1948 village and excerpts from the testimony and is handed out to participants at the beginning of the tour. The booklets and photographs from each tour are collected and are available online and in the group's information center. Zochrot also organizes lectures and study groups, has issued an educational kit for teachers, published a literary magazine, holds exhibits in its Tel Aviv office's gallery, and initiates architectural and urban planning–oriented projects, among other activities.

Autobiography of a City, the smallest of the groups, created an online archive of digital testimonies of pre-1948 generation Jaffa residents, especially Palestinians.[4] These residents are interviewed by the group's members, and their video-recorded testimonies are divided into excerpts, tagged according to keywords, and posted online. Within this "collected memory" (Young 1993: xi), each user's search is saved as a chain of stories that forms a unique path to the city's past. The virtual path in the archive can also be translated into a path in city space and used as a map for a walking tour. Artists were commissioned to use the archive materials for site-specific artwork, and in the future the archive is intended also to be used as a pedagogical tool for mediating memories of the pre-1948 city in local schools.

Baladna ("our homeland" in Arabic) is a youth association based in Haifa, led by students and student-organizers, and active in various Palestinian centers throughout Israel. It holds tours of destroyed Palestinian villages in which participants listen to a refugee testimony as part of its annual young leadership program for Palestinian youth in Israel. In addition to tours and testimonies, its after-school program includes creative and artistic activities, critical discussions about the writing of national history, and community-based projects. The group also trains youth to operate a news website and a monthly youth magazine, meets with other youth groups in the region and the world, and has initiated an advocacy campaign against a mandatory national service for Palestinian citizens of Israel in 2007.

I conducted fieldwork among the three groups over various periods from 2006 to 2013. I used participant observation and semistructured interviews, as well as discourse analysis of a variety of textual and visual materials. I held forty in-depth interviews and many shorter conversations on different occasions with activists from the three groups in their offices or in coffee shops, during activist events, and at conferences and exhibits in various localities around Israel. Interviewees included the founders of each of the groups, their staff members, dedicated activists, and casual audience members, as well as former members who had left the group and activists from other groups in the Israeli "peace camp." Additional interviews involved historians and scholars who studied the 1948 war and became involved in the public debates on it and funders, artists, and facilitators of memory projects who worked with the groups studied. I did participant observation on public tours and at lectures and artistic events as well as during external and internal meetings of the three groups. I collected and analysed different genres of texts: protocols or minutes from internal discussions and public events, mission statements and annual reports, booklets and other materials the activists handed out during tours, their online and physical archives of testimonies, educational toolkits, publications, lectures, newsletters, blogs, and websites. I also analyzed their use of visual media, including photos, maps, signs, and art projects that used video. I also read texts that were not produced by the groups, such as their mentions in the Israeli media and public debates and discussions of the history and memory of the 1948 war in political speeches, as well as their representations in school curriculum, literature, theater, film, art, and academic publications in Israel. The data I collected shed light on the motivations, strategies, and distribution of the activists' message and on the reactions and reception of their actions and claims.

I tried to hold all the interviews in interviewees' native languages, speaking Hebrew, my native tongue, with Jewish Israeli activists and colloquial Arabic with Arab Palestinian interviewees, but conversations with the latter often shifted to Hebrew, the language of the Jewish majority, which the interviewees spoke well. This reflection of the asymmetrical power relations between these languages and groups in Israel (Bourdieu 1991) preshaped the interaction with my informants: Even though I have studied Arabic for many years, my hegemonic subject position as a Jewish Israeli of Ashkenazi (European, non–Middle Easterner) descent was always present in my meetings with (Jewish and) Palestinian activists in Israel, shaping their approach and answers to my questions. I address the impact of my subject position in Chapter 3 in more detail and state that although it has granted me access to Jewish Israeli activism, it has also relegated me to observer rather than participant observer of Palestinian memory activism. This experience was, however, revealing about the ways in which Palestinian activists position themselves in relation to the Jewish majority, and as an outsider I was guided through internal debates and conflicts within Palestinian society in Israel that may not have been articulated in words to an insider. I point to signs that suggest that other things may be happening outside of my peripheral vision.

As mentioned, these activities by Arab Palestinian and Jewish citizens were initiated and maintained in one of the grimmest decades in the chronicles of the Israeli-Palestinian conflict. The first decade of the twenty-first century was marked by growing polarization, violence, and separation between Israelis and Palestinians. At the beginning of the decade, expectations and hopes of peace, sparked by the 1993 Oslo Peace Accords, were fading fast as leaders failed to see the accords through to their second and third stages after Prime Minister Yitzhak Rabin's assassination by a right-wing Jewish religious fundamentalist in 1995. The launch of the Al-Aqsa Intifada, a second upheaval in the Occupied Palestinian Territories (OPT) in 2000, and the killing of twelve Palestinian citizens by Israeli border guards during protests within Israel marked a new and violent chapter in the history of the conflict. Physical separation between Israelis and Palestinians was exacerbated with the erection of a separation barrier in the West Bank, ordered by the Israeli cabinet in June 2002. Reconciliation seemed out of reach; the word became an empty term.

The failure of Oslo and the events of the early 2000s caused major breaks within the Israeli left, which has constituted much of the peace camp that campaigned for Oslo (Hermann 2009). Having failed to end the occupation of the West Bank and Gaza or bring equality to Palestinian citizens inside Israel, peace activism in Israel was in deep crisis. It was also increasingly delegitimized in Israeli society (Hermann 2009). The Left was split: The majority of left-wing voters moved further to the center and right, embracing Prime Minister Ehud Barak's narrative that "there is no partner for peace on the Palestinian side" (Rabinowitz 2001a: 33–34); a minority moved further to the left, exploring new strategies of peace activism.

Guiding this search was a general shift from pragmatic solutions in the Oslo period to justice-based claims in its aftermath (Hill 2008). The central strategy of peace activism in the Oslo period, the binational "people-to-people" meetings, was now highly criticized by both scholars and peace activists who had taken part in it. These projects, which brought Israeli and Palestinians to meet in small groups, bloomed in the 1990s with the generous support of European and American funding. In the early 2000s, however, these meetings were criticized for reproducing the power relations between the two sides instead of changing them; their focus on breaking psychological stereotypes excluded political discussion of serious issues like the 1948 war and accountability (Challand 2011; Tamari 2005). A different approach to trust building was formed: no longer based on seeking consensus building in small group meetings but on one-sided acknowledgment of Israel's historical responsibility for Palestinian suffering, in both the past (particularly in the 1948 war) and the present (Challand 2011).

Similar historical justice-oriented claims have already been made in the region in 1998, around the fiftieth commemoration of the Nakba, by Palestinian intellectuals in the OPT, in Israel, and in the Arab world, calling for recognition of the Palestinian historical rights to the land (Hill 2008). The Far Left memory activists in Israel have been both responding to and reproducing these Palestinian claims and making their own claims to recognition of Palestinian displacement in 1948. They made *commemorative claims* (Berg and Schaefer 2009, 2) to remember the Palestinian displacement and to address it, through establishing and making public a commemorative record of the long-silenced Palestinian suffering in Israel. Claims of a second type for historical justice were also made: *transformative claims* for a profound social and political change of present society, derived from the "prolonged disaster of the past" (Berg and Schaefer 2009, 3; Torpey 2001, 337). These claims gradually expanded and became more concrete toward the decade's end (Gutman 2015).

The shift from a pragmatic, interest-based discourse in Oslo to a justice-based discourse in its aftermath was not limited to peace activism and civil society; it also appeared in the dominant political discourse on both sides of the conflict, albeit pursuing an opposite aim (Hill 2008). As a lesson from the failure of Oslo, each side now demanded public recognition of "an unpalatable and intolerable truth on the other side," as Hill put it (2008, 152), and called for acknowledgement of its own historical right for self-determination in the territory. The resulting zero-sum game of historical narratives and recognition claims reproduced the rival conflict positions and fortified the impasse between the two sides. It was thus that historical justice claims were utilized both in civil society and state leadership, yet the former tried to deploy them to advance future reconciliation, while the latter reproduced the conflict positions and hindered reconciliation.

Another discursive shift was catalyzed by the failure of Oslo: from a focus on the 1967 occupation of the West Bank and Gaza as the point of departure for the conflict and its resolution, to 1948 as the significant historical moment. This was a radical shift; 1967 marks the beginning of an occupation that can be removed (as attempted in Oslo) and is limited to the West Bank and Gaza (Shenhav 2010); however, an emphasis on the 1948 war that followed the establishment of Israel as the orienting event can be seen as delegitimizing the very formation of the

Jewish state. This shift in focus could be traced back to a discourse that was set in motion in the late 1970s with the publication of revisionist historiographies of the 1948 war by Jewish Israeli "new historians" and "critical sociologists" (Nets-Zehngut 2011; Ram 2007; for a review of the Palestinian discourse on 1948, see Hill 2005). The revisionist discourse was introduced by Jewish Israeli historians and sociologists who studied in the West and based their research on newly opened Israeli state archives of the 1948 war, thirty years after the events. These scholars reexamined the history of 1948 in academic publications and on the pages of *Ha'aretz*, Israel's left-leaning daily. Instead of a miraculous victory against all odds and five Arab armies, as their predecessors had portrayed the war, they described it as a more or less intentional campaign of a stronger and more organized Israeli military force, led by David Ben-Gurion's government, to expel Palestinians (Ram 1998, 2006, 2007; Pappé 1997a, 1997b, 1998; Cramer 2006; Morris 2007, 1990, 1988, 1987; Shlaim 1995, 1988; Flapan 1987).

The 1948 war began immediately after the United Nations declaration of Israel's independence on 14 May 1948, which terminated the British Mandate (1917–1948). But violence among Jewish and Arab residents of Mandatory Palestine had begun earlier, following the UN recommendation on 29 November 1947 to divide Mandatory Palestine into Jewish and Arab separate states. These mutual attacks were considered an intercommunity conflict until the armies of five surrounding Arab countries entered to fight the establishment of the Jewish state (Morris 2004, 13; see also Khalidi 1988). The war ended in early 1949 with Israel's victory (despite a great number of casualties) and expansion—over 260 square miles of former Palestinian land were conquered and transferred to Jewish farmers (Morris 2004, 367)—and in an enormous Palestinian loss, dispossession, and displacement. Between November 1947 and early 1949, almost 85 percent of the Palestinian population, around 770,000 Palestinians, were expelled from lands that became the State of Israel (Abu Lughod 1971; see also Esber 2008; Khalidi 1992; Morris 2004).

The war has been commemorated by Jewish Israelis and Palestinians (including Palestinian citizens of Israel) through mirroring national narratives: On Nakba Day Palestinians mourn the displacement and dispossession they experienced during and after the war; and on Independence Day Jewish Israelis celebrate their victory. In the dominant Zionist narrative, the war has been portrayed as similar to David's miraculous victory over Goliath (who stands in for the Arab countries who fought alongside the Palestinians, in this scenario; Auron 2013). In the Palestinian national narrative, the events of 1948 are viewed as a tragedy inflicted on unequipped and unprepared peasants who were betrayed by both Britain and Arab countries and subjected to an organized campaign of ethnic cleansing by Israeli military forces (Khalidi 1992; Abu-Sitta 2004).

These two opposing national narratives of the 1948 war and its outcome are constructed as a zero-sum game, between which one must choose. This construction presents a false symmetry between the two rival national communities, but the uneven availability of historical resources and disproportionate visibility of these histories tell a different story. From the 1950s onward, the Nakba was erased from the Israeli national landscape, history textbooks, and the dominant collective memory of Israel (Kadman 2008; Shai 2007). Palestinians within and outside Israel have been struggling against this erasure to maintain their memories and identity as rooted in their villages and neighborhoods in pre-1948 Palestine (Abu-Lughod 2007; Bresheeth 2007; Davis 2007, 2011; Slyomovics 1998). This connection between their national identity and their lost territories is at the heart of their national struggle. Against the severe lack of official documents—those that remain are scattered among different state archives (I. Feldman 2008)—there has been much private preservation of keys, ownership bills, pre-1948 identification cards, personal documents, photos, and documentation of specific villages and communities (Davis 2007, 2011; Slyomovics 1998), and nonwritten or spoken practices used to transmit memories of pre-1948 life and the war experience to future generations (Allan 2007). A surge in Nakba commemoration emerged around its fiftieth anniversary in 1998. The anniversary was marked by marches in the OPT and in Lebanon; a new publication of the history of 1948 by Palestinian historian Walid Khalidi featured in the daily pan-Arab newspaper *Al-Hayat*; a series on 1948 on Al Jazeera; art events, films, exhibits, and additional efforts to systematically record the testimonies of the remaining pre-1948 generation Palestinians, such as at the Khalil Sakakini Cultural Center in Ramallah (Hill 2005).

On the Israeli side, Israel's modern Jewish nationalism, Zionism, has always been infused with memory, from the Jewish Diaspora through Zionism in Palestine to the nation-state of Israel (Ram 1998). The Zionist narrative, which portrayed the settlement in Palestine as a return of Jews from the Diaspora to their biblical homeland, is deeply rooted in remembrance through the national landscape (Handelman

2004; Ben-Yehuda 2002; Katriel 1996; Y. Zerubavel 1995). Israelis are encouraged to hike, appreciate the new forests and ancient olive trees, and reenact the national myths (Katriel 1996; Y. Zerubavel 1995). The land has many national memorials and monuments dedicated to the Holocaust, war victims and heroes, and terror victims (Handelman 2004). A great deal of unofficial, individual, and local commemorations of Jewish victims and heroes takes place as well, especially through memorial books and films (Melamed 2013; Slyomovics 1998: xiii). Jewish fighters of the 1948 war are considered members of the founding elite of Israel,[5] Zionist heroes and pioneers, and their autobiographies and memoirs are housed in state and private museums and archives, as are state and military documents from the war.

In the 1990s, Jewish Israelis were more open to the new historians' breaking of some of the Zionist myths. In the following decade, however, the atmosphere overturned, as disagreement over who was accountable for the beginning and end of the conflict increased. Israelis and Palestinians further fortified their national narratives: each side casts its own people as both the victim and the hero and the other side as the villain or perpetrator, inciting one national identity and history against the other (Auron 2013; Goldfarb 2011).

To disseminate memories of the other in this context was a highly contested endeavor, and so the memory activists I studied drew on two sources of legitimacy. One was the already mentioned memory practices of the tour and testimony, which carried authority and legitimacy from their utilization by the state for national education. As one of Zochrot's founding members explained to me: "The practice [of the tour] is so strong that you can take advantage of it instead of inventing practices so different that would be mainly anti. [So we are] playing within the practice . . . connecting with the Jewish Israeli audience and understanding that just like the JNF [the Jewish National Fund] is posting signs [in national parks] around the country, so are we" (Yaron, Jewish Israeli tour guide and Zochrot founding member, interview 2009). I will return to memory practices later on.

A second source of legitimacy was the globally circulating paradigm of historical justice. Initially I noticed that members of the three groups often compared the Israeli-Palestinian conflict to other cases of postconflict reconciliation, in particular the South African transition from Apartheid. They connected their domestic work on Nakba memory to claims for historical justice that were made in postconflict cases and saw historical justice in general and truth and reconciliation in particular as a central path for bringing change to their region and ending the conflict. The activists describe a process that has three successive steps: airing the contested past in public and learning about the silenced Palestinian history, acknowledging the suffering of its victims, and seeking accountability and redress for them.[6] This model for reconciliation through airing the truth about a contested past—knowledge, acknowledgment, and responsibility—resembles the one used by South Africa's Truth and Reconciliation Commission, which was established in 1995 by the new government to discuss human rights violations under Apartheid.

Truth and reconciliation commissions are perhaps the best-known tool of historical justice following the South African transition from Apartheid, which became a paradigmatic case. Yet it is only one of the practices and institutions that have been developed to air and address a difficult past so that it does not come to haunt the creation of a better, more peaceful society in the future. Historical justice (Barkan 2000; Berg and Shaefer 2009) or transitional justice, as it has been termed more recently (Kritz 1995; McAdams 1997; Teitel 2000), is an expert-based paradigm that includes researchers, practitioners, and consultants. Historical justice highlights the significance of coming to terms with a difficult past in order to achieve a more equal and peaceful future. This approach gained prominence and popularity together with the growth of the human rights paradigm from the 1970s, the democratization of Latin American states in the 1980s, and the fall of communism in Eastern and Central Europe since 1989 (Wilson 2001). It has given rise to international debate on how to deal with the gross violence of the twentieth century, as well as more distanced atrocities such as slavery, colonialism, and the treatment of indigenous people (Barkan 2000; Berg and Schaefer 2009; Torpey 2003). In addition to truth and reconciliation commissions, numerous other practical tools and models were developed to assist the public airing of violent histories: from official apologies to international and local courts and tribunals, educational programs for peace, historical commissions, economic development, memorials, monuments, lustration, and the opening of secret archives (Barkan 2000; Berg and Schaefer 2009, 1–2; Bickford and Sodaro 2010; Olick 2007; Torpey 2003; Wilson 2001).

While I could understand the logic behind the appropriation of familiar memory practices as a source of legitimacy in Israel, initially I could not understand why, at a time of escalating violence and separation, these peace activists would make a giant leap and deploy a model that was designed for postconflict reconciliation before a transition to peace took place in their country. Moreover, in postconflict cases, the state was the one facilitating remembering of the contested past and its victims for its newly equal citizens. In the Israeli-Palestinian case, neither peace nor equality among citizens or governed noncitizens was exercised by the state, and the efforts of truth and reconciliation were carried out outside state channels. I also did not think that South African truth and reconciliation would possess legitimacy within Israel. In the post-Oslo period, most public linking of Israel to South Africa suggested that Israel was also practicing a type of Apartheid in its differentiating treatment of Jewish Israelis and Palestinians, rather than that a transition to quality and peace is near. Were these memory activists truly interested in changing Jewish Israeli awareness as they stated to me, or were they more oriented toward small circles of self-selected domestic and international audiences?

I learned that the activists have come to know historical justice and truth and reconciliation more closely through meetings with peace activists from postconflict countries such as Northern Ireland, Germany, South Africa, and the Balkans. These meetings were organized by their funders, mostly European foundations, which connected the activists in Israel to transnational networks of activists and intellectuals. In addition to serving as a source of legitimacy, the transnational claims for historical justice and the vocabulary of truth and reconciliation also served the activists in defining their position versus the state and in looking outside to activists, funders, and intellectuals around the world. This was also a viable example of how expert-based discourse and models for postconflict reconciliation travel the world, reaching unintended places, and shaping the vocabulary, strategies for political change, and claims of minority groups, civil society, and governments. This unique case study raised important questions about the possibilities the reconciliation discourse and models hold for grassroots efforts and discriminated groups as well as for cases of active conflict. This case study also enables an examination of the discourse and models' fundamental normative assumptions: first, that airing a contested past is indeed a crucial condition for reconciliation and for putting this past behind rather than perpetuating violence and polarization; and second, that producing such knowledge indeed leads to public acknowledgment and responsibility both in active conflict and in postconflict cases.

For the activists in Israel, the value of truth and reconciliation outside state channels and before the conflict's end stemmed from the promise of official recognition of the state that this model usually entails and that has vast significance for marginalized groups (Wilson 2001). In the eyes of the activists, such recognition of past wrongs can change the relations between the rival parties and lead to a resolution. And so, although the activist efforts in Israel were without any legal or state authority and were a history-writing agency more than a legal platform, the activists viewed them as an alternative route to peace. While negotiations in official channels were at a stalemate, they wanted to rebuild trust between Israelis and Palestinians at the level of civil society and through public discourse. This would create the necessary infrastructure needed to resume dialogue, which would hopefully lead to reconciliation in the future. The means were: make greater parts of Israeli society aware of the Nakba, acknowledge Palestinian suffering, and demand state recognition and accountability. Producing knowledge about this past through creating a record of testimonies, maps, documents, and tours was the first step.

What could have been the result of such actions during active conflict and outside—or even against—the state? Surprisingly it was quite remarkable, contributing to an extremely counterintuitive shift in Jewish Israeli awareness of Palestinian suffering during the 1948 war, yet it was not without a backlash of the state. From an unspoken "public secret" (Stoler 2009, 3) at the beginning of the decade toward the decade's end, the Palestinian experience of 1948, the mourned Nakba, appeared on the front page of every Israeli newspaper and in the headlines of national television news programs. It also proliferated through other mainstream channels: Jewish Israeli author Alon Hilu's novel *House of Rajani*, which critically discusses Jewish-Arab relations and land ownership before 1948, won the prestigious Sapir literary award (*Yediot Achronot*, 2008); a play based on a 1969 novella by Palestinian author Ghassan Kanafani, *The Return to Haifa*, was shown in the national Cameri Theatre; and nonfiction books, as well as documentary and feature films, by both Jewish and Palestinian filmmakers, came out in the second half of the decade.[7] No less controversial and polarizing, the Nakba has become visible to the majority of Jewish Israelis.

However, if the task of memory activism in Israel can be seen as a mission accomplished by this raising of Nakba visibility, its victory is not satisfying. Acknowledgment did not follow the knowledge production and wide circulation, which instead faced reactions of silencing and denial of Palestinian suffering. And in direct contrast to taking responsibility, the state reacted in repressive legislation, otherwise known as "the Nakba Law" (2011), which fines state-funded organizations that facilitate events of Nakba mourning during the national celebration of Independence Day. And so, instead of acknowledgment and redress, Palestinians in Israel suffered additional repression and diminishment of their rights.

This outcome could indicate a naive approach by experts and practitioners of the paradigm of historical justice and the model of truth and reconciliation worldwide. It shows that while the airing of a silenced or contested past can contribute to a new public debate, the prevailing asymmetries in power ultimately determine the debate's conclusion. In Israel, the debate has become a memory war. In addition to legislation, the reaction of the state also included investigations against human rights NGOs such as the memory activists' and reactionary changes to the school curricula in history and civics. This reaction has made clear that unlike the assumption of the globally circulating paradigm, making the contested Palestinian past of 1948 present is not necessarily an irreversible turn toward recognition and responsibility for past atrocities. Airing a contested past can instead cause further repression and denial and does not necessarily change the order or transform the dominant collective memory from the margins of society. In active conflict, the Israeli-Palestinian case shows, rather than the hoped-for enrichment of the public debate, bringing in a contested or silenced past can lead to silencing, denial, and constraints on public debate.

The failure of the knowledge-acknowledgment-responsibility model in this case of active conflict also raises the question whether it has in fact worked in cases of postconflict. While that question is beyond the scope of this book, based on the vast research of the South African case I can speculate that even in this paradigmatic example, state acknowledgment of suffering and a will to take official responsibility for it preceded the establishment of the TRC, where the contested past was aired in public. The model should therefore be restructured so that acknowledgment and responsibility become preconditions for the public production and circulation of knowledge on the contested past.

Zooming out of the Israeli-Palestinian conflict allows one to see a surge in memory of violent histories among grassroots and civil society groups around the world. In recent decades, individuals and groups have called for addressing past wrongs and for revising the official collective memory to include the memories of previously victimized and silenced groups. In Poland of recent decades, local groups have been using tours, tour guides, maps, testimonies, and the reconstruction of prewar Jewish sites to remember the immense Jewish population that lived in the country for centuries before the Second World War and is almost absent today. In post-Milošević Serbia, civil society groups created an alternative social calendar to remember the atrocities from the recent wars of the 1990s as war crimes (Fridman 2015). In Spain, the popular historical memory movement has exhumed mass graves to force an inquiry into the violence of the Franco regime; and in Argentina, a group established by sons and daughters of the "disappeared"—those citizens suspected of political dissent by the military dictatorship in 1976–1983 who were kidnapped and murdered, and whose bodies were never found—draw murals and mark the location of former detention and torture camps onto contemporary city maps to remind the public of their parents' fate and demand justice. The last two examples are of second- and third-generation memory activists who are linked to the victims of the contested past they remember through family ties. The first two examples are of activists of the same generation who are members of a state or society that victimized other groups. To paraphrase Marianne Hirsch, they offer an "ethical remembrance" of the other (2001) to their fellow society members. In light of this analytical division, Jewish Israeli activists in Israel can be seen as belonging to the second category of memory activists, offering an ethical remembrance of Palestinian suffering and displacement in 1948, while Arab Palestinian activists in Israel can be viewed as resembling the first category of activists who are decedents of the victimized group.

Memory-activist practices differ from more "traditional" and official commemorative practices by their interactive nature, their accessibility, and the aim to reach the participation of current residents of the sites where violent events once took place. As mentioned, they appropriate cultural practices as means to reframe the public debate on the past and to influence people's views toward present political issues and project a vision for the future. Like the groups in Israel, other memory activists often work in local spaces where the violent events have occurred in the past, where they organize tours, post signs, restore the physical environment, and publish maps and tour guides in order to document and produce knowledge on the past. Many of these groups also collect testimonies from current and former residents of these sites and house them in archives and information centers. Community-based educational and artistic work is often facilitated as well, on-site and online.

Unlike other agents in the field of memory, such as memory entrepreneurs (Jelin 2007), memory practitioners, and "communities of
memory" (Irwin-Zarecka 1994) whose interests and relationships center on the public commemoration of an atrocious event in the past,
these memory activists do not necessarily have a personal or professional stake in the events, and in any case they wish to go beyond commemorative issues. The political motivation behind memory-activist
initiatives varies, and while they can be used to advance less peaceful
and democratic aims, I trace them historically to a temporal shift in
international politics that is underlined by an effort to advance peace
and reconciliation worldwide.

The surge in memory of a difficult past among grassroots and civil
society groups today corresponds to a shift in transnational politics
from big visions of the future to a "coming to terms" with the difficult
past (Olick and Coughlin 2003; Torpey 2003; Barkan 2000). Instead
of celebrating past victories and heroic chapters of their shared past,
nation-states are called on to publically address the less glorious and
more atrocious parts of their history, to cultivate a memory that is
"disgusted with itself" (Olick and Coughlin 2003, 38). A new political
principle, the "politics of regret" (Olick and Coughlin 2003, 38; Olick
2007), grants legitimacy in the international arena to nations that ret-
rospectively inspect, regret, and address atrocious acts they inflicted on
citizens, rival nations, ethnic or national minorities, or colonial subjects.

This paradigmatic shift in transnational politics has presented a
challenge to social movements and peace activists, who are traditionally future oriented (Goldfarb 2009; Hermann 2009). Such groups,
which have often made an effort to bracket a contested and polarizing
past in order to highlight common ground, could no longer ignore
the contested past. Memory activism, when employed as a strategy
of peace activism that is oriented toward the past, brings in different
temporal relations as the foundation of its model for political change:
first the past, then the present and future.

Despite its growing visibility in recent decades, and particularly
from 2000, memory activism has been missing not only from studies of collective memory that still pay more attention to state-based
commemoration and to "official" political mobilization of the past,
but also from the literature on social movements and peace activism.
Social-movement theory in general is thought to be lacking a historical dimension, and as part of that lack also fails to acknowledge the
significance of the past for social and political intervention (Jansen

2007). Memory activism thus brings new empirical research and conceptualization that expand the boundaries of existing categories both of peace activism and of collective-memory politics and so is valuable in the study of conflict resolution and reconciliation processes. This book provides a historical and ethnographic review of memory activism and its practices through the pertinent case study of the Israeli-Palestinian conflict while pointing to a variety of examples around the world. It also develops the concept of memory activism as part of an integrative conceptual framework.

Collective memory is often studied as belonging to the powerful, assisting elites and political leaders in reinforcing their high status and power position. State and official memory and national history remain at the center of the field, despite new attempts to examine nonstate commemoration (see, for example, Jelin 2007; Bernhard and Kubik 2014; Fridman 2015; and Wüstenberg 2009, 2011). However, this book argues that collective memory can also serve as "weapon of the weak" (Scott 1985) and a tool for social and political change. As a counter-hegemonic force in society, Nakba memory activism in Israel assisted a marginalized group of citizens to intervene, albeit obliquely, on the level of culture, in state practices and public discourse.

Collective memory is the shared social perception of a group's past. Like Maurice Halbwachs ([1925] 1992), I study collective memory as a social construction that is created by a group in the present, framed by the time and place in which the group remembers. It therefore always reflects a specific sociopolitical context: present problems and understandings, visions for the future, group boundaries, interests, and power relations. I am committed to the work of scholars like Olick and Robbins (1993), Wagner-Pacifici (2010), Zolberg (1998), D. Levy and Sznaider (2006), Torpey (2003), Schudson (1992), and others who conceptualize collective memory as a process or performance, rather than as a symbolic system. The social construction of collective memory in the present is a dynamic process of selection, negotiations, mobilization, and contestations, rather than a coherent and consensual construction sustainable in time (Zelizer 1995; Schwartz 1982).

Processes of memory construction require "memory work," a key concept that refers to the production of an infrastructure of collective memory in order to "secure a presence for the past" (Irwin-Zarecka 1994, 13). Among other things, memory work is the process of framing the past, using available resources, in order to make sense of it in the present (4). This framing is composed of "overlaying" frames, materials, and tropes that have been used in the past and can be reused (7) as both meanings and our emotional and moral engagement with the past shift over time.

To capture such shifts in meaning through the overlayering of frames, I take inspiration from works like Zolberg's on the Enola Gay exhibit controversy at the Smithsonian's National Air and Space Museum (1998) and Wagner-Pacifici and Schwartz on the Vietnam Veterans Memorial (1991), and I similarly focus on the public debate and negotiation that are involved in the process of commemorating a contested past in a specific context.

However, unlike these works, the political debates and negotiations that are involved in memory activism often expand beyond the nation-state, although it remains an important site of memory. I join efforts to move away from the nation-state in memory studies and examine the global proliferation of ideas, politics, and memories, and trans-national memory politics. In so doing, not only do I ask how these processes of proliferation impact (and are themselves being impacted by) the nation-state, but more significantly I study the interactions between multiple actors and institutions that carry them: transnational networks of experts, practitioners, activists, artists, intellectuals, and funding bodies, among others.

The most important aspect that I take from collective-memory literature is "moral entrepreneurship," as Wagner-Pacifici and Schwartz (1991) explain:

> Attitudes and interests are translated into commemorative forms through enterprise. Before any event can be regarded as worth remembering, and before any class of people can be recognized for having participated in that event, some individual, and eventually some group, must deem both event and participants commemorable and must have the influence to get others to agree. Memorial devices are not self-created; they are conceived and built by those who wish to bring to consciousness the events and people that others are more inclined to forget. To understand memorial making in this way is to understand it as a construction process wherein competing "moral entrepreneurs" seek public arenas and support for their interpretations of the past. (382)

Different and competing moral entrepreneurs "seek public arenas and support for their interpretations of the past." Some of them, like communities of memory (Irwin-Zarecka 1994, 47–50), unite around the memory of an event in an effort to keep it actively remembered, while others, like memory activists, are more interested in advancing moral and political agendas that extend beyond commemoration.

Recent efforts to theorize the different categories of "mnemonic actors," as Bernard and Kubik have called them (2014), especially those operating outside state channels, created new typologies, yet memory activism remains a blind spot. If we group these typologies into three general "ideal types," we can see this quite clearly. The first ideal type of mnemonic actors, which is the most studied among scholars of nonstate memory, refers to individuals and groups who have personal experience or family ties that connect them personally to the historical events that they would like to publically remember. Among these are memory agents (as, for example, in Vinitzky-Seroussi 2009), memory entrepreneurs (in Jelin's definition, 2007), or communities of memory (Irwin-Zarecka 1994), as well as victim groups, former dissidents, and veteran groups. These are often portrayed as competing with each other over state recognition and legitimacy in what is perceived as a limited public space and a zero-sum game of mnemonic "assets" (Rothberg 2009). Memory activists are different from the first "ideal type" groups not only because their members may lack personal experience and stakes in the historical events to be remembered, but more significantly because their goals extend beyond commemorative issues. Rather, they aim to address a larger political issue and influence the dominant public debate in their societies, using memory practices as the means to do so.

A second ideal type of mnemonic actor is more pragmatic and expert based and less personally invested in the events to be remembered; these are memory practitioners, for-profit initiatives, and "pragmatic activists" (Wüstenberg 2011). These have been portrayed either as implementing transnational ideas and norms in domestic public debates or as mediating among different memory groups and the state in domestic struggles (Wüstenberg 2011). Memory activists are different from these "pragmatics" and experts because they strive not to mediate or commemorate but to make a stand and intervene in existing political discourse and public debate.

More politically motivated is a third ideal type of mnemonic actors, which were defined by Bernhard and Kubik as "political forces that are interested in a specific interpretation of the past" and who "often treat history instrumentally in order to construct a vision of the past that they assume will generate the most effective legitimation for their effort to gain and hold power" (2014, 4). Through a state-oriented political science lens, these agents are characterized according to their vision of themselves and their opponents and their style of interaction in the political arena: as warriors, pluralists, abnegators, and prospectives (Bernhard and Kubik 2014, 4). However, in Bernhard and Kubik's work, all these actors are rationally calculating their way to gain power rather than morally or ideologically invested in promoting a specific understanding of the past with the hope that this will lead to a new understanding of present problems and project a new vision for the future. While memory activists are political actors, they mobilize the past not for the aim of gaining power and status, but for advancing their moral and ideological visions. Like Wagner-Pacifici and Schwartz's conceptualization of moral entrepreneurs, memory activists "seek public arenas and support for their interpretations of the past" because they care about these interpretations, rather than use them instrumentally to advance their climb up the social ladder. Moreover, the silenced past that memory activists wish to make present and their interpretation of violent histories are highly controversial and more often attract public rejection and denial rather than granting the activists legitimacy and recognition in their society.

Instead of seeking political power as a goal in and of itself, the intervention that memory can perform opens a window to the meaning and nature of "the political." In the case of the Israeli-Palestinian conflict, my interrogation begins with the question, Why do Palestinian activists in Israel define their Nakba memory activities as "nonpolitical," when such activity appears to be extremely controversial and illegitimate in the larger society and expands the schism between their national group and state ideology? In Chapter 3 I explicate the strategic logic of articulating memory activism around the Nakba as nonpolitical and explain the importance of such consciousness-raising efforts for bringing about political change. In articulating nuanced distinctions among four different definitions of the "political," I argue for the real political work done by memory activism, not as simply building support for Palestinian statehood but as a pervasive strategy for raising consciousness among Jewish Israelis.

What the Israeli-Palestinian case makes visible about how memory can be used as a tool for social change lies not only in the nature of "the political" but also in the appropriation of familiar and dominant cultural practices for communicating a counterhegemonic message. These cultural practices can raise multiple issues and voices in a way that professional historiography and official history on the one hand, and social movements' repertoires of political action on the other, cannot (Horwitz 1999; Landsberg 2004; de Groot 2011). A central organizing idea of this book is its focus on specific strategies for and uses of memory that appropriate and redeploy what have come to be accepted as familiar memory practices—locally and globally—such as the survivor testimony and guided tours. I argue that the activist use of such cultural and commemorative forms may amplify or hinder the effectiveness of the dissemination of their claims among different publics.

This is most evident in the ethnography of a tour of Palestinian ruins in Chapter 1. Drawing on a history and genealogy of touring in the Zionist movement and of return visits among Palestinian citizens of Israel, the chapter reveals how tensions and contradictions inherent to the hegemonic use of the tour in Israel, as well as others that stem from its redeployment by activists, affect the audiences' response and anticipated transformation and carry intended and unintended consequences. In a tour of Palestinian ruins that is directed primarily at Jewish Israeli audiences, touring and visiting traditions clash as a Palestinian refugee testifies on the site's past. Jewish Israeli participants and the Palestinian refugee each come to this encounter with different mental maps of the specific site and the land as a whole, which inform their performance of their knowledge in each other's presence. Despite the intention of the tour organizers, neither side fully complies with the tour plan, causing confusion instead of the communication of Palestinian memories.

The survivor testimony operated a bit differently in Autobiography of a City's digital archive of Palestinian testimonies, in comparison to Zochrot's live testimony, as Chapter 2 elaborates. The activists, who are Jewish Israeli and Arab Palestinian artists trained in visual culture and what they term "storytelling" (Danon interview 2008), developed a mechanism for the production of oppositional knowledge (Coy, Woehrle, and Maney 2008). "The [primary] importation area of this state is stories. Building a very strong story is the heart of it. From here comes our work around narrative," Eyal Danon, cofounder of the group, said when explaining to me the motivation behind establishing this activist archive: using hegemonic practices as the means to produce counterhegemonic claims—in this case, in the form of stories. Yet I discovered that the activist mechanism was designed to serve what appear to be contradictory goals, as well as different audiences and funders. On the one hand, this online archive wishes to give voice to the silenced and marginalized Palestinian residents of Jaffa and on the other hand to problematize and criticize the very possibility that this testimony—of stories told by a witness to historical events, when used by the state and in general—can grant us access to a difficult past. The first stage of interviewing the witnesses proves to be quite fruitful in giving authority and legitimacy to the silenced residents, who can air their difficult experiences and memories. This was primarily because the activists combined a range of global and regional cultural practices and traditions in the interviews and their recording. However, in the second stage, when the testimonies were edited to story-size bites and archived according to different tags and search options, some of the authority and legitimacy were withdrawn, as the archive user was offered a meta-level reflection on the various, sometimes contradictory, possible versions of the past.

Indeed, the tactical logic of maintaining the public legitimacy and authority granted to cultural practices that have been used by the state for national education, in the activist production of countermemory, revealed an interesting potential for transformation, despite various contradictions and unintended consequences. Yet using hegemonic practices for counterhegemonic claims can also prove to be a double-edged sword. First, the inclusion of those who were previously excluded brings with it the risk of producing a new yet similarly exclusive interpretation of the past. Another problem that has been less commonly studied is depoliticization, which has been briefly mentioned and is discussed in length in the concluding chapter. Working in the realm of the cultural sometimes means choosing a tactical depoliticization in order to create distance from a public debate that is limited in order to open a space for new ideas and visions that otherwise would not have been conceived or accepted. Yet this is done with the aim of repoliticizing in the end and bringing these ideas to the political and public debate.

However, this movement between depoliticization and regaining political consciousness to reenter public debate is complicated and did not always work well in the activist deployment of the tour and testimony I studied. In Zochrot's activist tour, for example, Jewish Israeli participants are presented with a tour that resembles the hegemonic touring practice in their society, which since the 1980s is associated with leisure and experiential learning. In these decades, and unlike the earlier decades of nation building, the tour in Israel appears nonideological. Despite some objections and personal tensions with the dominant format, many participants in the early tours gave in to the depoliticized appearance of Zochrot's tour and learn things about Palestinian life and their displacement that they may not have encountered otherwise. Yet at the end, my interviews suggest, they do not necessarily connect what they have learned and experienced to a political claim or position regarding Palestinian suffering today and since 1948.

Memory activism's use of cultural practices also offers significant insight for the literature on social movements and collective action. Mainly, it expands the ways in which culture has been studied by social-movement scholars beyond the leading explanatory model of framing. While framing focuses on the discursive and rhetorical aspects of movement action, I derive a complementary explanation that includes nondiscursive aspects—an undertheorized terrain in the field.

Framing is a lens to understand activist efforts to construct political claims as part of a struggle over reframing the dominant discourse (Benford and Snow 2000; Snow, Zurcher, and Ekland-Olson 1980; Steinberg 1999). I use one conceptualization of framing, by Coy and his colleagues (2008), that seems particularly suitable to explain memory activism in Israel: the production of *oppositional knowledge* and claims against the dominant knowledge and claims. This production and dissemination of alternative visions to the dominant ones wishes to shift "the normative center of society" (Coy, Woehrle, and Maney 2008, 5.7) by questioning and subverting the common sense and envisioning alternatives (5.5). The strategy, which was developed in long-term studies of the American peace movement, includes four types of oppositional knowledge. It seems suitable for memory activism, because it similarly wishes to influence political debates that usually involve knowledge and interpretations of the past that touch on the fundamental organizing principles and moral assumptions of a society (5.6).

However, like many scholars of framing, Coy, Woehrle, and Maney assume that the whole process of transformation occurs discursively, through "a dialogue of ideas" or "interaction, disagreement and emergent consensus" (2008, 5.6). In other words, it is an essentially cognitive process, in which arguments and ideas are exchanged in the hopes that they will impact informed decision making among individuals in society. While the discursive medium can account for some of my findings regarding the activist efforts to intervene in existing public debate and political discourse, their means for this end offer an intervention through nondiscursive or rhetorical realms: the perfomative, embodied, material, and visual.

My findings, like some of the research on cultural memory, indicate that the use of cultural and commemorative practices such as touring, testimony, reenactment of historical events, and heritage preservation can complicate our "affective, empathic relationship to the past" (de Groot 2011, 588). Practices that involve the body in historical sites try to create a secondhand experience of historical events—or what Landsberg called prostatic memory (2004)—among those who did not live through them. These practices operate in multiple ways to solidify and fortify, unsettle, undermine, and upset dominant perceptions of the past (de Groot 2011). Taking into account the nondiscursive or rhetorical aspects of political action and transformation, through a genealogy and history of the practices of touring and testimony, reveals the setting in which activist claims are presented to audiences, the interaction in such encounters, and the audience's reaction. It shows that the interaction between activists and audiences is mediated by these cultural practices, which shape participants' previous expectations, habitual bodily gestures, embedded knowledge, and symbolic tropes. Cultural practices can therefore advance or hinder the effectiveness of the dissemination of activist claims among different audiences.

While my main arguments are shaped by, and in turn inform, contemporary debates in memory studies and social-movement theory, two additional fields of study are involved in my inquiry: peace and conflict studies, and scholarship on the Israeli-Palestinian conflict. Peace and conflict studies lends itself to a dual investigation: (1) I test the theoretical assumptions and models of scholars in the field who took an active part in developing the postconflict reconciliation paradigm, through ethnography of its implementation in practice in a case of active conflict; (2) and my findings inform a meta-level theoretical review of some of the field's dominant and influential set of accounts. As mentioned above, my findings suggest a reconsideration of some of the foundational assumptions of the expert paradigm. The extensive and interdisciplinary body of knowledge on the Israeli-Palestinian conflict is present in my investigation not only as historical background, for which I use various studies on the history, culture, public debate, and political discourse on the conflict. It also includes analyses of the structures and processes that have shaped both civil society and state organizations in the last decades. Yet in contrast to the common focus of scholars in this field on leaders, the state, official channels, and formal negotiations as central to studying the conflict and its potential resolution, I offer a new lens to the study of the conflict, as it is fought in the realm of public consciousness. I focus on the realm of culture and memory politics and reveal new avenues for political action and intervention in state practices, as well as the limitations and boundaries of the Israeli-Palestinian public discourse. The study of cultural memory and peace activism in this conflict offers an unorthodox approach to what appears an endless and intractable schism between the rival sides' understandings of the histories of the region and the conflict.

The first two chapters describe both state and activist deployment of the tour and refugee testimony. Each of the chapters focuses on one of the forms while examining a different activist group, describing its position and target audience. Chapter 1 is an ethnographic account of the activist tours of Zochrot, the largest memory group in Israel. The chapter probes how the tour, which was originally appropriated and deployed for Zionist national education, is now redeployed by a group of Israeli Jews to cultivate an understanding of Palestinian national history. Drawing on a history of touring in the Zionist movement and among Palestinian citizens of Israel, I show the intended and unintended consequences of a meeting, in the activist tour, between a Palestinian refugee and an audience of primarily Jewish Israelis. Although neither side fully complied with the tour plan, resulting in confusion rather than communication, participants testified to a successful transformation of attitudes. I interpret this response in light of tensions and contradictions inherent to the hegemonic use of the tour in Israel, as well as others that stem from its redeployment by activists. My findings suggest that the relationship between an activist group and its publics is enacted through cultural practices and forms and decided in the public sphere.

Chapter 2 shows how the genre of survivor testimony is utilized for a new category—Palestinians residing in Jaffa—in the digital archive of the Jewish Palestinian memory-activist group Autobiography of a City. This archive is analyzed within the local context of state utilization of Holocaust survivor testimonies and the formation of a paradigmatic form of recorded testimony in private digital archives around the world. Some of the issues scholars have attributed to "archives of suffering" worldwide and of Palestinian refugees as a test case are overcome in this activist archive. Yet tensions and contradictions between the activists' intent and the final product nonetheless exist. Primarily, the testifiers are given a voice and authority when interviewed, but this authority loses its value when their testimonies are placed in an archive that ultimately reveals the arbitrariness of any and all memory narratives.

Chapter 3 addresses the counterintuitive Palestinian strategy of memory activism in Israel: the redeployment of memory practices that were used for Zionist national education for the cultivation of a Palestinian national identity in Israel. Despite the striking similarity to Jewish Israeli activist deployment of these forms (the tour and testimony), the context, motivations, meanings, and stakes of these consciousness-raising activities of Palestinian citizens for their own society are different from those of Jewish Israelis, whose national collective memory is dominant and institutionalized. Palestinian memory activism is positioned within a two-front war—against the state's exclusion and within their own society. The case study of Baladna, an all-Palestinian youth association in Israel, illuminates the urgency and the immediacy of this type of memory work. It shows how the utilization of state commemorative forms can in some cases reach beyond state limitations, while in other cases it is bound to the existing order.

Chapters 4 and 5 address the state reaction: the memory war and the struggle over Nakba commemoration in Israel of the 2000s. Chapter 4 chronicles the shift in visibility of Nakba memory in Israel from a "public secret" at the beginning of the decade to a household term at the decade's end, ironically due to a repressive state reaction that tried to block activist and intellectual efforts to publically air this past. It reviews the state's reaction—most powerfully through legislation of the "Nakba Law"—that had a central role in this change. The chapter explores the relationships between memory and the law in democracies and how they might hinder or advance political change in this and other cases. Comparing the Israeli case to recent memory laws in France and Russia that ban contested memories of state violence in order to promote the dominant national memory, I find that such laws signal another stage in the process of reintegration of the silenced memory into public consciousness.

Chapter 5 presents the reactions in Israel to memory-activist efforts to strategically utilize truth and reconciliation outside state channels during active conflict. Their efforts reveal the limitations of these expert concepts in the context of an ongoing conflict. The Israeli case shows that historical accountability may simultaneously serve both the process of reconciliation and the perpetuation of the conflict. It is but one argument among many in a public struggle over narrating a past that has high stakes for the present and future. I proposes that knowledge of a contested past is best disseminated only after acknowledgment and responsibility are in place, both in cases of conflict and postconflict.

The concluding chapter offers lessons for other cases of active conflict. It maintains that both the production and dissemination of oppositional knowledge and the utilization of dominant cultural practices should be taken into account in the study of political activism. Along this line, a new model of knowledge-based political change is proposed, and novel directions for future research are drawn.

In addition to making an empirically grounded theoretical contribution, this book seeks to intervene in the Israeli public debate in which the memory war of 1948 still takes place by revealing the central tensions and arguments that continue to reproduce the conflicting positions, constrain public debate, and hinder any possibility of resolution in the near future. For me, the study and practice of memory are ultimately about and for the future. As memory activism demonstrates, visions of the future, as individuals and groups imagine them in the present, influence how the past is remembered, interpreted, and dealt with, and the past informs and impacts visions for the future.

1

The Activist Tour as a Political Tool

One sunny Saturday morning in spring 2008, I joined a group of thirty people who waited for a tour bus outside the train station in Tel Aviv. The majority of us were middle-class Jewish Israelis roughly between twenty-five and sixty-five years old. There were also a few internationals and a foreign filming crew working on a documentary on the Israeli-Palestinian conflict. We all had preregistered for this free tour through the organizer, an Israeli NGO called Zochrot, whose name means "we remember" in female plural form in Hebrew. We knew we were going to visit the ruins of a pre-1948 Palestinian village. From chatting in the train station I found out that for many, this was the first time they would be participating in one of Zochrot's tours. All of us were casually dressed, in hats and sport shoes or hiking sandals, carrying light food and water we had packed in advance. We looked like the thousands of other Israelis who go hiking in national parks and reservations every weekend. And indeed, after an hour or so, the bus dropped us off at the parking lot of a national park that was full with cars and hikers. Shortly after leaving the bus and stretching our legs we, joined by thirty to forty other tour participants who arrived by car, gathered around the tour guide, Amin. One of Zochrot's two Palestinian staff members, Amin explained in perfect Hebrew with a slight Arabic accent where we were going, what stops we would make on the way, and what we were about to see at these stops. For a Jewish Israeli like myself, everything felt quite familiar so far, resembling the popular script of the tour by foot as it has been practiced in Israeli schools, youth movements, scouting clubs, and family weekend trips around the country. There were only two indications that this was not a regular weekend tour. First, an elderly Palestinian in traditional attire, accompanied by his son, the son's wife, and three of his grandchildren, arrived in a private car and was greeted by the tour guide and Zochrot's staff members. Second, as the group started walking, we wandered off to an unmarked path in an otherwise well-marked and mapped park. Unlike the marked paths, lined by trees planted by the Jewish National Fund (JNF), Israel's land and forests agency, and seeded with archeological structures, along our path there were no signs, only wildly growing fruit trees, scattered stones, and cacti. There were no other travelers on this path, which together with the wildly growing flora suggested that it is not considered a destination for the ordinary weekend hiker. Our diversion from the marked path received curious and inquisitive looks from other hikers, who we soon left behind.

Zochrot's tour of Palestinian ruins continued to follow the tour format familiar to Jewish Israelis: following a tour guide on a path through nature, making stops along the way to hear the guide commenting on the landscape, explaining what had been there before. Yet some differences did arise: not only that the tour guide spoke first in Arabic and only later in Hebrew; the elder Palestinian also spoke alongside the guide; the man is a Palestinian refugee and a former resident of the site before its destruction in 1948. His mental map of the place, communicated through testimony, in combination with documents and photos, critical historiographies, and testimonies of other former residents, provided the foundational body of knowledge for this tour. Moreover, at central stops during the tour, signs prepared by Zochrot that carry the Palestinian place name in Arabic and Hebrew (sometimes also in English) were posted by the refugee's family, some of Zochrot's staff and volunteers, and willing participants. These signs resembled the JNF signs that are posted throughout this national park but had brighter colors.

The guide and refugee gave short oral presentations at every stop along the way. They had visited the site together at least once before to prepare for this one-time public tour of this particular site organized primary for Israeli Jews. In fact, the refugee's testimony was transcribed and translated to appear in a booklet handed out to tour participants at the beginning of the tour. The same knowledge on the site is distributed through two mediums: the written booklet and the spoken and embodied performance of live testimony during the tour. This suggests that Zochrot does not expect the written information to function independently from the refugee's presence and performance. Giving testimony is indeed a position that, in addition to providing firsthand knowledge, carries unique moral authority, especially when performed in situ (J. Feldman 2008, 69). It is a position and practice that Israelis are highly familiar with when the witness is a Jewish Israeli Holocaust survivor for example. But will they give the same legitimacy and authority to a non-Jewish witness, moreover, to a Palestinian who testi-fies about Jewish and Israeli violence, displacement, and dispossession? And how will the Palestinian refugee communicate a long-silenced memory to those whose parents and grandparent may have taken part in the war that caused his displacement and loss?

These and other questions suggest that this activist tour, which mimics the form of the tour previously used for Zionist national edu-cation, to portray not Jewish Israeli, but Palestinian ties to the land, is far from being simple and straightforward. The activist utilization of the tour carries dilemmas, tensions, contradictions, and ironies, some which are inherent to the hegemonic use of the tour in Israel, and others that stem from its activist employment in the political context of the 2000s.

Here we begin our close reading of how memory activists have been appropriating and redeploying locally familiar memory practices to pursue the postconflict paradigm of truth and reconciliation in the Israeli-Palestinian conflict. This close reading, which continues in the two following chapters, is of the activist appropriation of the tour and testimony by different groups of Jewish Israeli and Arab Palestinian activists since 2001; these are commemorative forms and practices that are locally rooted within Israel's dominant memory culture. The ex-amination not only includes cultural forms that have been dominant among Jewish Israelis but also considers similar, separate yet related, practices developed by Palestinian citizens. The analysis begins with the appropriation of cultural practices primarily by and for Jewish Is-raelis by the largest of the memory-activism groups I studied in Israel, Zochrot. Drawing on a history of touring in the Zionist movement and among Palestinian citizens of Israel, the intended and unintended consequences of a meeting between a Palestinian refugee and an audi-ence of primarily Jewish Israelis that is meant to receive that refugee's previously silenced memories is revealed.

Neither side fully complied with the tour plan and format, despite Zochrot's congenial facilitation. Nevertheless, the majority of partici-pants who joined Zochrot testified to a successful transformation of attitudes after participating in even one of the organization's tours. This response, which otherwise seems counterintuitive in light of par-ticipants' behavior and interaction in the tour itself, is explained, first, in light of the historical deployment of the tour as a tool for Zion-ist national education, and second, in relation to how activists have redeployed it in the political context of the last decade. My findings suggest that the relationship between an activist group and its publics is culturally mediated; this relationship is enacted through culture and cultural practices and decided in the public sphere.

Conquering the Land with Our Feet:
A Local History of Touring

> There is no better way to get to know the land than a well-planned trip. The trip links a person to his environment, he becomes attached to it and grows to love it. . . . The trip on foot is the most desirable. The impressions gained through close inspection of the environment while hiking become etched in a person's heart and have a great influence on him. (Vilna'i 1953, 5, cited in Katriel 1996, 8)

This pedagogical text, written by the established Jewish Israeli scholar and educator Ze'ev Vilna'i, was originally published in 1945 by the Youth Department of the Jewish Agency as part of the Pedagogical Library for Councilors series.[1] As the Zionist educator described here, touring the land by foot was perceived as central to cultivating personal attachment to the environment, and it was expected, additionally, that hiking will have "a great influence" on participants. From youth movement trips around the country in prestate Palestine to mandatory school trips in the national education system, to family weekend hiking tours organized by the Society for the Protection of Nature, tours by foot and hiking trips around the country are a central form of education, recreation, and symbolic communication in Jewish Israeli culture (Ben-David 1997; Katriel 1996, 1991; Y. Zerubavel 1995; Ben Yehuda 2002; Katriel and Shenhar 1990). Despite shifts in the imaginary links and ideological foundation of this form of secular pilgrimage over the years and a few critical debates within Israeli media, the tour remains today an almost consensual practice of mainstream Jewish Israeli culture,[2] and an important element in its complex of "public ceremonies and myth making practices" (Katriel 1996, 6, 12).

Yet this form or practice is in itself an appropriation that was shaped through an intercultural setting. The use of the organized hiking tour as a pedagogical tool was influenced by a secular European pedagogy and the ethos of a return to nature of German youth culture after World War I, expressed by its youth movements and their Jewish version, Blau-Weis (Katriel 1996). At the same time, it had somewhat religious elements in the Zionist movement's (secular) interpretation of the traditional Jewish longing to return to the sacred land of the Bible and pilgrimage (Katriel 1996). In the prestate years in Palestine and nation-building period as a state, the organized tour had two central goals: (1) to create and reaffirm a sense of belonging to the land both as the sacred biblical space and as a national homeland, and (2) to reconnect Jewish immigrants with nature, as well as with found traces of the land's past (Katriel 1996).

In the prestate days, Jewish youth movement tours also tried to show Jewish ownership of the land by using the imagery of "conquering the land with our feet" (Benvenisti 1998, 145; Katriel 1996, 6; Ben-David 1997; Lentin 2010, 67). After the establishment of the State of Israel, youth movements saw tours by foot as the best way to produce knowledge of the land (*yediat ha'aretz*), which fosters love for the land (*ahavat ha'aretz*; Naor 1989, 246, in Katriel 1996, 7; Katz 1985; Kadman 2008, 47).[3] For Zionist educators in the nation-building period, however, this "love" or attachment to the land that the tour by foot was supposed to cultivate was also a source of concern. These educators saw the lack of touring as a mark of lesser attachment and participation in the new Jewish state (Katriel 1996). Youth movement members were mostly Jewish youth of Ashkenazi decent, and those who did not hike in the same way—Mizrachi Jews and Palestinian citizens—were viewed as demonstrating a weak attachment to the land (Katriel 1996; Noy and Cohen 2005, 23). Later, in the more pluralistic Jewish society of the 1980s, what was viewed as a lack of interest in tours by some of the population, especially marginalized Mizrachi youth, was interpreted by education experts as an ideological stance that prevented full participation in the society, and was therefore something to be corrected (Stahl 1985). As tours became part of the mainstream secular Ashkenazi-oriented culture in the nation-state, pedagogues saw "a taste for touring" among non-Ashkenazi Jewish Israelis as an invitation to participate in the society through the production of its shared values around historical and archeological sites (Katriel 1996, 9).

But "distaste" for tours by foot may have existed not only outside the dominant Ashkenazi culture, but also within it. Katriel illustrates this by way of another form of commemorative and national education—Israeli settlement museums: "The paradox of having to consciously cultivate a sense of affiliation where it should have been a cultural given" may have been important for new Jewish immigrants in the Yeshuv but raised doubts among the next generations who were born in Israel and for whom "a sense of place was a cultural experience" that "the rhetoric of roots only threatened to undermine. The more markedly ideological these assertions became, the more potentially destabilizing they seemed to be" (Katriel 1997, 9). Native-born Israelis had, in Katriel's account, a lived sense of belonging to the land that was very different from the intentional cultivation of cultural roots through commemoration.

In the 1980s, the connection to the biblical past and ideological components shifted to accommodate ideas about personal growth and progressive and active learning. The tour by foot did not change its form but appeared as a nonideological activity, "a ritualized, pedagogically and recreationally oriented practice in its own right" (Katriel 1996, 10). However, the ideological foundation of the tour reappeared when the form was mobilized by both right-wing and left-wing groups, to make a political statement for or against the occupation of the Palestinian Territories since 1967, especially from the first Intifada onward.[4] Yet for the most part, as long as they appear nonideological, tours have remained an almost consensual activity that is a fundamental part of "growing up Israeli" (Katriel 1996).

A Palestinian History of Touring and Visiting

Although unregistered in the complex of practices and meaning making of "growing up Israeli"—that is, Jewish Israeli—Palestinians have also been strolling, touring, and visiting significant historical and national sites. Yet their restricted movement under martial law from 1949 to 1966 and the destruction of their pre-1948 sites by the state influenced their touring and visiting practices in a different way, giving these acts particular urgency and political significance. The literature has thus centered on one set of such practices over others: that of the return visit (Ben-Ze'ev 2004; Slyomovics 1998; Davis 2011). While Palestinians have been active in recreational hiking and strolling from the pre-1948 period (for example, Arab Girl Scouts' hiking tours, Hasan and Ayalon 2011) and until today (with growing difficulty in the West Bank as Shehadeh 2008 reported) return visits have received more scholarly and literary attention. Often these visits are analyzed through the lens of their national underpinning and commemorative dimension, although in the last decade or so some of these visiting practices have also incorporated aspects of leisure and active learning. In addition to return visits of Palestinian refugees with western passports to their village sites, or of Palestinians without immediate ties who instead follow "a mythology of place images and descriptions" (Slyomovics 1998: xx; see also Tamari 2003), internally displaced Palestinians who reside in Israel have been visiting the remains of their villages more often with their families. Some of the components of their post-1948 tradition have included picnicking, meeting others from the same locality, recounting their village's story during the annual Nakba Day and on weekends, and picking fruits and herbs and telling stories about their use (Ben-Ze'ev 2004). This tradition is unique to Palestinian citizens of Israel, who commemorate and transmit the memory of pre-1948 Palestinian places and communities when Israel celebrates its Independence Day (Ben-Ze'ev 2004; Slyomovics 1998, 17).[5] Around 1998, on the fiftieth anniversary of the Nakba and Israeli independence, Palestinian associations within Israel joined various commemoration efforts in the territories and abroad, in organizing group walking tours to the ruins of 1948 villages for Palestinians in general, not only for refugees. The majority of these groups mobilize around 1948 to raise awareness of specific and urgent political problems of Palestinian citizens in the present: the Arab Cultural Association (ACA) in Nazareth, which was led by Rawda Bishara Atallah and includes an archive and an information center, is associated with the Palestinian party Balad; the Sadaka-Reut youth movement holds tours in Jaffa to show the state of current home evictions and demolition of Palestinian residences; and the Association for the Defense of the Rights of the Internally Displaced Persons in Israel in the North of the country promotes the Right of Return of the internally displaced through tours, processions, and commemorative ceremonies.

In addition to the return tours of refugees to their lands, and the issue-driven tours described above, there are also a few initiatives that infuse tours of the ruins of 1948 villages with pedagogical and recreational elements, such as a weekend activity for Palestinian families. Central to them are the tours organized by the Association for Arab Heritage by Muhammad Yunnes and historian Mustafa Kabha, in the Triangle of Palestinian villages near Wadi Arah. Yunnes described the 150 core participants as teachers and civil society workers, as well as other professionals who reside in the center of the country. Very few of them come from refugee families. Some of them are interested in exploring nature, some in Palestinian folklore; and others are motivated by "ideology, identity, and a sense of belonging" (Yunnes interview 2009). Similar descriptions are given by Fawzi Nasser, an experienced tour guide and retired geography teacher from Nazareth, a descendent of refugees from the Galilee village of Iqrit. Nasser has been one of the first to hold tours of destroyed Palestinian villages, including for the Young Communist League of the Israeli communist party. Nasser relies on different sources of knowledge for each of these tours: publications by Israeli and Palestinian historians, documents, and photos, as well as a refugee from the site visited who sometimes joins the tour and testifies, or consulted to verify the information and confirm it with other institutional and human sources (interview 2012).

"The Arab [Palestinian] society has made a reproduction of the Zionist tours," stated Yunnes (interview 2009). "Once there was [going to] Tiberius and barbequing, . . . now they are looking for things of higher quality, in history, in heritage, and then [asking], why only with the Society for Protection of Nature [the state agency]?" Nasser also mentioned the similarity of his tours to those organized by the Society for Protection of Nature, describing both historical knowledge and love of nature and of hiking as equally important components of his tours (interview 2012).

Returning to Zochrot's activist tour with which the chapter opened and the meeting between Jewish Israeli participants and the Palestinian refugee's testimony, we can now see how these touring histories and practices present themselves in each other's presence. In this activist tour, which appropriates the format of touring that is central to Jewish Israeli culture, the refugee's memories are not only transmitted to Jewish Israeli participants through testimony but are more effectively performed unexpectedly through practices of return visits that are dominant among Palestinians.

Different Indexes of the Land

The older refugees who joined this and other Zochrot tours, who experienced the 1948 war as children, tend to be fluent in their telling of the past and often tell the same stories, sometimes even using the same sentences that were recorded and printed in the booklet that Zochrot handed out at the beginning of the tour. Yet a highly significant part of the refugee testimony is given without words, when the refugee stops along the way not in one of the preplanned spots where he is supposed to speak. The refugee suddenly steps out of the planned tour route and walks with purpose to a different spot to pick fruit or pull out weeds, to smell or taste. The group then stops on the route behind the refugee and waits for the speech or movement to resume without being sure of what is happening. There is confusion when the sequence of stopping and listening to the tour guide's or refugee's speech is not performed and the familiar tour format is interrupted. In some of the tours I attended, the refugee's son tried to make up for this interruption by picking up the abandoned microphone and resuming where the father left off. The son did not speak about what the father was doing at that moment but continued the explanation the father was expected to give in an attempt to correct the diversion from format and plan.

For the refugee, this stepping out of path and speech is not a break but a continuation of the testimony, only now through a sensory and embodied recollection of personal memories of the destroyed village. The practices of recollection he performs—smelling and tasting the vegetation on-site, and telling stories about them—are similar to those developed by Palestinians in Israel in return visits to their prestate village lands or neighborhood remains (Ben-Ze'ev 2004).[6] For Palestinians, the vegetation map of a destroyed village marks distinct regions, socioeconomic, and gender divisions of pre-1948 Palestinian society, which are negotiated from within, in a subtle way, in order to not interrupt the narration of a nationally shared experience (Ben-Ze'ev 2004).

Yet picking fruit and smelling herbs, as well as telling stories about them, is not foreign to the dominant tour format of Jewish Israeli culture. Botanical, historical, and cultural knowledge are also presented in that tour by a Jewish Israeli "interpreter-guide" (Katz 1985). This guide also picks up the fruit or herb, then raises it in the air for everyone in the group to see, and names it in Hebrew, in Latin, and often in Arabic, telling stories about its references in the Bible or Greek mythology and its uses in local traditions—such as Palestinian cooking or herbal medicine. The typical Israeli tour guide also practices some of the native ways during the tour of cooking coffee on a bonfire or tasting local herbs yet mostly relies on a textbook—plants or birds index, for example—to learn and teach about nature.[7]

These practices unite Jewish Israelis around a shared scientific knowledge of the land's flora, through the tour guide's legitimizing presentation of cultural and scientific knowledge of the native vegetation around the country, which also becomes part of the relevant scientific canon (Katz 1985). Thus similar practices that are part of these tours, specifically those that involve knowledge of the flora of the same territory, are related to two different indexes of knowing the land that combine embodied and sensory-based as well as scientific and textual knowledge.

However, while one index has been institutionalized in the Israeli state through its educational system, botanical gardens, natural parks, and museums, as well as tours, the other is still being carried by 1948-generation Palestinians through their physical sensations and in their memories. These memories are communicated through a sensory experience of taste and smell that is reactivated in every visit, yearned for between visits, and transmitted to the next generations through stories and traditional dishes (Ben-Ze'ev 2004).

Conducting the Palestinian-return visit practices in the midst of Zochrot's tour for an audience of Jewish Israelis disrupts its organized movement and speaking sessions to signal a memory of the pre-1948 village through the refugee's body and senses. It portrays knowledge and an attachment to the land beyond that which words can express in this bilingual and binational interaction of canonical practices of remembrance.

And so Jewish Israeli and Arab Palestinian national indexes of knowing the land, which underlie each group's dominant touring and visiting practices, constitute the meeting between the refugee and Jewish Israeli participants in Zochrot's tour. The latter were familiar with the legitimacy and authority of a Jewish Israeli tour guide who mediated the native flora and population to them through an exclusive ownership claim of the land. In the activist tour they encounter a native Palestinian who performs his knowledge and ownership of the land and communicates a long-silenced collective memory via dominant Palestinian memory practices of return visits.

While this meeting is highly significant to Jewish Israeli participants, it does not conclude in translation of the Palestinian index or transferring the refugee's memories to Jewish Israeli participants. Rather, this encounter brings more confusion than clarity to Jewish Israelis, who register other types of performance as effective in the activist tour.

Passive Witnessing and Visual Evidence

The organizers and many of the participants of Zochrot's activist tour express critical and cynical views in interviews about most commemorative practices that have been used to produce exclusively Zionist national history and identity. These include memorial ceremonies, museums, and monuments, but not the popular tour by foot. Perhaps this is due to their preliminary willingness to learn about Palestinian life in 1948, their deep fluency in the practice of touring, which is part of their Jewish Israeli habitus (Bourdieu 1991), the "nonideological" appearance of the tour in Israel since the 1980s, or the contemporary desire for authentic ties to the local past through material objects and sites (Nora 1996). Either way, Jewish Israeli participants who joined Zochrot report that the tour had successfully transformed their views on pre-1948 Palestinian life, and made them "see the whole country differently"—a recurrent statement made by many interviewees (for example interviews with Dalit, Nathan, and Ron in 2008; and with Batia, Frank, and Ariella in 2009).

Batia, for example, an activist in her thirties who grew up in a Kibbutz, was very critical of national ceremonies in general, even those organized by Palestinians in Israel to commemorate their displacement in 1948 that Zochrot participates in annually. However, she is very fond of touring: "It happens to me a lot that I walk in the tours of [Palestinian] villages and remember my tours of other sites before I *saw* the villages, a familiar memory," she said (interview 2009, my emphasis). "I did a lot of touring [before Zochrot]; my brother likes to tour. He is in the army and goes with his friends on many all-male tours [outside of the service], 'conquering the Gilaboon' [a stream that descents from the Golan to the Sea of Galilee] backward, and he sends many pictures in which one always sees a Palestinian house; the natural pool they swim in [is a Palestinian remnant]—and they are all strong guys; it's very powerful."

"'Conquering the Gilaboon' backward" is a phrase that refers back to one of the historical aims of the tour among Jewish settlers in Palestine and later Jewish Israelis: marking ownership of the land or "conquering the land with our feet" (Benvenisti 1998; Katriel 1996; Ben-David 1997; Lentin 2010).[8] During the activist tour Batia remembered her love of touring the country, when the physical movement of the body possibly calls to mind a difficult climb she took once or a swim in a natural pool she enjoyed before discovering that the Palestinian past is everywhere.[9] Her quote suggests that after this realization the tour is less enjoyable, and more of a reminder of past enjoyment that her younger brother still possesses. This is because back then the tour still contained the screen of Zionist ideology that blocked the whole picture from her eyes. After Zochrot lifted the screen, touring for her has not been the same.

Furthermore, unlike her brother and his friends, Batia was not sat-isfied anymore by the Israeli practice of touring as "conquering the land with our feet," when she watched it from the side, and sought a new way of touring, one that does not involve conquering. This reported transformation of perception shows Batia's alternating feelings of closeness and distance toward the institutionalized format of the tour. Specifically, the activist tour revealed that the exclusion of Palestinians and their lands is embedded in the dominant tour format.

A similar wish to tour differently was made by Dalit, an urban dweller in her early forties, with a postgraduate education in the social sciences. She found in the activist tour something that is missing in other familiar commemorative forms. "When I tour," she stated, "the passive position I take turns me into a witness, before deciding, I'm just a witness to what had happened. It doesn't go through the sublimation of a museum, aesthetization; it's like listening to a witness—which you do as well. To say: I heard, it exists, to acknowledge it. . . . [This is] unmediated information, unlike monuments that control [the infor-mation]. . . . Only pointing to it: you do not see it before, and you see it now" (interview 2008).

Unlike Batia's recollection of touring as an active and embodied activity, Dalit emphasized the passivity it enables—simply being there and listening, without deciding; Like Batia, her quote is also a call for a different way of touring, one that does not force participants to take a position, or engage or identify with an ideological stance as the institutionalized tours require. This position is better understood in the context of the local history of touring in Israel, during which the character of the tour by foot has shifted from an explicitly ideological tool for the creation of a Jewish national community to at least appear-ing as nonideological (Katriel 1996). In the contemporary context of the protracted Israeli Palestinian conflict, Jewish Israelis are constantly pushed by the state to engage with Zionist education and to identify as Zionists, as well as to take a Zionist stance in the political debate on the conflict. Zochrot, on the other hand, does not make any ef-fort during the tour to recruit new members and does not declare an affiliation to a political party or a specific political agenda. Instead it publicizes a learning tour that resembles ordinary weekend tours in Jewish Israeli culture and is conducted in Hebrew without any flags or other national symbols that are seen in demonstrations or protest marches. In this manner Zochrot's activist tour, which similarly to any other tour carries a specific agenda through its representation of the past, is presented as nonideological and less mediated while dealing with an extremely contested issue.[10]

Batia's and Dalit's approaches reflect the poles of a spectrum: on the one hand, those for whom, similarly to Batia, Zochrot's tour mostly echoes past touring, which stopped appealing to them after the revelation of its exclusive ideological construction; on the other hand, those who, like Dalit, still find in it a strong sense of authenticity and unmediated information when they strip it out of any locally prevalent ideological agenda.

The majority of interviewees expressed the latter approach. Many of them mentioned the ruins and the image of the refugee pointing to them more than any other component in the tour as to what was most transformative for them: "There is something strong emotionally in those places; to see these ruins, it does something [to you]," Ron, a staff member of an international human rights organization from Jerusalem told me as we were walking on a half-marked trail toward the end of one of Zochrot's tours (2008). In an interview I conducted in 2008 in Tel Aviv, Ariella noted, "The stones are an extremely strong testimony [*edut* in Hebrew, which also means proof or evidence]." Frank, a graphic designer from Jaffa, explained that pre-1948 Palestinian life was "already in the individual collective memory of everyone, [in the] subconscious, [and it takes] very little to deal with it [i.e., make it conscious]—just pointing a finger, you pass ruins, and it has an effect. People understand it no matter what [their] political identification [is]" (interview 2009).

Pointing to ruins, scattered stones, or pieces of tile is a way of documenting what usually has no other documentation when refugees visit their destroyed village site. Slyomovics described this gesture as "a tangible survivor from, a relic from the mundane would of vernacular architecture" (1998, 11). A recurring and haunting image in Palestinian villages' memorial books is a black-and-white photograph of a Palestinian man in the 1980s pointing to the ground or out of the picture to a place that, according to the captions, was his house, his ancestors' graves, or his mosque (Slyomovics 1998, 10).[11] The same gesture of the refugee in Zochrot's tour serves as intelligible evidence of dispossession and loss, connecting the material relic with the testimony. It also raises questions about the absence of other forms, especially written documentation that can account for the loss in legal and formal channels (Slyomovics 1998, 10).

Alongside their critical distance from other forms that may articulate Zionist national ideology and pedagogy, in Zochrot's tour, a Palestinian refugee pointing to ruins had reportedly made the greatest impression on those in the group. These Jewish Israeli participants viewed it as "unmediated information," which gave them credible visual evidence; to them that seemed less pedagogical and ideological than the original tour. Once again, and similarly to Vilnai's quote earlier in the chapter, participants attributed this strong impression to the tour's "direct" contact with the land. However, such an experience stands in opposition to the early use of the tour and other forms of national commemoration that continue today to push Jewish Israelis to take a Zionist stance regarding the conflict (even if it seems artificial to them). Ironically, it was only as a result of not being pushed to cultivate or engage with any sort of national memory that the Jewish Israeli participants who joined Zochrot's were able to experience the tour as a pedagogical tool. Only in this depoliticized manner they could learn about Palestinian ties and ownership of the land and most important, to *see* the land differently, that is, to see inclusively and not exclusively. This, in fact, may be the result of applying the current status of the dominant tour in Jewish Israeli culture: as long as it appears nonideological, it seems "unmediated," and thus its representation of the past tends to be successfully accepted.

Let us now return to the questions I raised earlier—will Jewish Israeli participants in Zochrot's activist tour give legitimacy and authority to Palestinian memories of prestate life as well as of displacement and dispossession; and how will the Palestinian refugee communicate a long-silenced memory to them? The organizers' aim of facilitating translation and transmission of Palestinian memories to Jewish Israeli participants was partially achieved, although this happened counterintuitively and not in accordance with original plans. Instead of translation, the meeting with the refugee generated confusion among Jewish Israeli participants when the familiar format of touring in Jewish Israeli culture was interrupted by the practices of a return visit in Palestinian culture. Jewish Israeli participants draw primarily on their relationship with the Jewish Israeli culture of touring, expressing distance and closeness to the familiar practice, and calling for a pacified and more inclusive practice of touring without conquering the land.

The various locations and histories through which the tour has traveled, the "force fields" (Stoler 2009, 14) and distinctions in which it was entangled originally, both reverberate and take new forms and meanings when reused by memory activists in the 2000s. The case of Zochrot's activist tour demonstrates the significance of culture as a mediator between activist groups and their publics, a relationship that has not been fully explored in the literature on social movements and peace activism. As the case of Zochrot's tour demonstrates, the appropriation and redeployment of popular cultural practices for the distribution of oppositional knowledge and claims to the dominant ones (Coy, Woehrle, and Maney 2008) may amplify or hinder the effectiveness of their dissemination among different publics. The mediation of activist agendas by cultural practices will be made even more visible in the following chapter, in which I juxtapose the appropriation of live testimony in Zochrot's tours with recorded and archived testimonies of 1948-generation Palestinian citizens in a Jaffa-based activist archive.

2

The Activist Archive of Survivor Testimonies

In one of the video segments in the online archive of digital testimonies of the Jaffan association Autobiography of a City, Abu Subhi is interviewed by his grandson, Sami Abu Shehadeh, a Jaffan historian and activist. The interview takes place in the grandfather's backyard, while the two are sitting on plastic chairs, facing each other. Abu Subhi states that young Palestinians from his grandson's generation make him furious when they ask if there were Arabs in Jaffa before 1948. Abu Shehadeh laughs and answers: "How should they know, if you and other people in your generation don't tell your stories? Schools don't teach this story." When Abu Subhi repeats his statement, his grandson elaborates his response: "How would they know if schools don't teach that and *people don't talk about it*, and no movies [exist], and even if there was [a film], they wouldn't show it at schools. This issue is very important! When someone hears and knows that this city was glorious and flourishing, that it had good, respectable people, that it had industry, agriculture—one's sense of belonging becomes stronger" (Sami Abu Shehadeh in Abu Subhi interview part 25, my emphasis).

Abu Subhi listens with a frozen impression until the "glorious and flourishing" part and then looks down and to the side and starts whistling a tune, inhaling from his cigarette as if not paying attention. He clearly does not like to hear his interviewer-grandson's speech, especially as the sentence "and people don't talk about it" is directed at him and his generation of Palestinians who have been living in Jaffa since before 1948. His grandson is placing the blame of continued silences and lack of knowledge among the younger generation on him and his peers. Moreover, he goes further to connect this lack of knowledge to his generation's "sense of belonging," critically reflecting his views on the work of memory and collective identity.

The rebuking of the interviewee's statement by the interviewer in the middle of a video-recorded testimony is a rare scene in digital testimony archives. The moral authority attributed to witnesses who lived through traumatic events, and their unique perspective, which is valued as an important addition to the historical and legal records when other sources are missing, grant the "survivor witness" respect and consent that bracket disagreement or critique (Moyn 2011; J. Feldman 2008; Allan 2007). Yet here the interviewer is critiquing, even blaming the witness for the silences in remembering Jaffa as it was in the prestate period.

Moreover, because it is believed to capture "raw memory" and "deeper reflections," the act of giving testimony is attempted to be recorded in the most undisruptive or the least mediated manner (Shenker 2010, 43). In trendsetting digital archives in the West, where testimonies are recorded on video, this is done by placing the testifier in domestic bourgeois settings, assuming that he or she would feel most at ease in his or her own home or a home-like environment, while also giving authenticity to his or her speech act. The testifier, who usually lived through traumatic historical events, is filmed in these archives against a soft background, and within a frame of medium or tight close-up that focuses viewers on the speaker's face alone or on his or her face and hands (Shenker 2010, 43). The interviewer is unseen and mostly unheard in the resulting product, instructed to let the testifier talk without frequently interrupting (Shenker 2010, 43).

Autobiography of a City combines dominant conventions of digital testimony production with the Arab tradition of storytelling in the testimonies its members recorded about Palestinian urban life before and during the 1948 war. Some of the Western conventions, such as the domestic setting, are adopted, while others, as the excerpt of Abu Subhi's testimony demonstrates, are not. This is due partly to Autobiography's engagement with the local tradition of storytelling that existed in prestate Palestinian localities. It involved a meeting of elders in public spaces in which they told stories in speech and in song while drinking coffee or tea, smoking, and eating (Allan 2007). This tradition is referred to in Autobiography's focus on stories (rather than monologues or chronological accounts) and the resemblance of the interview to a friendly conversation among two or more people. Unlike the local tradition of storytelling, the stories are recorded inside the testifiers' house, as city space is still designed to express primarily Jewish Israeli identity and history.[1] The public meeting of elders who share stories and recollections no longer exists within the fragmented Palestinian population of Jaffa. This meeting is recreated in the archive when various stories told by 1948-generation Palestinian residents are brought together. However, the combination of these two somewhat conflicting conventions of documentation and representation of the collective past, globally circulating and locally rooted in Arab pre-1948 communities (Allan 2007), results in an archive of testimonies that both adhere to some of these conventions of representation and subverts them.

This examination of an activist archive of testimonies continues our close reading of how Israeli memory activists in the 2000s have been appropriating and redeploying locally prevalent memory forms and practices to disseminate contested Palestinian memories with the aim of influencing public debate. Like the redeployment of the popular format of touring by Zochrot, refugee testimonies as a dominant cultural form have been utilized by memory activists in the 2000s to give visibility and audibility to the Palestinian memories of 1948. Like the tour, testimony is not simply a report of past events, but a performed speech act that targets a listener (Felman and Laub 1992, 5; Papailias 2005, 23), a constructed and narrated nonfiction storytelling about past events. Testimonies are utilized and made intelligible to various audiences around the world today when they take after a globally circulating formulation, which has been shaped with the great influence of Holocaust survivors' testimonies in war trials (MacLagan 2006), as well as earlier oral history projects in Europe and the United States (Perks and Thomson 2006).

After World War II, testimony became a pervasive and powerful tool that is produced today in the context of numerous historically specific injustices and human rights violations such as colonial violence, forced migration, genocides, and national confrontation (truth commissions for example; MacLagan 2006). In Israel, recorded and live Holocaust survivor testimonies are still to this day a central pedagogical tool for national education (Ben-Amos and Hoffman 2011; J. Feldman 2008). As a result, the globally circulating and local conventions of video-recorded survivor testimonies that were described earlier (domestic background, etc.) are highly familiar to Israeli citizens.

Exploring motivations behind Autobiography of a City's archive of digital testimonies exposes its character and social function in the context of the local and global conventions of survivor testimonies and archives. It examines the strategies and exposes the labor behind the group's collection and production of digital testimonies, comparing this practice to Zochrot's performance of live, on-site testimony. As our inquiry unfolds we see how this activist production undermined not only the hegemonic state deployment of testimonies for cultivating only Jewish Israeli identity, but also the practice of testimony itself. I find that this dual purpose creates a central tension in Autobiography's activist archive: on the one hand, the activists are committed to appropriating and redeploying survivor testimony for empowerment and solidarity among the marginalized Palestinian community in Jaffa; on the other hand, the activists are very critical of the use of testimony as a source of knowledge and access to the past, as well as a building block in the construction of an exclusive national history and collective memory. While partly fulfilling the goal of empowerment, this tension ultimately restricts the effect of the activist archive.

Appropriating the Survivor Testimony in Autobiography of a City's Archive

> Collective memory is the basic code of operation that we are working according to from birth to death; therefore the possibility to subvert it is very significant because it touches on the very foundation. This is *the* place in which to operate. . . . The [primary] exporting product of this state is stories; building a very strong story is at the heart of it. From here comes our work around narrative. (Eyal Danon, cofounder of Autobiography of a City, interview 2008; my emphasis)

Autobiography of a City is a memory-activism group that uses visual, creative, and technological knowledge for the production of high-quality video-recorded testimonies and a smartly accessible online archive. It was formed in 2000 through the Ayam Association for Recognition and Dialogue as an online archive of video-recorded testimonies. The testimonies are of residents of the Jewish Arab city of Jaffa who remember city life before and during the 1948 war, which dramatically transformed city space and its population. Behind the project are cofounders Sami Bukhari and Eyal Danon, a Palestinian citizen and a Jewish Israeli who are artists, curators, and youth educators. A group of Jewish Israeli and Arab Palestinian artists who live or work in the binational city of Jaffa acted as the board, and two Palestinian staff members operated the archive. As the opening quote indicates, their focus on collecting testimonies stems from the central role of memory and narratives in the Israeli state and society. Yet they are redeploying this commemorative form to raise awareness of memories and narratives that the state has excluded from the national collective memory, namely of the 1948-generation Palestinians in Jaffa.

In addition to their focus on narratives and stories, the group acknowledges the significant role of the visual medium in shaping collective memory (Danon interviews 2008, 2009). Most of the group's founders and members are artists who use video and still photography in their artistic work and have dealt with the topics of commemoration, storytelling, and national history writing in other artistic projects—in a highly critical manner. However, art is used not only because it is the founders' and members' vocation but as a field that enables the dissemination of oppositional knowledge (Coy, Woehrle, and Maney 2008) in the form of contested memories (Danon interview 2008). Group members view the autonomy that is attributed to the artwork and artistic field as a privilege that gives them room to act: it provides them the freedom needed to deal with difficult topics, enables them to get funding that would not be given to political projects on Palestinians in 1948, and allows the group to mobilize the produced knowledge outside the art worlds.[2] In Danon's words, art allows the group to "take advantage of artists' talent and skill of using the visual—the tool of propaganda—to deviate from the bourgeois artistic narrative and field and intervene in other fields, in the public space and on the web" (Danon interview 2008). This artistic talent can be used for creating "counterpropaganda" by portraying and telling stories that were silenced and excluded from the official history using similar means for their production and distribution as the ones used by the state.

In the group's online archive of digital testimonies, the artistic skills and narrative construction meet a systematic method for producing and archiving knowledge about the local past. The group has developed a method of classification that is based on keywords and an online search engine that offers the user multiple links between segments or stories from video-recorded testimonies. Danon stated that the stories collected are not filtered using any historical or other criteria, "because we are not an academic project, and because we are interested in ambiguity, contradiction, and multiplicity" (interview 2008). However, the group's semiprofessional archival work makes it harder to discredit their product and disqualify the knowledge they produce and archive. This activist production of knowledge of the past blurs the lines between professional historian and amateur: unlike amateur or "local" historians, who create private oral history archives in other cases (Papailias 2005), the Jaffan activists are well versed in scholarly theories, methodologies, and critical ideas about history writing and the politics of memory. Their social background and milieus are similar to those of many historians and intellectuals on the Israeli left, but they are not bound to the academic norms of knowledge production.

Through their production of knowledge on the silenced past of prestate and 1948 Jaffa, not only do Autobiography's members seek to shape the prevalent collective memory of Jaffa and of Israeli society through manipulation of narrative forms and visual conventions of representation. They also aim to recreate a Palestinian community in the city. Built by the well-educated among the younger generation of Palestinians and Jewish citizens in the city, this internal and local archive provides Palestinian residents in particular a space to tell their story that does not exist elsewhere. As the Palestinian population of Jaffa is highly fragmented, and meetings among its elders where storytelling traditionally took place no longer exist, Autobiography of a City brings the elders' stories that its members collected in separate interviews to meet again in the archive (Bukhari interviews 2008, 2009; Danon interviews 2008, 2009, 2011). The hope is that this would be followed by the creation of a shared identity, stronger social ties, and cooperation among the residents (Rabia interview 2009). In other words, the virtual archive was built to assist the recreation of a real-life community and serve, to some extent, as its blueprint.

The stories that Autobiography collects and archives are captured in ways that "glocalize" collective memory: bringing together transnational and national conventions of digital survivor testimony production and the locally rooted, Arab tradition of storytelling. Paying attention to the labor invested in the process of producing these digital testimonies of Jaffa's elders and placing them in the archive tells much about the globally circulating and domestic conventions of testimony production and their activist appropriation in Israel for the last decade or so. Similarly to other institutional and private archives, the multiplicity of factors involved in this production creates dynamic representations and forms of storytelling (Shenker 2010, 54).

Producing Testimonies

The testifier in Autobiography's archive is an older man or woman seated on a sofa in the interviewee's living room or on a plastic chair beneath the fruit trees in his or her backyard. The living room is a mix of bourgeois and Middle Eastern styles: an ornamented sofa and coffee table against the background of decorative objects on a chest—among them a Jewish menorah in one of the Palestinian houses. Coffee or tea and refreshments are sometimes visible on the table or being served during the interview (in one interview an older woman serves food and pleads with the interviewer to eat), a mark of Arab hospitality and of a genuine setting for a friendly visit. Some testifiers are dressed more casually and smoke cigarettes while leaning against the armrest of a couch; others, dressed up in button-down shirts and jackets, remain seated tall without moving too much. The appearance and demeanor of the testifier seems to depend on the familiarity of the testifier with the interviewer and his family. In various interview segments of elder Palestinians at least some degree of familiarity is apparent. This is evident, for example, when one testifier, Georgette, after naming some of the people she knew from 1948, tells her interviewer: "your parents know them for sure." Together with the interviewer she then tries to identify another woman, "the one who is married to the electrician . . . who has a cat" (part 8). The frame of the camera changes from one interview to another but is usually a medium close-up, from slightly above the head to the knees. It shows not only the face but also hands and upper body gestures and gives more room for nonverbal expression than the tight close-up of the conventional digital archive.

More than an interview between two people—only one of whom, the testifier, is visible in the conventional testimony segment in dominant digital archives—Autobiography's testimony segments often resemble an informal (or less formal) conversation that involves a number of people. First, while in the conventional testimony the interviewer is silent, to allow the answers of the testifiers to be edited into a monologue in the final product, here the interviewer's voice is heard throughout the process as elaborated in the following paragraph. Second, additional voices of unseen figures are heard answering the questions directed at the filmed interviewee, while others are seen crossing the room behind the interviewees' backs. This indicates that the setting is familiar and even social rather than the conventional intimate setting, occupied by a single testifier, an interviewer, and a video-recording crew. An audience of relatives, friends, and neighbors is present in the Jaffan interviews, and the interviewer is a familiar person that the interviewees know through family or social ties. Another difference from the conventional survivor testimony interview is that Autobiography does not isolate the testifier from his or her surroundings: during interviews in backyards, noises are heard coming from street traffic, hip hop music from a passing car; dogs barking and other voices are heard in the background, sometimes turning the interviewee's head in their direction (for example, in the interview with Mahmud Bukhari).

Similarly to the conventional testimony recording, the interviewers, usually Autobiography's Palestinian cofounder Bukhari accompanied by Danon, go mostly unseen (for example in segments from the interview with Abu Subhi). Yet they are often heard, not only asking questions but also commenting, repeating the testifier's sentences for emphasis, joking, and noting. Bukhari is a local (as is Abu Shehadeh), as the friendly attitude of some of the interviewees toward him and his casual participation in the conversation demonstrate.

His and other interviewers' questions often seem to be guiding the testifier to affirm a certain collective perception of the past that emphasizes the agency of Palestinian residents who left the city or stayed in it after 1948. However, the testifier does not always comply right away. "Were there many casualties?" "Were there a lot of bombs in Jaffa?" the interviewer tries to refocus Abu Eli on his story about the Israeli paramilitary groups' bomb attacks in Jaffa in 1947–1948. The story was interrupted by Abu Eli's wife, Georgette, who, seated on the other side of the living room, recalled a story about a bomb hidden inside a milk jug. As the camera moved from Abu Eli to capture Georgette, her story was followed by another story about a well-educated Palestinian woman who married a British soldier and moved to Britain. "Yes, a lot of bombs exploded," answers Abu Eli. "That was the reason behind people's fear at that time?" the interviewer tries to guide Abu Eli to the desired answer. "Yes, but that happened before the British withdrawal"—while the mass flight of Palestinians from Jaffa was when the British had left in April 1948. "[But] people saw that there were bombs?" the interviewer insists. "Yes," both Abu Eli and Georgette agree, Abu Eli also nodding his head strongly. A similar attempt to guide the testifiers to give agency to the Palestinians who left Jaffa— the fear that the Israeli bombing had spread to the Palestinian population, encouraging them to flee—is evident in other interviews, for example, with Mahmud Bukhary, Sami Bukhari's father (part 6).

Sometimes the testifier lets him or herself be guided, as in a segment of the interview with Georgette and Abu Eli (segment from 6 August 2007). Her personal story of how, after being orphaned from her mother in 1947, she was told by her ill father to go on a boat to Greece with her sister in 1948 ("my sister was fourteen and I was eleven, where would we go alone?") is interrupted in the middle by the interviewer's question that points to the collective historical context of that moment: "were there a lot of people leaving via the port?" She accepts the guidance and answers, "yes, I saw/witnessed that"—taking on the role assigned by the interviewer as a witness for atrocities Palestinians experienced in 1948—"I saw two or three terrifying scenes," she said and then described scenes in which she was not hurt but witnessed other Palestinians getting hurt. In her story she connects the circulation of rumors of the Deir Yassin massacre near Jerusalem, one of the major atrocities inflicted on Palestinians in the 1948 war, to the fear that guided Palestinian Jaffans' actions during that time.

Other times the interviewee does not comply, as seen in another segment of Georgette's testimony, where she tells a different story about the same episode. She is asked: "Do you remember Um Eli [her mother-in-law] during the war? The bad things that happened to you or your relatives and neighbors during the war, things that you saw or heard about?" Georgette, looking up, thinking, starts to answer slowly: "We didn't go out of the house much. I saw the situation in Jaffa when we left Malakan [her neighborhood before 1948]. . . . The quarter was empty, all the shops were damaged. You can't even see a cat in the street [smiling]. We came to the monastery and stayed there until the Jews entered the place." The story continues to describe how Georgette and her sister immediately recognized among "the Jews" a familiar person who took care of them: an Israeli soldier ("the first face we saw") who was the brother of Georgette's sister's sewing teacher. The soldier was one out of a group of Jewish soldiers who entered the monastery, but he nonetheless assured the sisters that they were safe with him. Palestinian families and community leaders were an additional source of comfort as they brought them food and looked after them (Georgette, part 8).

Sometimes remembering the past is collective and collaborative, and the interviewer takes an active part in the effort of the testifier to

recall the names of people and places referred to in the story. As someone who grew up in this community the interviewer is expected to
know these people and places, as the following segment demonstrates:

> Georgette: There was another Greek woman with us, Helena.
> Abu Eli, not seen in the frame: Was she working for the consul?
> Georgette: No, Helena, Helena, the wife of the electrician, living
> near" (pointing her arm in the direction)
> Abu Eli: Abu-Abdullah El-Faran . . .
> Georgette and the interviewer: Oh, yes.
> Georgette: Across from his house. The one with the cat.
> Interviewer: Oh, yeah, the neighbor of Abu Shehadeh.
> (Georgette is nodding and smiling) (Georgette interview, part 8)

Such collaborations are not part of the prevalent formulation of
survivor testimony in prominent archives in Israel and the West or are
at least not seen in the final product, because the transmission of "raw
memory" from survivor to an audience is supposed to be unassisted as
well as include all relevant details.

Moving from formulation to content, the narrative of many testimonies in the Autobiography of a City archive is of the everyday life
and urban landscape before 1948, including leisure (cinema and res-
taurants they could not afford in their youth, dancing, and even places
where prostitution took place), holidays and family events (the Rama-
dan evening feasts, weddings), food and its preparation ("it was fresher
than today, in generous amounts, and tasted better," Abu George and
his wife recall, part 3), how housework was conducted (cooking, laun-
dry), description of the market, money, trade, and the arts and crafts-
manship. Often these are presented as a nostalgic portrayal of a peaceful and simple (even if not wealthy) life in a multicultural atmosphere
of good relations between Jewish, Muslim, and Christian neighbors
before 1948.

According to this narrative, the vibrant and multicultural city life
was interrupted by Jewish aggression and military actions in 1947 and
1948. Mass fear among the unprepared urban population led to subsequent flight from the port of Jaffa mainly to Gaza and Lebanon.
However, the nostalgic lens of prewar life is not always put aside when
describing war events. This is evident in Georgette's story mentioned
above, for example. When she is asked if she saw or heard any "bad

things" that happened to her relatives and neighbors in the 1948 war, she tells a story about continuous solidarity with a Jewish soldier and with Palestinian neighbors helping each other with food and shelter (Georgette interview, part 8).

The conventional framing of survivor testimony usually conceals the work and design that goes into the production of digital testimony and presents itself as providing direct access to the survivor's experience. In the archive of Autobiography of a City, however, the voice and comments of the interviewer, the larger frame of the camera, and the interruptions in the background make the process of producing testimonies more transparent to the archive user.

This is crucially important because testimony's production practices, chosen in order to accommodate specific purposes and audiences, shape the testimony itself. These practices portray expectations from a testifier and define who is a good witness. These expectations are infused into the testimony, as Ness Godin, a Holocaust survivor and a tour guide at the American Holocaust Museum in Washington, DC, demonstrates: "if I get too emotional I cannot bring the message . . . you know, this [is] what people have to think about" (quoted in Shenker 2010, 46). Similar expectations are embedded in human rights archives of digital testimony and the testimonial form they produce, where sad and sentimental stories together with the presentation of survivors' bodies are expected to elicit empathy from the audience (Rorty 1993, 122; MacLagan 2006).

Indeed, there are contradictory expectations that the testimony would be at once dramatic and memorable and move the listeners, and yet would also be communicated with emotional restraint; that it would encapsulate "the force of events not fully understood" (Papailias 2005, 23) in a linear story with a clear and coherent message (Shenker 2010). A "good witness" knows how to tell the story in a way that fits the institution's goals and produces a product that can be used for pedagogical purposes (Shenker 2010). A "good" testimony should usually include the visceral surplus of atrocious memory and evoke emotions that enhance the authority of the story, and the pathos of the archive, as long as it can be contained in a coherent rational narrative told in chronological order and with restraint (Shenker 2010).

Autobiography's testifiers, however, tell most of their stories without an explicit visceral expression of traumatic loss, even when the stories are dramatic and make atrocities vivid, without catharsis or redemption. There is anger and nostalgia more than melancholia, and various moments of smiling and laughter but no crying. There is no concern that anything or anyone would lose control or stop the interview. As a participant in a conversation more than an investigator, the interviewer also expresses some emotion in response to the stories, for example by clicking his tongue as an expression of empathy with suffering (Abu Eli interview, for example). Some interviewees tell their story in a more controlled and collected manner than others (for example, Bukhari, part 6)—which a Palestinian memory activist called "like a history book" (Lina interview 2009). Others tell it like a traditional tale—especially with regards to details of the mundane procedures of pre-1948 housework and daily routines, which they animate with their upper body and hands, and describe as magical moments of unity and bliss (Georgette, part 3; Abu Subhi on coins, part 31).

The Moral Authority of the Testimony: Live and Recorded

> The witness is a kind of food processor . . . the witness puts the kid in touch with the reality, that it really happened. . . . Their job is to explain simple things . . . not historical analysis. This makes it easier for the child to understand that these are not just things written by a writer. (Yosi Levi, organizer of Israeli youth journeys to Poland, quoted in J. Feldman 2008, 67)

Like the tour, the survivor testimony is considered a symbolic vehicle more than a source of new historical information (J. Feldman 2008, 67; Moyn 2011). As the quote suggests, the testimony is a living monument to a scholarly historical record that embodies both the victims' lived experience and the group's political identity (Wiztum, cited in J. Feldman 2008, 67; Allan 2007). Israeli youth trips to Poland, a popular practice that mounted in the 2000s, are accompanied by a Holocaust survivor that gives testimony in situ. The survivor-witness that accompanies the group is speaking *for* the dead, not *of* them, an authentic incarnation of the facts (J. Feldman 2008, 67). Despite the great difference in context and past experience, the survivor's authority in on-site testimony on youth trips to Poland as well as in Zochrot's activist tours of pre-1948 Palestinian villages is similarly based on his or her physical presence, hence the "story cannot be divorced from the person of the storytelling" (J. Feldman 2008, 67). The physical presence of the testifier as a source of authenticity and authority, however, becomes less and less available as members of the survivors' generation become fewer. Digital archives try to maintain this presence with audio-visual documentation.

This authority of the in situ "I/eyewitness"—the storyteller who is also an incarnation of the events (J. Feldman 2008, 67–68)—is maintained in the testimonial form of digital archives around the world through the requirement of telling only events the testifier himself or herself experienced or witnessed. Personal stories rather than political statements or historical contexts are supposed to maintain the "uniqueness of the performance of a story which is constituted by the fact that, like the oath, it cannot be carried out by anyone else" (Felman and Laub 1992, 206).

Although testifiers are guided implicitly by the message sought by the archiving institution, they might act differently than expected both in the recording studio and on-site, being guided by the resolves and audiences of the testimony (Shenker 2010) and the assignment of "supreme moral authority" (J. Feldman 2008, 69). Acting differently can mean, for example, giving a moral or political lesson beyond the personal story, exceeding the time allotted for the testimony recorded, or not addressing the requested topics and periods (J. Feldman 2008, 69; Shenker 2010). Such segments would be more easily edited out in digital media than when performed live (J. Feldman 2008, 69; Shenker 2010). Yet "editing" exists on-site as well. For example, if there are conflicts or disagreements between the guide and witness on a Poland youth trip, they would never be settled in public but only behind closed doors; the witness's authority is not to be undermined in front of the audience (J. Feldman 2008, 69). This is also evident in Zochrot's tours.

The powerful embodied experience of performing testimony in situ, which is considered to be an extremely effective and authoritative way of transmitting the memory of the survivor on the trip to Poland (J. Feldman 2008), is lost in the recording studio. However, the testifiers' firsthand experience of the situation is expected to carry with it to the recording the moral weight of what Linell and Rommetveit have called "epistemic responsibility" (1998, 466). "Epistemic responsibility" is the moral obligation to share unique knowledge of suffering, and to make others secondhand witnesses to it (Katriel 2009, 156).

In the activist tour, Zochrot passes on the moral duty to remember Palestinian suffering and loss in 1948 from the I/eyewitness, the Palestinian refugee who gives testimony during the tour, to a Jewish Israeli audience. This audience, decedents of the perpetrators in the Palestinian testimony, is supposed to remove its national historical narrative and take the universalistic position of a moral witness for humanity (although this often takes place prior to participation in the tour). The self-designated culpability in Zochrot's tours uses pre-1948-generation Palestinian testimonies in situ as a powerful form of memory production and transmission for the difficult task of turning "citizens who do not know (and may not wish to know) into bystanders who must make moral choices" (Katriel 2009, 156; see also the discussion on the Nakba as a "public secret" in Chapter 4).

In the online archive of digital testimonies of Autobiography of a City, the moral duty to share one's experience of suffering is internal to the Palestinian community first, as the monologue of the interviewer Abu Shehadeh at the beginning of the chapter highlights. A local stance rather than a universalistic one may be sufficient for the archive user to transcend the dominant Jewish Israeli national narrative and become a secondhand witness to the events of 1948 in Jaffa. A communal conversation can take place through the mediation of the archive, as well as a conversation on the archival materials. Both in the activist tour and in the activist archive, the redeployment of survivor testimony is expected to "create a space for a broad-ranging intergenerational dialogue at the familial and societal level" (Katriel 2009, 165). Such dialogue, however, may be hindered by the activists' dual engagement. Their redeployment of the authoritative status of the witness and dominant norms of representation seek to undermine not only the exclusive deployment of Holocaust survivor testimonies by the state to cultivate only Jewish Israeli identity, but also the form of testimony and the tradition of storytelling themselves, as the next section elaborates.

(De)constructing the Activist Archive

I have already mentioned some of the group's central aims, primarily giving voice and authority to 1948-generation Palestinian residents of Jaffa, transmitting their memories to the next generations, and reuniting a fragmented community. However, in their creation of an activist archive in Jaffa, Autobiography's members set out to achieve another goal that has not been discussed thus far. This goal is disseminating their own critical message regarding the selective and exclusive construction of historical knowledge through popular commemorative forms and conventions of representation, in the nation-state as well as outside state channels. This message is conveyed through revealing the mediation and manipulation embedded in the form and practice of the testimony, in particular in the context of its appropriation and institutionalization in Israel. And so, unlike the other archives of testimonies, this activist counterarchive has a dual commitment: to the hegemonic practice of testimony that gives authority to the witness, and to a radical manipulation of it.

The inclusion of both of these elements in the Jaffa project allows the group to speak to several audiences at once: funders (primarily municipal and private art funds); artists, the artistic community, and its audiences; interviewees who take part in the project and their familial and social circles; and other Jaffa residents; as well as students, scholars, and educators who seek the knowledge stored in the archive. Each of these audiences "has to be influenced differently," Danon asserts (interview 2008).

Maintaining a variety of voices, interpretations of the past, stories, forms of storytelling, and interests is one of the key ways Autobiography accommodated the dual standing and addresses different audiences. Danon's abovementioned statement that the group does not filter the stories it collects from interviewees because it is interested in "ambiguity, contradiction, and multiplicity" (interview 2008) testifies to its commitment to a variety of voices and personal perceptions of the shared past rather than giving preference to a single coherent narrative.

Such diversity exists even in the most controlled process of producing unified digital testimonies in dominant archives but has a central role in Autobiography's activist archive. As mentioned, the production of survivors' testimonies in digital archives in the West is shaped by the interaction of institutional and individual practices, and framed by a variety of different goals and preferences, which are often obscured in the outcome (Shenker 2010). Despite attempts to control and restrict the outcome, this multiplicity of interests and acts creates constantly evolving representations and forms of storytelling, rather than "fixed capsules of memories" preserved for the next generations (Shenker 2010, 54). The activist archive in Jaffa is less unified and controlled than other archives that bracket both the context and the labor invested in the production of survivor testimonies. This presumably increases the degree of dynamic representations and relations between different ways of making a silenced past audible and visible in this archive in comparison to the dominant archives.

However, the most profound manifestation of a variety is apparent in Autobiography's archival system. This system of classifying, storing, and retrieving information is designed to produces multiple narratives of the local past. The search capability of the archive consists of movements between thematic keywords that link excerpts from different testimonies. "The keywords are the foundation stones of the archive; each of them is a junction for the meeting of different filmed stories" Danon explained (interview 2011). The keywords are offered to the user at the beginning of his or her search as an animated stream from which to choose, and they also pop up and change according to the specific topics raised by the testifier during the screening of each filmed story-size segment. In addition to the thematic keywords that classify testimony segments and guide the search through them—for example, "1948"; "the Ajami Neighborhood"; "education"; "property"; "father"; "memory"—each segment is also classified according to its relevance to the following categories: time, either pre-1948, during 1948, or after 1948; space, either in or outside Jaffa; genre, whether in an interview, in art, or in documentary (most segments are interviews); name of author-producer (usually Bukhari and Danon or "the Jaffa Group"); and date of production. Each interview is indexed by two Palestinian staff members, young Jaffan women who also lived in Western Europe during their academic studies. The indexing identifies every thematic word expressed in each interview. In the future, the founders hope, as more and more words will link stories together, this archive will be broader and offer more possible search routes, as well as a greater variety of different stories on the same event (Danon interview 2011).

Each search in the archive connects different story-size segments into one narrative on the past, which can be saved in the archive or deleted. The user can therefore create different narrations of places and events from a chain of stories of Jaffa residents, as well as view other users' saved searches—different chains of stories linked through keywords—in the archive. This search mechanism manifests the variety of possible constellations of memories of Jaffa in 1948 that users may extract from this archive. Each search indicates not only what residents remember taking place before and during 1948, but also the endless ways of remembering the past through stories, ultimately exposing the arbitrariness of archival knowledge and undermining its masked, sheltering authority (Derrida 1998).

The search mechanism of this activist archive also enables some interaction between users who observe each other's saved searches, as well as between the user and the testifiers through the particular story segments the user accesses in the archive. Such interaction is always extremely important against the reification of the survivor by the archiving institution, and even more so in a community-based project of empowerment and acknowledgment. Yet it is one of the things that are explicitly and implicitly constructed and rechanneled in the recording and transmission of the memory when it is transferred from the interview to the archive: the interaction diminishes in the separation of giving testimony and listening. In Autobiography's online archive, however, it potentially reappears when the testimonies are placed together, as the archive is designed for nonlinear reading. A listener searches stories and the testifiers regain an audience. It is, nonetheless, a reconstructed interaction between different bits of testimony (like the interaction of files in the archive that I. Feldman 2008 examines), which is limited to what the users encounter in the search.

Moreover, the interaction in archives is also based on a search that is inward looking, to knowledge housed as a model *for* reality, rather than outward looking, for a representation *of* the past (Halpern 2005). Similarly to other archives, the index determines the conditions under which the interaction between stories will take place, allowing or prohibiting connections between them. This gives the Palestinian members of the group who are in charge of the indexing work in Autobiography's archive a crucial role in the production of knowledge on the local past and on recreating the interaction between storyteller and listeners. This is another form of empowerment and speaking not on behalf of Palestinians but by and for Palestinians (whose memories construct a shared memory of the city) that Autobiography's archive seeks to bestow on Jaffa residents.[3]

The plurality of stories in the archive, production factors, and audiences, however, also suggests the possibility, even the likelihood, of contradictory outcomes. Contradictions exist first, in this archival body of knowledge about the past, as different testifiers tell different stories on the same event or place. A single testifier may also change his or her tone or version during an interview, as was demonstrated earlier. Second, a foundational contradiction stems from the dual commitment of the group to redeploy a dominant institutionalized form of collective memory while also critically reflecting on its inherent and institutionalized reproduction of differentiation and exclusion in Israel. The presentation of critical self-reflection on national and transnational forms of history writing requires a second layer of distancing and displacement of the testifier's memory in the archive. If the testifier gains authority and legitimacy in the first layer of testimony production, as the carrier of a unique firsthand experience that should be heard in public, what is his or her role in the second layer, in which a meta-level "lesson" about the form of testimony is transmitted to the archive user?

In the group's 2011–2012 blog, this second and critical layer is introduced to the archive user explicitly, using the metaphor of a virtual tour of the city: "In our main product, *www.jaffaproject.org*, we offer a unique free virtual tour, in different layers of information told by different people. The [idea] is *to [emphasize] the rule of the receiver in any [storytelling]* by providing the visitor the position of *an active participant in the [editing] of the narrative* he or she [is] now viewing."[4] The emphasis here is not on the testifier but on the receiver, the archive user who is authorized or at least gains access to view and edit the narrative of the story-size segments he or she chooses to watch. Bringing forth the role of the receiver of *any storytelling*, as the quote states, raises the user to the meta level of an archivist who appropriates the form and selects the content. It turns the user's attention from the unique lived experience of the testifier to the randomness of encountering and composing a narrative of the past from testimony segments.

Moreover, the unique experience of the past is now attributed to the user of the archive, whose choices of random video segments compose a different narrative in each search, creating a unique virtual tour of the city:

> Given the structure of the virtual space, the surfing tourist is provided by floating tags that represent the terminology used by the people telling the story of the city. clicking on a term takes you to a *random* video, photo, or text that this term is used at, and while receiving the information the website offers you other tags used in the same piece you are viewing, allowing you free choice to tour how much as you like and wherever you like, thus allowing you to take an active rule and *explore what kind of story your choices reveal*. Each visit, thus, becomes a *unique particular virtual tour*. You are invited to tour the site [in] different times and *think about the experience of hearing* [a] *different story each time about the same place*. (Autobiography's blog, my emphasis)

The invitation to "think about the experience of hearing [a] different story each time about the same place" suggests that there is more than meets the eye in this archival search: the discovery that a single version of the past does not exist, but rather different stories and narratives are discovered in each visit, should raise further questions among users about what access to the past we can really gain. This description elaborates another self-proclaimed statement in Autobiography's blog that it explores "the connection between narrating, editing and medium," which announces its preoccupation not only with narratives of the past but also with forms of mediating this past through editing and medium: a meta-level reflection on the testimonial formulation and archival medium.

Multiplicity and diversity in this activist archive are therefore both a tool of empowerment and inclusion and a vehicle of criticizing the possibility of accessing a blocked and traumatic past through the dominant formulation of testimony. As a tool of empowerment and inclusion, it strives not to advance a single version of the past while excluding others, as the state did. Rather, the group records various experiences and memories, especially by those whose voices were silenced in the dominant collective memory and concerning everyday life, which is not considered historically significant in the national historical record. Coining these versions "stories" and combining the dominant testimonial formulation with the traditionally Arab form of storytelling attributes to this effort the capturing of local voices through communal traditions on the one hand. On the other hand, however, this multiplicity of stories is placed in the archive in a manner that takes away from the authority of these local past experiences as an authoritative historical account outside the house and beyond the family circle. When placed in the archive, each story is retrieved almost randomly to serve as a possible building block of any number of narratives on the past, which are part of an endless variety. The authority (in terms of knowledge and moral authority) of the testifier in the interview is replaced by a user's authorization to "edit" and experience the archiving mechanism and learn a lesson about the arbitrariness of accessing and recalling the past through testimonies. It renders each voice and story in the archive less authoritatively and uniquely revealing, ultimately stressing the fictional and arbitrary nature of testimony as a means for constructing a collective memory.

Conclusion

The present moment is an interesting time to examine the production of digital testimonies and the labor invested in private archives of testimonies. Citizens increasingly "expect documentary collections to provide them with a touchstone for their identity, a sense of place, and a repository for cultural memory" (Papailias 2005, 21; also in accord with Nora's argument in Chapter 1). This allows nonhistorians to attempt to compensate for silences in the national archive by filling in its gaps through producing new documents, such as oral history in the Israeli case study, or designating new categories of artifacts as historical documents (ruins in Zochrot's tours, for example; Papailias 2005; Berkhofer 2008). However, the expansion of archives to include the experience of groups that have been excluded from it does not necessarily escape the risk of supporting the positivist vision of "archival totalization" and reifying these groups' identities (Papailias 2005, 21). Here the challenge of the Israeli memory-activist endeavor is raised again: How can one make visible and audible a silenced group through an authoritative and legitimate national and transnational formulation (survivor testimony) that was used to exclude the silenced group in the first place? How might an activist testimony archive avoid reproducing this problematic attribute again?

The local production of testimonies by and for the community in Jaffa, together with the multiple factors (purposes, practices, and audiences) that come into play in the production of testimonies in the digital online archive of Autobiography, managed to escape some of the problems scholars have had with the transnational construction of survivor testimonies and "archives of suffering" (Allan 2007). Unlike paradigmatic digital archives, less of the labor put into the production of testimonies in this activist archive is concealed in the outcome. This is the result of two factors: (1) the presence of the interviewer as taking part in a conversation between neighbors replaces a formal interview by an external expert-investigator and an elaborate filming crew; (2) the archival structuring of knowledge about Palestinians in Jaffa before and during 1948 is made evident in the search of testimonies in the online archive. While the form of survivor testimony is used to give authority and legitimacy to the testifiers' unique experience, the critical reflection in the archive on the selectivity and exclusion embedded in the construction of historical knowledge through testimony puts those in question in order to deliver a critical message about the arbitrariness of memory narratives.

These memory activists have a dual commitment: to use a familiar and dominant form in order to document and legitimize silenced memories of a marginalized community on the one hand, and to critically reflect on this form's inherent power of exclusion and differentiation between groups on the other hand. In this process, the testifiers are given voice and authority when interviewed and de-authorized when their testimonies are placed in an archive that reveals the arbitrariness of memory narratives, through an additional degree of distancing and displacement from their lived memory as recorded in the interview.

An understanding of how memory activists in Israel have been re-deploying the practices of testimony here and of the tour in the previous chapter in relation to their transnational and local history to produce truth on Palestinians in 1948 cannot be completed without pointing to the differences of this production between Jewish and Palestinian citizens. The next chapter describes the structural and cultural context against which memory activism is conducted within Palestinian society. It examines how internal and external motivations, constraints, and distinctions shape the collective memory and political claims that they entail. This exploration reveals the marks of silencing and exclusion that the history of Palestinian citizens in Israel carries and how it deeply affects their efforts to make it visible and audible in the last decade in particular.

3

Similar Practices, Higher Stakes

Palestinian Memory Activism in Israel

The experience of Palestinian memory activists in Israel is different from that of Jewish Israelis, whose collective memory is dominant and institutionalized in Israel. As high as the costs and risks of exclusion from Israeli society are for Jewish Israeli memory activists who remember Palestinian suffering, they are even higher for Palestinian citizens, who are already excluded and are therefore more exposed to formal and informal state sanctions.[1] Their efforts are perceived as a memory war against the state's silencing and denial.

Yet the struggle in Israel between dominant Jewish Israeli and marginalized Arab Palestinian collective memories is only one front of the memory war over the representation of the Palestinian experience of 1948 in public discussion of the conflict and its possible resolution. On another front, an inner battle takes place between Palestinian currents in Israel that focuses on who will shape the collective memory and unique identity of Palestinian citizens. I examine Palestinian memory activism in light of these stakes and motivations, focusing on how activists position their production and transmission of Nakba memories inside and outside Palestinian society in Israel.

The story of Baladna, an all-Palestinian youth association in Israel, is a striking example of a case in which Zionist commemorative practices have been adapted for Palestinian use. Baladna ("our homeland" in Arabic) was established in 1999 by Nadim Nashef, a student organizer and former director of education-oriented NGOs and of the youth section of the Balad party. The aim of the group, which officially registered in 2001, is to educate and empower Arab Palestinian youth in Israel (both Christian and Muslim) in order to prepare them to be leaders in their communities. As part of Baladna's young leadership program, participants take tours of destroyed Palestinian villages, where they listen to a Palestinian refugee's testimony on the local life before and during 1948. Learning their own history is seen by the organizers as critical for developing and strengthening their sense of a Palestinian communal identity, and the program is geared to enhance their solidarity and political participation. Since the early 2000s the group has organized yearlong after-school youth programs in different locations in Israel, starting with the Palestinian urban centers of Haifa and Nazareth, and the more peripheral towns of Rahat (in the Negev) and Kfar Kara (in the Triangle area, east of the Sharon region). They also hold meetings with Palestinian youth groups in Jordan and the West Bank and send representatives to attend youth NGO conventions abroad.

The tour and testimony Baladna facilitates for Palestinian youth in Israel illuminate how, for those on the marginalized side of the conflict, the use of hegemonic cultural practices (tours and testimonies) carries different meanings, goals, and stakes than Jewish Israeli memory activism. Some of the aspects of this Palestinian utilization of dominant cultural forms can point beyond state limitations, while others are bound to the existing order.

The differences between Jewish Israeli and Arab Palestinian memory activists are also reflected in the special challenge that the research posed for me as a Jewish Israeli participant-observer of an all-Palestinian group in Israel that intends to engage in a dialogue on 1948 mostly among themselves (i.e., Palestinian society in Israel). This has relegated me to observer rather than participant-observer and produced an ethnography that is based primarily on the activists' description of their work through a three-generation framework (detailed later on) and the ways in which they position themselves and their memory work in relation to both Palestinian and Jewish Israeli formal politics and political culture in Israel. I point to signs that suggest that other things could be happening outside of my peripheral vision, namely a strategic distinction from state institutes that declares memory activism of the Nakba to be a "nonpolitical" activity.

More specifically, within the highly political context of the two-front memory war on the events of 1948, I examine all-Palestinian memory activism in Israel as a cultural liberation effort that is part of a general claim for cultural autonomy. As with the strong grip of Zionism in commemoration and documentation of the past in Israel, where power and culture are intimately connected, liberation involves disconnecting the two, at least symbolically, as Goldfarb argues (2011, 58). One attempt to disconnect culture from power is one-sided memory work that does not include Jewish Israelis. Another effort is manifested in an assertion that their memory work is apolitical. This assertion, based on a threefold definition of "the political," distinguishes Palestinian activists' work both from politically affiliated Palestinian parties in Israel and from state institutions.

A third aspect of the disconnection of culture and power is manifested in Palestinian citizens' silences about the past and their tendencies toward disbelief of both Jewish and Arab Palestinian scientific-historical knowledge produced by formal institutions and national ideology. This requires a careful knowledge production of "reliable information" (Kabha interview 2009) that could serve as a basis for building trust and increasing community-based participation and is another way in which memory activists distinguish their work from formal politics and state education.

A Two-Front Memory War

> A computer program that erases memory hasn't yet been
> invented. . . . This is why [Palestinians in Israel] got
> engaged with memory, because it is the only tool that is
> open for [them to] use. (Tamer, Palestinian activist with
> Autobiography of a City, interview 2009)

One of the major battlefields of the memory war between Palestinian citizens and the state is the school curriculum of Palestinian and Jewish schoolchildren in Israel. In the 1990s, history curricula of Jewish Israeli schools included more critical and inclusive textbooks, citing "new historian" Benny Morris and the Palestinian perspective of the 1948 war (2000, 2002; for Palestinian curriculum see Al-Haj 2002). Yet in the 2000s the exclusion of Palestinians from the national history curriculum, both for Jewish and Palestinian schoolchildren, prevailed.[2]

A booklet explaining key terms in Palestinian history from 1948 onward, titled *Belonging and Identity*, was distributed among Palestinian schoolchildren in Israel in 2005 as a response to a state educational program called "100 Terms in Jewish Heritage, Zionism and Democracy" for Jewish, Arab, and Druze schools.[3] The booklet was created by Palestinian scholars led by Asad Ghanem, then head of the Political Science Department at Haifa University and head of the Ibn Khaldun Association, which produced the booklet together with the Center against Racism. It was endorsed by the monitoring committee for Arab education and by heads of Arab municipalities. According to Ghanem, "not only did much of the curriculum" initiated by then minister of education Limor Livnat (of the center-right Likud party) "have no relevance to Arab schoolchildren, but it was designed to exclude their history and narrative. Our booklet is trying to rectify that. . . . They cannot know who they really are and where they live unless they are offered this kind of information."[4] The state program was canceled in 2007 by the next minister of education Yael (Yuli) Tamir, from the center-left Labor party.

Yet even with the cancellation of the program, contested topics in the national history of the state were studied solely from a Zionist perspective in Jewish Israeli schools for the rest of the decade. In 2009, Minister of Education Gideon Sa'ar (Likud) excluded the Palestinian experience of the 1948 war from the study of Palestinian schools in Israel as well.[5] The minister banned a dual-narrative history textbook coauthored by Jewish Israeli and Arab Palestinian teachers and historians and ordered a rewriting of the main civic studies textbook to be less critical of Israel.[6] The battle between academics and curriculum advisers (both Jewish Israeli and Arab Palestinian) and the Ministry of Education was inflamed in 2010 by the right-wing NGOs the Center for Zionist Strategy and Im Tirtzu (If You Will It, in Hebrew), which published reports accusing university professors and the authors of high school textbooks in history and civics of anti-Zionist bias.[7] On the side of left NGOs, Jewish Israeli high school teachers who use Zochrot's educational kit were interviewed in *Ha'aretz*. They nonetheless stated their *pro*-Zionist approach as the reason behind the inclusion of Palestinian history in their classes.[8]

This open and public memory war between Palestinians and the State of Israel on the representation of the 1948 war in official channels—in which not only the fight over the curriculum but also "many small things eroded the [Zionist] narrative," as some activists believe (for example, Tamer interview 2009)—is not the only memory war on 1948 that Palestinian citizens participate in, however. This public battle conceals an important front within Palestinian society in Israel that formed in relation to its repositioning and shift in political discourse following the Oslo Peace Accords.

This shift started in conversations among Palestinian intellectuals related to the communist party in Israel, Rakah, and manifested itself in the internal discourse of the political leadership in the end of the 1990s and beginning of 2000s and in the formation of the National Democratic Alliance (NDA; Rekhess 2002, 21). It marked a shift from claims for multicultural coexistence of Jews and Palestinians as truly equal citizens of Israel to demanding rights as a national collective, including intrastate cultural and political autonomy (Rekhess 2002, 21–22). Marginalized and excluded from most realms of Israeli public life—politics, economy, culture (Rekhess 2002, 21–22)—and losing hope for achieving equality with Jewish citizens, Palestinian leaders, intellectuals, and activists have stated the demand for political and cultural autonomy within Israel (Zaydani, in Ozacky-Lazar and Ghanem 1990; Bishara 1996; see also Jamal 2007; Masalha 1992; Haidar 1997, 198; Manna 1995, 81; Rekhess 1998, 114, 2002, 12–14).[9]

Three public documents published in Hebrew between November 2006 and May 2007—*The Haifa Declaration, The Future Vision,* and *The Democratic Constitution*—authored by intellectuals and civil society organizers,[10] articulated this shift to the Jewish Israeli society. In all these documents the Nakba is presented as foundational to Palestinian identity (Jabareen 2014, 31–32). With the move to claim intrastate cultural and political autonomy, the war on the memory of 1948 also began to take place within the Palestinian society in Israel, as a central channel for shaping the direction it would take as an autonomous national group. As Tamer, a Palestinian activist who collaborated with Autobiography of a City explained:

> The change will come from there [memory] because if Palestinians in Israel would in the future become less marginal in the realms of politics, it requires a different background (that's composed of knowing the Palestinian past). In the meantime, the war is on the consciousness, to build an identity, to maintain it and make it stronger. Everyone in Palestinian society does it, and so there's a big war on it, on *which* memory it would be. (interview 2009)

Several political groups take part in this internal memory war with the hope of shaping a unique identity for Palestinians in Israel. The popular Islamic Movement wishes to emphasize religious elements in a shared Palestinian identity, versus other streams led by secular intellectuals (Rekhess 2002). The decision of the Islamic Movement's northern section not to participate in the Israeli election, "as if they are not seeking power and rule but truth and religion," Tamer interpreted, gave the movement prominence among many Palestinians in Israel whom the intellectual-based secular parties could not reach (Tamer interview 2009). Among secular Palestinians like Tamer, many of whom came out of the communist party, Rakah, Balad is a leading voice that pushes for the construction of a national identity as a mechanism of modernization and means for solidarity rather than an end in itself (Bishara 1995). However, the communist Jewish Palestinian stream, Hadash, received most of the Palestinian votes in national elections during the 2000s.[11]

Palestinian Memory Activism and the Generational Framework

Palestinian memory activists of the Nakba in Israel have been part of the discursive shift from claiming multicultural coexistence to claiming collective rights and cultural autonomy for a national minority. Palestinian memory activists were bred in peace organizations, in particular binational education initiatives like the Neve Shalom-Wahat al-Salam school and the Givat Haviva Education Foundation (like Jewish memory activists) as well as in youth movements and summer camps of the Palestinian political parties. These activists belong to a secular elite that is accustomed to meeting Jewish Israelis with similar attributes, local and transnational positions, goals, and self-selected audiences. Their memory activities stem from the call for cultural autonomy, as they focus on community-based commemoration to learn and teach their own history and cultivate a collective memory for Palestinians in Israel. Baladna manifests this as an all-Palestinian group whose activities are conducted without the involvement of Jewish Israelis as organizers or audiences.

Among other aspects, the communal context is evident through the generational framework of Nakba memory, according to which memory activism is located in and targets the third generation with the assistance of the first pre-1948 generation who experienced the war. "There was a generation of the Nakba, there was a generation that was afraid to talk about it, and now, when you live relatively well, there are kids who want to know why—[even if] they stopped talking about it [i.e., on the Palestinian side]—there is still war," Yasmin, a youth counselor in Baladna outlined this framework (interview 2009). This focus on the third generation as the potential agents of change corresponds to an image of this young "Stand-Tall Generation," as Dan Rabinowitz and Khawla Abu-Baker have called it (2002), which formed around the October 2000 events. It signifies a redemptive rise of Palestinians in Israel out of trauma and silence and into speech and action. After the dreadful experience of 1948 of the grandparents' generation, marked by shock and silence, followed by the fear of the parents' generation to discuss it under martial law and in its spirit after it ended (a generation that nonetheless led the Land Day protests in 1976), a new cohort was born in the 1970s and 1980s who took a political stand in the Oslo aftermath and was visible in the demonstrations of October 2000 in Israel (Rabinowitz and Abu-Baker 2002).

A parallel generational story about silence and discovery exists among Jewish Israeli memory activists, highlighting an almost complete erasure of the Nakba by the state, which made the younger generation discover only today what their grandparents participated in and what their parents knew but suppressed. In both societies, however, there have always been exceptions to this generational division. In private Palestinian schools, the national and personal history of the Nakba was present in speech or gestures throughout the decades (Kanaaneh and Nusair 2010), and Jewish Israelis and Palestinian members of groups on the left, most notably Matzpen, have always talked about the expulsion of Palestinians in 1948 as a pivotal moment in the history of the conflict. Moreover, the generational story highlights a rise of secular elites and their version of a Palestinian national identity based on the idea of cultural and political autonomy, while the emergence of a religious identity resulting from the rise of the Islamic Movement in Israel from the 1980s is ignored, despite its popularity in other Palestinian circles (see, for example, Rabinowitz and Abu-Baker 2002, 12).

The "Stand-Tall Generation," marked by the young men and more so by the young women who led the October 2000 demonstrations in Israeli universities, is made up of college students whose parents have threatened to stop their financial support if they become too politically active and who broke traditional gender boundaries. Rabinowitz and Abu-Baker call them "Yuppies" (2002, 8, 69). Baladna's counselors and youth in Haifa and Nazareth are their slightly younger brothers and sisters who are also, for the most part, secular students.

But the majority of Palestinians in Israel, including youth, do not participate in these memory activities, as will be detailed later (Amal interview 2009; Amr interview 2009; Tamer interview 2009; Danon interviews 2008, 2009; Bukhari interviews 2008, 2009). The younger generation is split. Many of the youth already identify with the dominant group of Jewish Israelis, speak Hebrew, engage with the dominant Americanized Israeli culture, and have moved away from a Palestinian identity, culture, and history, which are less legitimate and less available in the larger society. Others identify with Palestinians in the Occupied Territories. However, both identifications reach their limit when the youth is rejected by these "others" or excluded by both parties, a situation that was defined by Al-Haj as "double peripherality" (1997; see also Rabinowitz 2001b; Rabinowitz and Abu-Baker 2002, 70–71). This state of multiple exclusions calls for a new identity that would accommodate their specific history and position as third-generation Palestinians who are citizens of Israel.

The limits of existing identities are what brought some of the youth counselors to Baladna during their academic studies and what they see as a serious crisis for youth today (Ali interview 2009; Yasmin interview 2009). (Baladna also offered the counselors student funding in return for community work similar to that of non-Palestinian organizations.) Other counselors were previously politically involved with Balad's or the communist party's youth groups. And the vast majority previously took part in the expanding civil society network that Baladna joined in 1999.

Similar Practices, Different Meaning: The Story of Baladna

In winter 2008–2009, during the Israeli attack on Gaza in response to the firing of Qassam rockets from the Gaza Strip by Hamas, Baladna's youth counselor Yasmin, an articulate undergraduate student from Haifa, conducted the following inquiry with her group: "We started with the war on Gaza, presented what one sees in the newspapers and on the Internet in Israel and in the Arabic media, [asking the youth] where do they locate themselves, what would they want to hear [in the media], and what does it [actually] say about them. Thinking back, does their family live in an existing village or a nonexisting village? What is their family story, including those whom nothing happened to [in 1948]; are they living in the same place? Are they talking about it? Did it have an influence; did you hear about it? How were you educated at home?" (interview 2009). Similar questions guide the youth program throughout the year. "In school you never get to it; we are studying everyone's history but ours," Yasmin explained (interview 2009).

This example of looking back to 1948 from the present state of the conflict typifies Baladna's memory activism and the role of this past in it. To reflect on the events that brought Palestinians to their current situations, the past is directly connected in Baladna to the present state of conflict, occupation, and discrimination against Arab Palestinians in Israel and outside. Tracing the refugees who reside in a refugee camp in Gaza, seen in the media coverage of the attack against the background of vast destruction of infrastructure and casualties, back to their pre-1948 villages in Israel links different contemporary experiences of suffering and loss among Palestinians. Refugees in Gaza and Palestinians residing in Israel are linked back to a shared experience in 1948 Palestine. The year 1948 is both the shared history and the dividing line between different Palestinian histories of oppression, and Baladna focuses specifically on the experience of Palestinians who reside in Israel and are its citizens, rather than on the refugee-camp experience that epitomized the general Palestinian struggle for statehood (Allan 2007).

Cultivating a particular "Arab Palestinian with Israeli citizenship" perspective within the larger Palestinian national identity is Baladna's goal. This goal is preconditioned by learning one's own history, building solidarity with others in the same situation, and taking responsibility for change within one's communities (Nashef interview 2008; Ali interview 2009; Hala interview 2009; Yasmin interview 2009).

The study of the Palestinian experience of 1948 thus takes a central part in Baladna's program yet is transmitted through two state-oriented cultural forms, which have successfully cultivated a Zionist national identity among Jewish Israelis. Tours and testimonies are employed in a similar manner to Zochrot and Autobiography of a City (as well as other political and nonpolitical Palestinian organizations) in addition to discussions, creative projects, and community-based initiatives.

Why would a Palestinian identity project use the same cultural forms that have been used to exclude Palestinians in the first place, the same exclusion that made such a project necessary today? The answer is: for similar reasons that Jewish Israelis use them.

Underlying the deployment of tours of destroyed Palestinian villages are the same qualities attributed to this cultural form by Jewish Israeli activists in Chapter 1: first, the transformative potential of their embodied experience, as Nashef noted: "The tour connects you emotionally more than reading a text or analyzing what happened, which is more rational. When you see a half-ruined church, I assume it is more effective" (interview 2008). Baladna youth counselors agree (Yasmin, Ali, and Mahmoud interviews 2009) and add to the pedagogical merit of the tour a second attribute: increasing group solidarity: "Tours are the experiential part of Baladna, they [the youth] always hear, 'when we visited there, do you remember, we were told that this happened,' and it gives them a sense of belonging and makes it easier to remember all the history when they experience it" (Ali interview 2009). The transformative effect of tours is also visible in other areas: "We see a change in them [i.e., the youth] when they go through it, in all topics, not just this one. In most cases we can change their opinion" (Ali interview 2009).

Refugee testimonies are presented during the tour and in documentary films by filmmakers and other Palestinian activists.[12] Personal stories and inquiries into family history of both the youth and their counselors (who often go through a journey of personal learning together) are encouraged but not mandatory (Mahmoud interview 2009; Ali interview 2009; Hala interview 2009). The testimonies highlight everyday life and mundane experiences rather than heroic or victim-oriented stories and give preference to ordinary people, especially women—an inclination similar to other memory-activist groups in Israel.

Listening to a multiplicity of such stories, including their own family history, is supposed to highlight the richness of everyday life experience, which the counselors connect to the experiences of women more often than of men. This micro-level lens replaces the more common and authoritative macro lens on the events, which, according to the counselors, are often told in a detached and rational manner (or what Lina calls "talking like a history book," interview 2009). It is also an alternative to impersonal slogans, which are considered "less interesting" and less memorable (Yasmin interview 2009; Amal interview 2009; Danon interview 2011).

While the testifiers are well respected—as a source of firsthand knowledge, as carriers of a unique perspective, and as symbolic figures that embody the suffering of the whole people—Baladna teaches the youth to critically assess various views and perspectives of the past. Similar to the Autobiography of a City archive, testimonies embody not only an ethical duty to document and remember, but also a variety of versions of the past that are used as a pedagogical tool for vivid yet critical learning. This is especially true in the case of family stories, which are traditionally considered to be a suspicious historical source in academic circles, but whose benefit lies in their variety—having many versions, experiences, and views to choose from (Yasmin, Mahmoud, and Ali interviews 2009). "I knew many personal stories, and it is also interesting, but not essential and fundamental regarding the whole history thing. [It is] things people say . . . and nothing more. Nothing that helps research the Nakba, [because these are] stories that are similar in most places . . . not new things. Most of the stories are alike in the [estimated] 530 villages; they were destroyed and displaced in the same way," Hassan asserted (interview 2009).

In addition to tours and testimonies, creative and artistic projects as well as a final community-based project are employed by each of the youth groups. This project is specifically a community-building activity; it is chosen, designed, and conducted by the youth within their local community. In the past, these projects have included, for example, a collection of traditional recipes gathered from family members and a study of how the traditional head scarf for men, the kufiya, has been transformed from a symbol of solidarity with the Palestinian struggle to a popular fashion accessory around the world, denoting—even in Israel—a detachment from its political context.

The transformative experience of the tour and the "epistemological responsibility" that is anticipated to be transmitted by live and digital testimonies, which Chapters 1 and 2 articulated, are supposed to assist a general change that ties together the youths' identity and their community: from fragmentation and identity crisis to community building and empowerment. This change is anticipated to derive from giving agency and acknowledging other Palestinians in the youths' and their families' position, which will lead the youth to take responsibility for his or her community (Nashef interview 2008). This path is quite different from the Jewish Israeli activist project that aims to evoke responsibility for the suffering their own society inflicted on "the other side" of the conflict, even if it is presented as part of "our" shared history, by Zochrot, for example. Community building is an unintended consequence of Zochrot, albeit a central one for participants' engagement. Community building is also quite different in the archival effort that Autobiography of a City has been pursuing; not only is it a local endeavor for Jaffa residents, but the group has also been reconstructing a community mainly through a virtual structure (the online archive of stories) before similar ties and interaction have been—or can be—tangibly formed.

In any case, where national community building is as central to memory activities as it is for Baladna, it would seem to involve constructive elements and a positive content rather than stressing critical distance. Yet Baladna's study of the Palestinian experience in 1948 is conducted with caution, inseparable from a general discussion of national history writing that deconstructs both Jewish Israeli and Palestinian national narratives. This means "knowing that there are lies on the Jewish Israeli side, and knowing that are also lies on the Palestinian side," as Yasmin bluntly put it (interview 2009).

An example for this critical discussion is one of the program's key sessions, in which youth are joined by their parents and asked to list the ten most influential historical events for them. They consult their parents and the Internet. The list usually starts with either the first Zionist Congress in 1897 in Basel, or with the Arab Revolt in British Palestine in 1936–1939 (Yasmin interview 2009; Ali interview 2009; Hala interview 2009). The variety of possible historical trajectories that the youth and parents finally produce, albeit small, not only suggests that Palestinian and Israeli histories are tied together but also proposes that there are more than one, or two, views of the history of the conflict and of the occurrences that precipitated the current situation of Palestinians in Israel.

However, following this and other activities that consist of the more deconstructive elements of the program—questioning the history they had known and the available national identities—family histories and community work are brought in as a constructive element, "so they will know who we are," Yasmin explained. "After you hear about the history not everything is clear; [a lot] is undermined" (interview 2009). The construction completes the journey to the past: "There is now, there is history—so they will have the whole continuum, the [full] circle, and then they will decide" (Yasmin interview 2009).

More specifically, the year concludes with community work, through a project each group designs and raises funds for from local businesses. This project is considered to be a favorite activity of the participants. "For the whole year we have been talking and talking, and now we can give back to the community," said Omar, a high school student from Yasmin's group in Haifa.

All members of this specific group I interviewed and observed during sessions seemed to have absorbed Baladna's messages and principles, which they repeated almost word for word. The knowledge they gained about their history of 1948 raises consciousness and is crucial to knowing who they are today. If they had to choose how to teach history at Israeli schools, they would prefer to give both Jewish Israeli and Palestinian stories, so that the students (sometimes presented as "we") would have a choice between several views (group conversation 2009).

But in addition to these statements, there were signs that other things were happening. Some of the youth stated their difficulties in obtaining family stories from their parents. One girl said that the way your parents raise you is not the central influence on your education, but "there is the kindergarten [and] the surrounding environment" that influence a person's education as well—for better or worse (Hala interview 2009). While the generational framework of reference that I have heard from their counselors and other Palestinian memory activists exists in her quote, she also expressed the uncertainty and difficulty of being a member of the third generation that, according to this framework, has to build a new structure of knowledge on the past as a basis for its identity. The quote suggests that these youths tend to grow up with contradictory messages inside and outside of the home and therefore are faced with confusion and a general mistrust of fundamental sources of education and socialization, such as the education system, the neighborhood, and the media.

This is also an obstacle for memory activism. According to Palestinian memory activists, many Palestinians, including parents and youth, "do not know and do not want to know" about the Nakba, as Yasmin explained, regarding middle-class urban youth in her groups in Haifa: "Why would they know? . . . Everything is going well for them; they go to the best private schools; why would I need to know? Only when I took the bus and a woman shouted, 'Dirty Arab, get off the bus!' he suddenly wants to remember" (interview 2009; see similar statements in Rabinowitz and Abu-Baker 2002, 69). "From being told not to deal with this so many times, we [finally] want to deal with it. We are tired of listening to old wives' tales and seeing the images on TV. [They are] like soap [operas]," she added without stopping for breath (Yasmin interview 2009).

Her quote is revealing. While the necessity of memory activism was explained by Yasmin and her fellow Baladna counselors as a response to the individualizing and fragmenting effect of liberal capitalism, which brought a crisis of national identification to Palestinian youth in Israel, the generational story gives memory activism a redemptive effect that ties it back to the national struggle while also increasing Palestinian agency. And yet, it was surprisingly described as nonpolitical.

How can Nakba memory be nonpolitical in the context of a two-front memory war on Palestinians in 1948? There are at least three answers to this question, as the next two sections explain.

Three Definitions of the Political

As described in Chapter 1, there are other Palestinian groups in Israel who conduct tours of pre-1948 Palestinian villages and use refugee testimonies that do not fall under my definition of memory activism. Most of these activities are held to propel a specific political cause by formal organizations or ones related to a political party, such as the Association for Arab Culture in Nazareth, the Reut-Sedaka movement in Jaffa, and the Association for the Defense of the Rights of the Internally Displaced Persons in Israel in the North.

In this context, Palestinian memory activists are unique in stating that they organize "nonpolitical" tours (Hala interview 2009; Yasmin interview 2009; Amal interview 2009; Amr interview 2009). I have heard this statement from Palestinian activists from Baladna and Autobiography of a City, as well as from historian Mustafa Kabha and community organizer Muhammad Yunnes, the founders of a unique initiative to conduct monthly family tours to destroyed villages in the Triangle of Palestinian towns near Vadi Arah. Kabha stated: "It is completely nonpolitical—a history that is unrelated to a political identity—[but to] the family, the natural environment; there are no flags and no [other national] symbols. People come to know, it builds consciousness, [but] it doesn't need to lead to a political position. The [touring] group doesn't have a political identification. We insist that it will not be connected to any political party" (Kabha interview 2009). However, it provides people with "a foundation for their connection with the land, and a narrative that constructs a national movement" (Kabha interview 2009). So, what is "consciousness," and what is "political" and "nonpolitical" in recovering Nakba memories for national identity among Palestinians in Israel against the background of a two-front memory war?

The competition between Palestinian parties and movements in Israel to mold the dominant memory of 1948 according to their political vision of a Palestinian identity gave public Nakba activities a specific connotation within this society. Engaging with Nakba memory in public means, predominantly, a mobilization of this past in a specific direction for Palestinian *partisan political interests* (Tamer interview 2009). "I am not a political person means I am not affiliated with a political party,"Tamer, who collaborated with Autobiography of a City, explained (interview 2009). Yasmin, Baladna's youth counselor, noted that at the beginning of each year when new youth join the program, which they assume to be mainly about the Nakba, their parents say: "Don't let them go to political demonstrations!" (interview 2009; a similar concern was reported by another counselor, Mahmoud interview 2009). A nonpolitical commemoration of the Nakba therefore means an activity that is not affiliated with a political party or movement; nor does it include the cultural repertoire most associated with political protest in Israel (demonstrations, marches with flags, etc.), as Kabha's statement demonstrates.

Similar to the definition of the *political* among Palestinian memory activists in Israel, a second meaning of dealing with the Nakba in public is referred to as *enraging the state* and in return suffering its sanctions. "Political means to make Israel angry," Tamer clarified. "Many Palestinians are still afraid following the martial law period, that [if] she is a student, [she] will not get her degree because the Shabakh [Hebrew abbreviation for the General Security Service, or Shin Bet] controls everything" (interview 2009).

Therefore, stating that memory activism of the Nakba is nonpolitical does not mean that the activists do not value its significance as consciousness-raising for political change. It means that they position themselves outside of the competition between political parties on shaping the collective memory and identity of Palestinians in Israel and present their work to Palestinians as not directly threatening the state.

These distinctions seem to be strategic, as Amr from Autobiography of a City stated, for example:

> Our project can draft [Palestinian] people, [because it is] not propaganda; it can accommodate some of the population that is seeking a sense of belonging, identity, common ground, to feel solidarity in opposition to the polarization that existed until now. Precisely because of the fear of talking politics, we came up with the approach of "Lets tell our story [in a way that] is also less threatening for the other side"—not a narrative that stands in opposition, but giving a stage [to individuals]. On the other hand,

> this multiplicity of narratives in Jaffa is a case study to other cities, mixed or not, and [Palestinian] villages. (interview 2009)

The political purposes of achieving "solidarity," "a sense of belonging," and "identity" are attempted by Palestinian memory activists through presenting a variety of personal stories rather than via national ideology, or "propaganda." The latter, represented by a premolded, single Palestinian national narrative, is prevalent in both the external (Israeli Palestinian) and the internal (of Palestinians in Israel) memory struggles. Palestinian memory activists view a single Palestinian national narrative as closely related to the two connotations of the political mentioned above: serving partisan political interests, and raising fear of threatening the state and Jewish Israeli society. Instead, their memory activism favors an inclusive community-based work of collecting personal stories in various localities to construct a collective memory and identity from the ground-up and from the local to the national (Amr interview 2009; Danon interview 2011; Kabha interview 2009).

Rejecting the need to fit a variety of existing memories into a particular national narrative, the activists offered distinctions between their political goals and the political outside of their memory group. Hala, Baladna's program coordinator in 2009, told me that Baladna's work is apolitical, which Yasmin, a youth counselor, clarified as "something social and not proper political." She said she joined Baladna because it is the only place in her city, Haifa, that offers social engagement without a partisan political affiliation. According to her, the absence of partisan political affiliation allows the youth groups to raise questions that are not limited by a commitment to a specific political camp, questions that other organizations do not approve of discussing (Yasmin interview 2009). The frequent use of the words "propaganda" as well as the will to expose "lies on both sides" (Yasmin interview 2009) seemed to demonstrate the activists' and their audiences' suspicion of political statements that mobilize the past for partisan purposes within Palestinian society in Israel.[13]

This distinction necessitates a third meaning for the political to describe what the activists are doing. This meaning is *community-based consciousness-raising*, which is intended to increase solidarity among Palestinian citizens. The corresponding media through which to mobilize the youth toward this political goal are often the arts, which are seen as an alternative strategy to the political partisan education about the Nakba and to Nakba representations that enrage the state. Creative and artistic projects are described as "not politics as we know it but also political" (Amr interview 2009) or "not partisan political but actually political" (Ali interview 2009). These projects focus on raising questions to be "opened and debated, [through engaging youth in] interviewing [people] and understanding that they can bring change, and that it [i.e., the dominant narrative] is just an opinion" (Amr interview 2009). Here, *political* means raising consciousness toward a critical assessment of reality more than toward a specific content, because this reality is seen as infused with different opinions, ideologies, and interests that are presented as fact-based truth.

However, the distinction of Palestinian memory activism from partisan political activism, which also organizes tours and listens to testimonies, not only is strategic but also stems from a structural shift and carries a cost. The expansion of Palestinian civil society organizations in Israel in the 1990s was based on American and European funding by private foundations and EU institutions that required grantees not to be affiliated with a political party, as well as to demonstrate pluralist values such as gender equality and dismantling of primordial identities. The foundations' selection of activities to fund did not necessarily fit the needs of Palestinians in Israel, nor did it fit the needs of those in the Palestinian Territories in the 1990s, when funding gave preference to creating and advancing processes rather than institutions (Challand 2011; Tsachi interview 2009; this has changed today, however). The European normative approach of postnational pluralism fit with the values of Jewish Israeli activist groups, a society already in the process of deconstructing the dominant Zionist identity, much more than those of Palestinian organizations that are still claiming national recognition. Tsachi, a Jewish Israeli activist with Autobiography of a City and other organizations, who experienced the "NGOization" of both societies in the last two decades (Dana 2015; Herzog 2011; Payes 2003), compared the effect: In Zochrot, for example, "there is adequacy between the [group's] values and the European funders' [values]. But encoding the European code is tougher for Palestinian organizations. The rule of the EU that there would be no involvement in formal politics is a misunderstanding of how the Palestinian society in Israel works—all the cultural power comes from there [i.e., formal politics]" (interview 2009).[14]

The surge of civil society organizations within Palestinian society in Israel since the 1990s has not only broadened the range of political and social initiatives; it has also divided similar activities and their audiences to political and apolitical entities. "It is a challenge to separate themselves [from political parties], sometimes doing the same activity under two separate hats," Tsachi explained. "In the last decade they learned how to play the game and managed to separate themselves but lost so much—the audience, the participation, the identification" (interview 2009).

Within Palestinian society the informal political affiliations of many of the nongovernmental organizations are well known or anticipated even if their members deny such affiliation. In the case of Baladna, for example, which was founded by a former Balad member, Nashef, as a separate organization, people still expect its youth program to push a national approach similar to Balad's youth group (which Nashef had previously directed). At the beginning of each school year, the youth who enter the program expect Baladna "to only talk about the Nakba" and thus also "say things they thought Baladna wants them to say: extreme speech, that nationality is the most important and not religion," Yasmin described (interview 2009). Ali, Baladna counselor and a member of the communist party, explained the differences and similarities between Palestinian nongovernmental associations and parties: "A party has a political line and political activities—election, the traditional May 1st celebration, and other things that Baladna does not do, because it has a social line. But there are views regarding history and ideology that bring all political parties closer together and also affect the associations and institutions: It is a culture that exists" (interview 2009).

This political culture persists despite structural constraints because of the need to fight the war on memory and identity on the binational front. This connection of culture and power—as in Tsachi's assertion that "all the cultural power comes from" partisan politics—is characterized by acting within the accepted boundaries of formal politics and of civil society in Israel, while using available means to resist and push these boundaries from time to time. Goldfarb calls this the "politics of legitimacy" (2011). Yet as the next section stresses, memory activism is unique for acting not only within the order's political culture but also as distinctly separate from it.

Baladna as a Cultural Liberation Effort

After examining the positioning of Palestinian memory activists within the political and structural context of their society, this section analyzes all-Palestinian memory activism in Israel as a cultural project that confronts the state. It analyzes their efforts to learn about the Nakba and remember it as a liberation effort within the general claim of Palestinian citizens for cultural autonomy in Israel. Where power and culture are intimately connected, as with the strong influence of Zionism on Israeli state education, commemoration, and documentation of the past, liberation involves disconnecting the two, at least symbolically, Goldfarb argues (2011, 67). One attempt to disconnect culture from power in Israel is one-sided Palestinian memory work. While Baladna's activities reveal the entanglement of Palestinian history with the history of Zionism and the establishment of Israel, its members and other Palestinian memory activists learn it for themselves and discuss it among themselves as part of a larger effort for political and cultural autonomy for Palestinians in Israel.

Distinguishing their activities from those conducted by partisan Palestinian parties and groups affiliated with them, even if initially stemming from funders' requirements, also helps to disconnect power and culture. The threefold definition that Palestinian memory activists give "the political" corresponds to Goldfarb's conceptual typology of power: (1) the Weberian legitimacy and coercion of formal institutions (affiliation with political parties); (2) the Foucauldian truth regime of decentralized power (enraging the state by discussing the Nakba; Foucault 1984); and (3) the Arendtian interactive and deliberative production of something new in public (community-based consciousness-raising; Arendt 1958; Goldfarb 2011, 33). As discussed, Palestinian memory activists distinguish their work from the first two connotations, which they view as "proper political," and link it to the third, which they declare apolitical.

In this respect, their statement is not dissimilar to those made regarding artistic and social projects in socialist Poland in the second half of the 1970s, which Goldfarb studied, in which artists and activists separated themselves from the politics of legitimacy and coercion of the party-state, and from its ideological truth regime, and spoke and acted independently within the existing order (2011, 55, 62). "The most radical political challenge was to be anti-political," Goldfarb wrote about the movement leader Lech Wałęsa's statement that the dissident Polish movement Solidarity is not a political organization, just a trade union (2011, 59). In a party-state, Solidarity did not act to maintain the existing order through pushing the boundaries of what was considered legitimate but instead attempted to withdraw from it and act as if Poland of the 1970s were a democracy (Goldfarb 2011, 59).

In Israel, a democratic state where ideology and power do not always correspond,[15] the activist assertion that Nakba memory activism is apolitical nonetheless concerns a similar wish to separate their work from the legitimacy and authority of the state and its political institutions, as well as from the dual narrative framing of the conflict—a withdrawal from the discriminatory order and a liberation effort from both official positions of the rival sides of the conflict.

Nonetheless, this withdrawal and liberation effort from existing frameworks and institutional constraints is taking place alongside a more pragmatic politics of legitimacy that acknowledges them and utilizes them for change. This acknowledgment comes to light with the activist awareness of the interweaving—instead of separation—of the two sides' national histories, the mirror manipulation of the past for present political claims, and the legitimacy and authority that hegemonic memory practices carry (tours and testimonies). Like in the Polish case, this activist appropriation and redeployment of dominant cultural forms in Israel produces something that contrasts with the ideology of the state. However, the state can also use the cultural autonomy that is reflected by the activist utilization to prove its democratic capacity, support of free speech, and general tolerance (Goldfarb 2011, 58), while in reality these were severely limited in the 2000s.

A debate between the strategies of the politics of legitimacy under coercion and that of withdrawal from the discriminatory order was observable in a renewed debate among Palestinian partisan parties during the events of October 2000. It concerned a claim for political autonomy through boycotting the Israeli elections and establishing a separate Palestinian parliament within Israel (Rekhess 2002, 15). The national awakening among Palestinians in Israel that followed the October 2000 events raised calls for its mobilization toward an alternative political channel that would "serve as a means to prevent our masses from being dragged along in a struggle limited to the confines of the Knesset alone."[16]

However, even those who supported the idea stated that the aim was not "to cut themselves off from the state" but simply was "the only integrative way in which they can live in this state," as then Knesset member (MK) Azmi Bishara from Balad wrote (1999, 115, cited in Rekhess 2002, 17). Bishara's quote is indicative of the limits of the debate about political autonomy, stopping at adopting what would appear to be a line of detachment from the state. Going further could result in losing rights and perhaps even their Israeli citizenship, which enable Palestinians in Israel to make such claims in the first place. It would provide "an excuse for the authorities to perpetuate discrimination and deprivation," as the opponents to an independent parliament argued (Rekhess 2002, 17).

Palestinian memory activists, funded by external foundations, function outside the scope of the state's education system, formal politics, and cultural institutions. They exist within a constrained political culture that still has the freedom to use legal and cultural means available in a democratic state. These means include the cultural forms used by the state to cultivate Zionist identity; but this is more difficult for Palestinians, who are bound by their ethnonational membership and their status as second-class citizens. And this citizenship, second-class or otherwise, can always be lost.

However, what distinguishes memory activism from formal political initiatives is the idea that collective memory as a medium for consciousness-raising is the only weapon available for Palestinians in Israel that the state cannot disarm, as the earlier quote in the chapter states. Engaging the public with it in separation from state institutions, calling it a social rather than political endeavor, can be interpreted as a variation on the politics of legitimacy through mere naming as apolitical, but it can also be viewed as a withdrawal from the state and a secession from the ongoing negotiation within the boundaries of formal politics.

If collective memory and historical consciousness are the only remaining forms of resistance that the state cannot seize, and if these forms can be utilized outside of state structures and institutions, then the "weapon of the weak" (Scott 1985) is not only the daily push to change political positions until some concessions are achieved; it is also an attempt to create a free debate and creative cultural work outside the boundaries of this order, as Goldfarb asserts (2011, 55, 62). This cultivation of memory is liberating but also very fragile, since it lacks institutions in which to be rooted. And the vision of activists regarding such future institutions, namely museums and archives, uses the exclusive, ideology-oriented Israeli state institutions as role models, as shown in the next section.

Institutionalizing National Memory without a State

> For a people to have an archive it has to live in a safe place; if the Jews didn't have a state, they would not have built Yad Vashem. (Lina, Palestinian activist with Zochrot and Baladna, interview 2009)

Borrowing memory and documentation practices that the state uses was first and foremost a means for memory activists to be heard and convince both sides. However, the inequality in available sources and institutions made this very difficult. The production of Palestinian history and collective memory was confined to the available sources, namely a limited number of testimonies and sites of ruins. These sources were not only a small percent of what could have been preserved as historical evidence, but testimonies are also disregarded as less credible by Israeli historians (see Chapter 4). "The Palestinian narrative suffers a huge lack of documents, and oral history is the only alternative. The Jews built a collection of oral history in the 1950s [Holocaust survivors' testimonies in Yad Vashem]. The Palestinians did not [collect], and they lost a lot, because many [of the witnesses] have passed away," historian and activist Kabha noted (interview 2009).

This comparison of Nakba oral-history collections with the model of the national institute of Yad Vashem, one of the largest archives of Holocaust survivor testimonies in the world and central to Israel's Zionist national ideology, reiterates the quote from Lina at the beginning of this section. Her statement further demonstrates that a national archive is not only a symbol and a house (Derrida 1998) for a nation's shared past that is recognized worldwide, as Yad Vashem has been for Jewish Israelis. For Palestinians, it also signifies the problematic state of their national territory, in which their authority and legitimacy as a collective are rooted. It is difficult to build a national archive in the air, when it is not allowed to be planted in the ground.

Palestinian documents from 1948 and earlier have disappeared or been destroyed, and what is left has been archived in different countries (I. Feldman 2008). Collections of testimonies, maps, photos, and objects are stored in Internet websites, living rooms, private archives, memorial books, and films. There are many more of them now, but they are not safely preserved or housed in any central institution.

Kabha himself is leading a significant effort to construct a national Palestinian archive in Israel, in the Umm el-Fahem Art Gallery, for which he has been collecting resources for two decades. The archive was inaugurated with a vast photo exhibit in 2008 and contains photos and documents of the destroyed Palestinian villages in the Triangle, as well as refugee testimonies. Lina acknowledged this development but expresses a desire for something that is "more like Yad Vashem, like Holocaust archives." "There needs to be an archive that has influence, that has visitors, [and] schools and schoolchildren brought in; the place would become alive and people would donate their documents. . . . [Today] some don't trust [a Palestinian archive], but if they see it is well handled [they will]. People are thirsty for something like this; there is almost nothing" (interview 2009).

Not everyone shares this reported "thirst." Palestinians in Israel are not all eager to contribute their stories, documents, and photos to a national collection. There are, in fact, two opposing strands, for and against the urgency to self-document. On the one hand, scholars and activists report an eagerness to tell personal stories among some 1948-generation Palestinians and to engage with such stories among younger generations of Palestinians in Israel. People preserve and document inside the family as well, for future claims (I. Feldman 2008). On the other hand, there is still silence among older Palestinians, as well as degrees of distance and interest among younger generations in recalling the traumatic loss (Tamer interview 2009; Danon and Bukhari interview 2008; Danon interview 2011; Yasmin interview 2009).

The elders' unwillingness to talk has many reasons and is only partly due to the limitations of the channels offered to them for sharing their stories publicly. As mentioned in Chapter 2, the transnational and "Zionist" formats of tours and testimonies can be limited in capturing local ways of preserving and communicating long-silenced memories inside the family and close milieu, if aired at all under severe restrictions and threats. However, the local memory practices of 1948 that Palestinians in Israel developed under intimidation are also not always used to externalize people's personal memories—at least not in return visits, nor in storytelling. "Some 1948-generation Palestinians in Israel talk about their village and visit it, but others do not, even if it is close to their new house in Israel," said Lina, who records refugee testimonies for Zochrot and other groups. "[They say:] 'It is no longer ours'" (interview 2009).

Even taking part in the post-1948 tradition of visiting the village sites on Nakba Day, or participating in the annual Return Procession "doesn't mean that Palestinians talk [about the Nakba] on other days of the year. I don't think [they do] so; it is very hard to talk about the trauma," Lina maintains (interview 2009). The interviewer's rebuke on the 1948-generation's silence in the opening of Chapter 2 is another example of this unwillingness to talk publicly, even when local projects offer a space for personal stories (Abu Subhi interview, part 25, Autobiography of a City digital archive).

Among those who agree to testify, there are gendered silences. From Lina's experience in interviewing Palestinian refugees in Israel and abroad, men and women bring different memories and do not speak about the same things. "Men talked more about heroism and fighting and slogans, and until he [i.e., the testifier] arrives at talking about himself he talked about the history like a textbook. Women are more connected to themselves and their stories are stronger; they tell the truth more, not giving speeches or thinking about every sentence. They are more emoted, [talk] from the feminine place—few men have cried before me, [versus] more women. [Women have] stronger memory; they made sure they remember small details. They worked then in the house and outside; they remember everything—the men only worked outside," she elaborated the differences. Her emphasis on the strengths and advantages of women's memories of everyday life is part of the already-mentioned effort of memory activists in Israel to capture (and give voice to) the memories of ordinary people who are not usually heard in the public sphere. This emphasis manifests for example in screening a short film by Raneen Jereis that features women's testimonies about 1948 as part of Baladna's program, to highlight the strength of women despite their ongoing exclusion from public life.

Indeed, women's memories represent the secular gender equality that Baladna wants to promote in the pluralist Palestinian society it envisions for the future. It is also, however, a vehicle of national memory meant to symbolically portray the emotional baggage of the Nakba that the 1948 generation has carried and give its members agency and honor (Yasmin interview 2009). Similarly to Lina's quote, for Baladna's and Autobiography's activists, highlighting daily life, family ties, and emotions in women's testimonies is seen as more authentic and closer to reality (and thus to "the truth") than the more template-like stories of heroism that highlight "battles, blood, and power" (Yasmin interview 2009) in what is perceived as less personal testimonies by men and officials (Amal interview 2009; Danon interview 2011).

Do gendered and generational silences and people's refusals to contribute personal items to Palestinian archives also signify a wish to withdraw personal memories and experiences from any formal structure, including a national Palestinian project within Israel? The final section summarizes the observations and raises questions regarding the possibilities of building trust and participation within a context of a general distrust and disbelief in formal politics and institutions, Jewish and Palestinian, in Israel.

Conclusion

I observed that Palestinian memory activism of the Nakba in Israel is based on a threefold definition of the political. Yet it can also be analyzed as a three-dimensional strategy that distinguishes itself from other initiatives as nonpolitical:

1. a Weberian politics of legitimacy—accommodating a structural constraint, on the one hand, that stems from NGOs' external funding norms, and using hegemonic memory practices to grant authority and legitimacy to Palestinian memories of 1948;
2. an Arendtian community-based cultural liberation project— acting in separation from state structures and from Jewish Israelis despite the entanglement of the two peoples' histories and memories to cultivate a unique national identity for Palestinians in Israel;
3. a knowledge-production project of "reliable information" on the Nakba, which supplies neither ideology nor scientific (historical) truth to people who see their context as a Foucauldian truth regime from outside and from within their society.

I want to expand on the third part of the strategy before concluding the chapter's findings. The silences that were described in the previous section mark the general mistrust Palestinians feel toward information that comes from state agencies—the education system (including history curricula and academic research), media, and formal politics— which they see as arenas of Zionist ideology. The Arab media, however, did not traditionally offer them anything less ideological, and so a general disbelief has spread from disregarding knowledge produced by state institutions toward self-criticism of the Palestinian political organization and Arab media (see, for example, Ben Zvi and Bir'im 2009; Copti and Buchari 2003). Such an approach underlines the effort of Palestinian memory activists to distinguish memory work of the Nakba from the contested state-based Zionist historical narrative (see Chapter 4) but also from any national ideology or "propaganda." Kabha, one of the first documenters and researchers of the Nakba in Israel,[17] defined this effort as aimed "to give reliable information without symbolic and emotional aspects" and described how it is done: "In constructing a larger narrative from these little voices one has to create a puzzle, not select one [voice]" (interview 2009). He is trying not to involve symbols—or "anything too emotionally symbolic on its various aspects"—and stated that, like Baladna, he does not care as much about building the historical database or record, because it can develop on its own (Kabha interview 2009). He finds it more important to assure that the knowledge of the past is not distorted, on the one hand, and that people are not using it to be "stuck in the image of a victim," on the other hand (Kabha interview 2009)—another symbol of national narratives, certainly the Jewish Israeli one. According to this, "reliable information" is free of national symbols and emotions and is not committed to a professional historical record (even by the historian Kabha, who produces it in addition to academic research). Amr from Autobiography of a City similarly stated that the Jaffa project is "more accessible because we intentionally don't have a political statement. We are not historians, we haven't been professionalized, [but we are just] simple artists within our own medium" (interview 2009).

Political consciousness, the third definition of what is considered political, is to Palestinian activists the alternative product to political partisan power within Palestinian society and the alternative to the production of knowledge in state institutions. In the new historians' debate with "old historians," for example, which became centered on the question of whether or not the Palestinians fled their homes or were expelled by Israeli military forces, there was not for the most part a change of political consciousness among most Jewish Israeli scholars toward considering Palestinian displacement in 1948 a crucial matter for any conflict resolution. In fact, it was the opposite, as "new historian" Benny Morris's shift of political view demonstrated (Shavit 2004; see Chapter 4). But "reliable information"—not scientific and not of national ideology—which is delivered through an experiential learning anticipated from touring, is expected to raise the consciousness of participating Palestinians with or without a personal connection to the displacement of 1948, against the background of a general distrust of other sources of knowledge.

However, the self-selection of participants prevails in this society as it does among Jewish Israelis, and not all Palestinians wish to be exposed or contribute to this knowledge and experience the anticipated transformation of consciousness. Despite the assumed autonomy of memory activism of the Nakba, the more a Palestinian national narrative was publicly developed in Israel in the 2000s, the more it was opposed and sanctioned by the Jewish Israeli majority. It was banned and undermined, making it more urgent but also more risky for Palestinians to participate in its production.

The first half of the book described how the three memory-activist groups have appropriated and redeployed two hegemonic memory practices in Israel, tours and testimonies, for contested memories. The next half of the book analyzes these efforts in Israel as part of a larger memory-activist effort to implement the transnational strategy of truth and reconciliation. In addition to mapping the various levels of truth and reconciliation work in Israel, it examines how the challenges that its application raises in cases of active conflict such as the Israeli-Palestinian conflict may help overcome some of the problems that exist in its deployment in postconflict cases.

4

The Shift

The Nakba Law and the Memory War on 1948

> Seven years ago I didn't know what the Nakba was;
> now it is in the newspaper, and not only the name;
> the paper writes what it is! (Nathan, participant
> in Zochrot's tours, 2009)

Although the Palestinian experience and memories of 1948 in Israel
are still far from receiving official or public acknowledgment, everyone
now *knows* about the Nakba—a change that seems to have taken place
in a brief period somewhere between 2005 and 2007. From the historians' debate of the late 1980s and the 1990s to the memory activities of
the 2000s, the Nakba has gradually entered the mainstream channels
and drawn the attention of the majority of Israelis (Ram 1998; Pappé
1997b). This shift began before an amendment that became popularly
known as the "Nakba Law" was proposed in 2009. However, the extensive coverage the national media dedicated to the process of legislation—from the first version of the law that was preliminarily approved
by the Constitution, Law, and Justice Committee of the Knesset in
May 2009 to its acceptance, after substantive revision, almost two
years later, on 22 March 2011—ensured a widespread dissemination
of the term Nakba and what it stands for, as the opening quote notes.

The memory war on 1948 exploded into the center of the public debate immediately after the law was first proposed in 2008 by MK Alex
Miller from the coalition's right-wing party Yisrael Beiteinu. Miller's
proposal criminalized commemoration of the Nakba during Independence Day or the day of the establishment of Israel, sanctioning individuals who violate the law to up to three years in prison. The proposal
was preliminarily approved by the Ministerial Committee for Legislation and Law Enforcement on 24 May 2009, an act that evoked enraged
responses across the political spectrum in the media, and an appeal by
center-left Labor ministers Yitzchack Hertzog, Shalom Simchon, and

Avishai Braverman against the bill. The Israel Democracy Institute, a leading independent research center, called the bill "anti-democratic, unconstitutional, and extremely detrimental to freedom of expression and to peaceful demonstration in Israel" and stated that if it passed, "it is not likely to increase the 'loyalty' of Palestinian citizens of Israel, but rather could lead to an increase in separatism and extremism among this population" (Kremnitzer and Konfino 2009). Zochrot was asked to respond in an op-ed on the mainstream news website Ynet.[1] The authors of these different responses to the bill elaborated on what the Nakba is, testifying to the state of popular public knowledge about it when the law was proposed. In later responses to the legislative process, such elaboration no longer appears, suggesting that it is no longer needed as the general public became informed about the Nakba.

The proposal was rejected, but the Ministerial Committee for Legislation and Law Enforcement discussed amendments to it such that instead of incarcerating individuals the law would fine state-funded institutions for similar actions: "mark[ing] Independence Day or the day of the establishment of the State of Israel as a day of mourning," or "reject[ing] Israel's existence as a Jewish and democratic state; contain incitement to racism, violence, or terrorism; support armed struggle and terrorism by enemy or terror organizations against Israel; or support acts of vandalism or physical desecration that dishonor the Israeli flag or the symbol of the state."[2] The finance minister will have the authority to impose the fines after receiving a ruling from the ministry's legal counsel and a team of professionals from the Justice Ministry and Finance Ministry.[3]

None of the law's versions included the word Nakba, but referring to acts of mourning during Independence Day points directly to a post-1948 tradition of Palestinian citizens who visit their destroyed village lands on the national holiday, because it was the only time during the year they were allowed to move freely throughout the country in the martial law period (1948–1966). The Israel Democracy Institute noted the law was directed specifically at preventing financial support for Nakba Day events conducted by Arab Palestinian citizens by entities that receive money from the state (C. Cohen 2014).

The public debate mounted again in 2011, when a revised version of the bill had been approved in a second and third reading in the Constitution, Law, and Justice Committee of the Knesset on 14 March 2011 and shortly thereafter, following a heated discussion among the MKs, passed in the Knesset plenum to become an amendment to the

Budgetary Foundations Law.[4] During the same Knesset plenum, on 22 March, another contested law was discussed and approved that implicitly discriminates against Palestinian citizens: The "Acceptance Commissions" bill that allows small local communities to set up admission committees, could now legally prevent Palestinian citizens from living in small community localities.

Thirty-seven MKs voted in favor, and twenty-five voted against the Nakba Law. Half of the MKs, 60 out of 120, avoided the decision by not showing up for the vote, including central members of the coalition: center Kadima party leader Tzipi Livni and five of its MKs, center-left Atzmaut head Ehud Barak and its MKs, and most of the ruling Likud party MKs, including Prime Minister Benjamin Netanyahu, Education Minister Gideon Sa'ar, Finance Minister Yuval Steinitz, and Culture Minister Limor Livnat. These absentees were criticized in an editorial in the daily left-wing newspaper *Ha'aretz* and called on to "wake up before it's too late," as their silence "encourages the instigators of racism, creating a convenient fertile ground for them to continue their disastrous activities."[5]

At stake was Israel's democracy, as both left and right speakers and columnists asserted, albeit for opposite claims. During the committee's vote MK Miller called the legislation "an important proposal that was written in the spirit of the Israeli Declaration of Independence and presents an important *national answer to the varying threats* that try to exploit the principles of our state's democracy in order to fight against it and refute its foundations."[6] Arab Palestinian MK Hanna Suweid from the opposition left-wing Hadash party asserted that the law would actually damage Israel's democracy by limiting the freedom of expression and putting collective blame on Palestinian citizens. "Commemorating the Nakba does not mean that I deny the existence of the State of Israel," he said. "I say this as someone who for some years commemorates the Nakba. I am not the happiest person on this day, but to go from this to the criminal accusation that I want to deny the existence and independence of the State of Israel as a Jewish democratic state is an imposition of guilt, collective guilt without any proof."[7]

Both Miller and Suweid judged the law in relation to Israel's democratic government, but each emphasized a different, even contradictory, aspect of it—for Suweid, Israel's democracy should enable Nakba commemoration for Palestinian citizens, while for Miller Israel's democratic character is exploited to pose threats to its foundational national Jewish character in the shape of Nakba commemoration by

Palestinian nationals. MK Herzog (Labor) criticized the practical aspects of this "threat" during the commission's vote, stating that the laws would sanction the already poor Arab municipalities in Israel, and that it "highlights a subject that's less and less common in the Arab public and gives it greater importance."[8]

Various intellectuals and prominent public figures, including Israel Prize laureates, petitioned against the Nakba Law, and responses of left-wing and Palestinian politicians in Israel, as well as some center-right MKs, condemning it filled the newspapers. Most of these responses called the amendment antidemocratic, harmful for free speech, and one that silences Palestinian citizens' history. One 24 March 2011 op-ed, however, titled "The Palestinian Narrative Has Won," by *Ha'aretz* contributor Oudeh Basharat, a Palestinian citizen, stated that the law at least recognized that the Nakba exists and expressed a wish that it would start a discussion on what happened to Palestinians in 1948.[9]

The legal organization of Palestinians in Israel, Adallah, and the Association for Civil Rights (ACRI) appealed to the Supreme Court, arguing that the law is unconstitutional (HCJ 3429/11; delivered 5 January 2012). But the court used an American legal doctrine to determine that it cannot yet judge the law, as "the questions that this law raises will only become clear with its implementation."[10] Throughout this period, the term *Nakba* became a common idiom, as it appeared in daily newspapers and television broadcasts reporting on the legislation process and the reactions to it from left and right. Today the focus on 1948 and the one-state solution to the conflict that is sometimes associated with it are carried out not only by the radical Left but also by center and right-wing public figures (see Sheizaf 2010).[11] The "public secret" (Stoler 2009, 3, 148) of Palestinian displacement and loss in 1948 is publically discussed by everyone.

What Brought the Change?

The Nakba Law is seen by many, including some of the activists, as the state's reaction to the growing awareness and visibility of Palestinian history and memory of 1948; more specifically they view it as the state's effort to prevent the inclusion of the Palestinian expulsion in 1948 in debates about the conflict and its resolution. Supporting this opinion is the fact that a similar bill was brought to the table in the previous three Parliaments by right-wing MKs Zvi Handle and Arye Eldad but was not taken any further,[12] suggesting that there was no need to worry about Nakba commemorations before, although Palestinians in Israel marked Nakba Day and Land Day annually then as well. Viewing the Nakba Law as the reaction of the state suggests that the activities of the Israeli memory activists and their predecessors, the "new historians," and supportive Jewish Israeli and Palestinian civil society and human rights groups, have had quite an impact, despite the growing national sentiment in Israel in the 2000s (Kabha interview 2009; Tamer interview 2009; see Chapter 3). In fact, it is fair to say that the public debate on the history and present state of the conflict since 2007–2008 has been increasingly focused on the Palestinian side and on the construction and development of the Palestinian historical narrative rather than on the Zionist narrative, which is already developed and well-studied (Lubin interview 2008).

To be sure, the mobility and equality of Palestinians in Israel have not changed,[13] but their collective representation shifted when the war of 1948 as a pivotal moment in their national history and identity entered the public debate in Israel. Despite repeated attempts to delegitimize Palestinian citizens through political rhetoric, parliamentary investigations, and legislation that might yield severe sanctions,[14] the surge in national sentiment of the 2000s erased neither critical voices nor the platforms that enabled these voices to develop and bring this change of focus: the academy, literature and the arts, and civil society. These fields have disseminated knowledge on the Nakba within Israel and abroad: From the revisionist "new historians" and "critical sociologists" of the late 1980s and 1990s, the retelling of 1948 has expanded in the 2000s to studies and debates in many other academic disciplines such as geography, urban studies, literature, film, and political science. Artists and filmmakers who take part in the global interest in post-colonial identities have brought the Nakba to local and international art venues and film festivals, and young best-selling authors such as Eshkol Nevo and Alon Hillu have conveyed it to the mainstream Israeli reader.[15] Human rights associations and activist groups have themselves learned about and distributed within the Radical Left political community both the knowledge of the historians and memory activists as well as the message of dealing with this past for the future resolution of the conflict. In most fields and professional circles of Jewish Israelis, however, there is still today huge resistance to the idea, but "at least there is a conversation," as one memory activist noted two years before Basharat's column (Tsachi interview 2009).

This counterintuitive shift of attention in Israeli public debate in the midst of active conflict and increased nationalistic sentiment raises questions about the role of the Nakba Law, and "memory laws" in democracies in general, in bringing this transformation, which contrasted the law's original aim of blocking the public visibility of the Nakba. Although it has not been implemented yet, the law nonetheless presents a threat to—or at least has a chilling effect on—various entities that are asked to host commemorations of the Nakba, like universities, binational schools, and local municipalities. Right-wing NGOs like Im Tirtzu and politicians on the right called to implement the law starting in May 2012, around Independence Day, in their continuing efforts to exclude Palestinian citizens and their Jewish supporters whom they perceive as disloyal to the Jewish state.[16] In June 2012, MK Miller proposed a new version of the Nakba Law, against the recommendation of the Knesset's legal adviser, Eyal Yanon, which fines academic institutions that host Nakba events. Such events began to be held annually in 2012 at Tel Aviv University and the Hebrew University but were canceled or forbidden in Haifa University, which, like Hebrew University, has a large percent of Palestinian students. Held not during Independence Day but on or around Nakba Day (15 May), these events—an exhibit and demonstration at Hebrew University and an annual memorial ceremony at Tel Aviv University—were preceded every year by public calls to prohibit them and sanction the universities that allow them. They eventually took place alongside protest by right-wing student groups, which sometimes heated up and led to police arrests.

After focusing in previous chapters on the activist deployment of silenced memory to bring change in public consciousness, we now turn to the state's reaction—most powerfully through legislation, in this instance—that had a central role in this change. Exploring the relationships between memory and the law in a democracy, I ask how they might hinder or advance political change in this and other cases; what the law is expected to do in battles over the inclusion of contested pasts and violent histories in the national collective memory; and whether these expectations are fulfilled.

Some of the central debates regarding laws that regulate collective memory of contested and violent pasts have been taking place in or regarding France, Russia, Spain, the Ukraine, and Rwanda in the last decade. I am focusing on the first two cases, where a growing number of such laws and legislation initiatives have taken place since 2000, many of which were received with a huge outcry and protest that eventually led to their cancelations; others remain in place. These debates on memory laws are a fruitful source from which to draw lessons for the Israeli-Palestinian case of memory legislation because they too are an effort of the state to block public calls to air a contested past. But first we should understand what memory laws are.

Memory Laws: Between Free Speech and National(istic) Education

Two types of laws in particular try to control the public perception of a contested past: (1) laws that *forbid* the positive perception, denial, or justification of a violent past such as genocide, ethnic cleansing, or mass violence; (2) laws that *enforce* a positive representation of a violent past and criminalize negative views that stand in opposition to the official memory. While laws of the first type have gained legitimacy (but see Teachout 2006), memory laws of the second type have raised great controversy and criticism within and outside the legislating countries because many saw them as antidemocratic.

If we look more closely at the relationships between national memory and the law in general, a central tension becomes apparent that challenges liberal-democratic politics: national laws often accommodate the national majority and exclude minority memory and experience (Rothberg and Ildiz 2011), while liberal-democratic legislation tries to accommodate all citizens equally. Indeed, even in the absence of memory laws that fortify a positive perception of the nation-state regarding a difficult past, national laws are usually shaped in line with the hegemonic perception of the national past and, in turn, fortify this perception.[17] For example, hate crime laws are shaped according to the dominant perception and collective memory of certain atrocities in the nation-state's history and democratic tradition (for a German-American comparison see Savelsberg and King 2011), and laws that dedicate memorial days, national ceremonies, and archives assist the educational system in disseminating these perceptions and memories in the society (E. Zerubavel 2003; Nora 1996; Durkheim [1912] 1995).

Memorial-day laws powerfully demonstrate this point. These laws "remind" the dominant national community of its shared past in order to reactivate the society's identification and solidarity every year through the social calendar. Officially, memorial-day laws set the rules of public conduct in these occasions for public institutions, media programs, and businesses, yet they also reflect and in turn shape the narrative of the past that is being commemorated in these specially assigned days (E. Zerubavel 2003; Durkheim [1912] 1995; Nora 1996). Some such laws designate a broad and general theme to be molded into particular narratives by local branches of educational and national institutions according to specific social and political contexts, interests, and sensibilities (Vinitzky-Seroussi 2001). In many cases, however, these laws include predetermined specific narratives about the nation and people and by so doing centralize and unify national commemoration around the majority, while excluding national minorities (Anderson 1991; Nora 1996; Gellner 1983). In Israel, for example, significant events in the national history of Arab-Palestinian citizens—such as the Nakba, Land Day, and the events of October 2000—have always been excluded from memorial-day laws or laws that establish memory institutions or archives.[18]

What, then, is the "added value" of memory laws to the safeguarding and fortification of the majority's national history and culture? How does the active banning of minority groups' memories in these laws differ from simply ignoring them in memorial-day laws that systematically propagate the dominant national memory? Analyzing the legislative process and public debate in different cases of memory laws, I found that both types of laws (memorial-day laws and memory laws that fortify the dominant perception) are in fact stages of the same process of reaction to calls to address violent histories and difficult memories. While memorial-day laws often pertain only to the majority's victimhood and suffering and exclude minorities' suffering, memory laws actively ban contested memories of mass violence by minority groups as a step further in reaction to existing attempts to break the official silence about violent pasts. Such memory laws are therefore another stage in the process of return of the once-lived, long-silenced memory into public consciousness and debate.

In light of the tension between the law and national memory and history, the critics of memory laws in the cases I studied argue that constructing the memory of the past or determining the historical record is not the task of the law. They say assigning such responsibility to the law limits freedom of speech as well as the freedom of academic research and the freedom of occupation for historians and history teachers (Nora 2008; Garton Ash 2008; Wartanian 2008). However, a variety of legal techniques have been used in practice for collective memory construction, sometimes for oppositional goals and outcomes, especially in the international and regional level in comparison to the national level. These tasks were taken up by courts (Osiel 1997), legislation of hate crime laws, and official apologies and redress (Savelsberg and King 2011; Torpey 2003; Barkan 2000), as well as memory laws. However, in comparison to courts, for example, memory laws can be viewed as a one-sided form of legal intervention in the perception of the past. While trials expose conflicts between different views and claims, memory laws reveal the force of silencing other interpretations by the state. And yet, as we will see, even this force cannot silence what has already been aired in public. A basic paradox in memory laws gives room to counter-memories and contestations: The state uses the legal system to maintain a positive perception of its violent past and to block counter-hegemonic interpretations, yet these interpretations gain visibility and publicity in the process of legislation and become better-known to the larger society (and the world) than they were before the legal intervention.

Examining two cases of memory legislation in the last decade and a half raises interesting similarities regarding the motivations behind memory laws, their function in practice, and their consequences regarding minority rights and democratic public debate. From these examples we can better understand the Israeli Nakba Law as a reaction to the return of Nakba memory to public consciousness.

The French "Colonialism Law"

One of the most industrious European countries in creating memory laws is France, who by the early 2000s already had three laws of the first type: the Gayssot Act, which criminalizes Holocaust denial, enacted in 13 July 1990 (and which expands the freedom of the press law from 1991); a law that acknowledges the Armenian genocide from 29 January 2001; and the Taubira Act of 21 May 2001, which recognizes slave trade as a crime against humanity. None of these laws, however, discussed a more recent and troubling past: the colonialization of Algeria. Unlike the crimes committed during the Vichy years, for a long time recognition of the violence and injustices committed during the Algerian War (1954–1962) was not advocated publically by interest groups (Lo¨yto¨ma¨ki 2013, 221). As Lo¨yto¨ma¨ki shows, the state was able to keep "juridical 'amnesia'" and official silence regarding French crimes during its wars of decolonization owing to the amnesty laws that passed after the Algerian War and a restrictive definition of crimes against humanity (Loÿtoˮmaˮki 2013, 221).

What finally broke the silence in the realm of law was, paradoxically, a 2005 memory law of the second type that attempted to guard against such a break: a law that acknowledges the contribution of "repatriates" in the former French colonies in North Africa (Algeria, Morocco, Tunisia), as well as other parts of the world (Law 2005–158, passed 23 February 2005). In the context of Algeria, the law recognized the efforts of *pied-noirs* (French settlers in the colonies) and Harki—Muslim Algerians who fought with the French in the Algerian War of Independence (Crapanzano 2011).[19] A great controversy arose regarding section 4 of the law, which required high school curricula to "recognize in particular the positive role of the French presence overseas, notably in North Africa." The law passed in a parliament led by President Jacques Chirac and his leading, right-leaning party, the Union for a Popular Movement (UMP).

The section stirred a huge outcry: forty-four thousand people signed petitions calling for its cancelation; a thousand or so historians, intellectuals, and culture figures sent petitions and statements; and parliament members from the socialist and communist parties publically condemned it. One petition stated that the law enforces an official lie about massacres that sometimes went as far as genocide, as well as about slave trade and the heritage of racism. A crisis in foreign relations soon followed. Interior Minister Nicolas Sarkozy had to cancel a preplanned visit to the French Caribbean in fear of mass protest, and the French ambassador to Algeria made a special gesture by attending for the first time the official commemoration ceremony of the massacre in Setif in May 1945, in which tens of thousands of Algerians who protested for independence were killed by the French colonial army (forty-five thousand, according to the official Algerian version, or fifteen to twenty thousand, according to French historians). The ambassador called the massacre "an inexcusable tragedy"—a contradictory term as far as determining who is responsible for the killing. The gesture was accepted, yet the president of Algeria, Abdelaziz Bouteflika, declared that his country never stopped waiting for a French admission of all its actions during the colonial government and Algeria's War of Independence.[20]

The domestic and external objections led to the cancelation of section 4. In December of that year, President Chirac asked for a reexamination of the law, which according to him was "dividing the French," which would lead to a new version.[21] Later Chirac ordered the removal of section 4 of the law. But the protest already sparked a larger criticism against memory laws in general.

France's most notable historians organized under an initiative by renowned historian and public intellectual Pierre Nora titled Liberté pour l'histoire ("Liberty for History") and published an appeal against the law. "It is not up to the state to say how history should be taught," historian Pierre Vidal-Naquet was quoted as saying in the *Guardian*.[22] The state should not be allowed to intervene and impose "an official version of history, in defiance of educational neutrality" and the freedom of historical research or education, Professor Gerard Noiriel and others further maintained, according to the same *Guardian* article. Education rather than the law should write history or determine an imperative to remember, the historians argued (Garton Ash 2008).

Left-leaning parliament members protested the damage to freedom of speech and criticized the attempts of interest groups to "confiscate history for their own ends," in the words of Noiriel, according to the *Guardian*; the section was apparently tabled by MPs with close ties to France's community of former Algerian settlers lobbying for Harki and *pied-noir* rights. MRAP, an antiracism group, said that above all the law showed "contempt for the victims."[23]

In January 2006, France's Constitutional Council, its constitutional court, stated that laws "should serve to set mandatory duties and rights, not to be an incantation."[24] Legal scholar Stéphanie Gruet interpreted this statement as implicitly critiquing France's excessive use of memory laws (Wartanian 2008), which indeed was terminated in 2012. On February 28 the Constitutional Court found the Armenian genocide denial law, which brought about a crisis in French-Turkish relations, to be unconstitutional and declared that there will be no further memory laws in the future (Curran 2015).

What can we learn about memory laws from this case of failed legislation? Raffi Wartanian, who studied the French case, inferred that memory laws of both types are circumstantial and triggered by specific occurrences in the present (2008). The section against Holocaust denial, for example, was added to the freedom of speech law in 1990 after defamation of the Jewish cemetery in Carpentras ignited a surge of support for outlawing Holocaust denial. These laws are reactive rather than preventative, a patch rather than a solution to the contemporary ailments of racism. Additionally, France's memory laws are unequally tailored for groups with power and visibility, such as the Jewish community; the Armenian community, which is the largest in Europe; or, in the case of the "Colonialism Law," France's community of former Algerian settlers. In other words, these laws should be understood in the political context of their legislation, such as the debates of that time on Turkey's candidacy to join the European Union.[25] The political context includes pressures to air or to silence contested pasts by influential minorities and interest groups, external states, or international bodies such as the European Union.

While some may view memory laws as contested symbolic gestures that spark heated debates and threaten to polarize society, others might consider them as means for increasing social solidarity in immigration countries. Indeed, in France, like in other Western democracies that attract a large number of immigrants and refugees, memory laws are supposed to assist the official policy of integration through inclusion of minority histories in the official historical record and collective memory (Wartanian 2008). However, by acknowledging the experiences of some minority groups and excluding others, they often result in polarization, frustration, and humiliation of the excluded groups (Noiriel quoted in Henley 2005). In some cases, exclusion of a social group from the official collective memory can exclude it from political participation and active citizenship (Rothberg and Ildiz 2011); in other cases, misrecognition of suffering can lead to violence (Barkan 2013).

With this knowledge on the attributes of memory laws in France, we can return to the difference between the exclusion of minorities from the general laws that make up the national collective memory in the state's calendar and the exclusion of a specific minority group in memory laws, like in the colonialism law.

Wartanian (2008) argues that unlike the three memory laws that have passed before 2005, which deal with crimes against humanity and which carried only a declarative value, section 4 of the 2005 law does not acknowledge the crimes of French colonialism in Algeria and was created to disseminate this interpretation of the national past in the pedagogical infrastructure of the state. In other words, it is a new step in fortifying the national memory against the collective memory of those who suffered from state violence, something that was not necessary before, when this memory was simply ignored in the memorial-day laws. In 2005, the silence of French colonialist violence in Algeria in state laws was not enough to stop the surge in calls to address this past, and an active enforcement of the national memory that excluded these memories came to the rescue in section 4 of the law.

However, section 4 did not outlive the domestic and external outcry and was canceled by the president out of fear that it would further divide the French and steal votes from his ruling party. Since then no law that recognizes Algerians' suffering has been enacted.

With the constitutional court ruling against memory laws, the French historians felt that their problem was solved and shifted their support to the struggles against memory laws in the Baltic countries and Russia since 2009. The Russian case that is elaborated in the next section is even more interesting in comparison to the Israeli case, as both concern laws that have been passed despite public protest and were part of a wider campaign to maintain a positive memory of the national past against countermemories and claims.

The Russian Legal Processes against the "Falsification of History"

In Russia, a law first drafted in 2009 appears to resemble the laws against Holocaust denial in Western European countries but is in fact aimed at forbidding any criticism of Russia's actions during World War II. Laws against Nazi propaganda and symbols already existed at the time this law was proposed, and a list of banned extremist literature that included Adolf Hitler's *Mein Kampf* has been maintained by the Ministry of Justice.[26] Yet a law pertaining to similar offences was proposed in the Duma in 2009 on the eve of the sixty-fourth anniversary of the Allies' victory in WWII (8 May) and approved around the same date five years later.

The proposal was immediately overshadowed by another legal initiative: a historical truth commission that President Dmitry Medvedev ordered to convene on 15 May 2009. The official mission of the commission was evident in its full name: the Commission to Counteract Attempts at Falsifying History to Damage the Interests of Russia. Yet there was another goal behind the commission, as well as the law—they were both designed to block the surge of Eastern European narratives about World War II as part of a larger attempt "to politicize history and to prevent the emergence of any historical narrative that would belittle the image of the Soviet Union, the legal predecessor of today's assertive 'new Russia,'" as Kora Andrieu explained (2011, 213).

The law's very first draft received negative reactions as well, although surveys showed that 60 percent of Russians supported a law on the falsification of history (Koposov 2010). One of the initiators of the law proposal, Duma deputy Irina Yarovaya from United Russia, told the progovernment newspaper *KM*, "We will not allow the rewriting of history; the Soviet soldier will remain a liberating soldier, protecting peace in the face of the fascist plague." The paper praised the bill because it would make the scientific community "hit the brakes" and "filter the conclusions" (Gortinskaya 2013). As the paper suggested, the law was directed against revisionist historiography and critical views of Russia. It was an attempt to produce an ideological consensus regarding the positive and liberating role of the country in ending the Second World War as a basis for contemporary national identity by silencing critical voices both within the country—such views are held by the liberal creative class, pro-West intellectuals, and civil society groups—as well as from abroad, by postsocialist countries.

Russian historians were divided: Some supported such a law, or hoped it would bring an opening of the archives; others saw it as severely limiting their scientific freedom (Koposov 2010). They received the support of external organizations such as the French Liberté pour l'histoire, the American Historical Association, and the American Association for the Advancement of Slavic Studies, as well as from Italian historians in the form of a petition.[27] Other intellectuals and civil society leaders commented against the law, as I elaborate later on, but did not have the power to change the legislation. While a commission is limited to making recommendations to the president, a law can be enforced by all judges to condemn anyone who is "traducing the past."[28] The commission met twice, supported the production of some leaflets, and was disassembled in 2012. The debates about the law proposal were only the beginning of a long and volatile, yet successful, process of legislation.

Both the law and the commission came at the end of a decade or so during which postsocialist countries have exposed and condemned the practices of the Soviet occupation as part of their transition to democracy and nation-building efforts. Such revelations and condemnations of the crimes of Stalinism, which showed that the Soviet regime was oppressing rather than liberating, in addition to scholarly publications on the violence of the Red Army in the countries it occupied during World War II (the mass rape of women, for example), conflicted with the national sentiment of Russia (Koposov 2005). The postcommunist countries' condemnation is addressed in the title of the first draft of the law against the "rehabilitation of Nazism in the newly independent states within the territory of the former Soviet Union." Indeed, it was to be enforced within the borders of the USSR as defined on 22 June 1941, both on Russian citizens and on citizens of today's independent countries that were then part of Soviet territory. The law enforces a range of sanctions on these new states if found guilty.

Domestically the Second World War is, in the minds of some, the only historical event that can unite the Russian people today (see, for example, Andrieu 2011, 214), and so countering the growing contestation of the dominant and positive perception of this national past was the task that the lawmakers tried to fulfill.

Another legal initiative related to memory preceded the law: a 2007 law that gave the Kremlin vast authority over history textbooks, after President Vladimir Putin complained in 2006 that the current ones present a negative perception of the Soviet past because their authors were funded by foreign foundations (Andrieu 2011; Koposov 2009). Unlike these books, a teachers' handbook titled *The Modern History of Russia, 1945–2006*, which was published that year, recounted Stalin's numerous achievements and presented him as the most successful USSR leader and as a "'contradictory' figure, evil for some but a hero for others" (Andrieu 2011, 212). And yet, Stalin is too controversial to be the basis of the collective memory that unites the Russian nation in comparison to the victory in World War II (Koposov 2009). According to Russian historian Nikolay Koposov (2005), the victory over fascism was a uniting collective memory in the Soviet regime and became a founding myth in post-Soviet Russia—in both regimes, however, the positive perception of Russia and the allies' victory in the war obscures the memory of Stalinist terror (Koposov 2005).

The first two versions of the law outlined an expansive memory law that criminalized rehabilitating Nazism and "distorting" the verdict of the Nuremberg Tribunal, with a penalty of three to five years in prison (Koposov 2009, 2010).[29] However, it was unclear how the law would be executed and what version of the past is "the right one." It was unclear even to Duma members how to translate the vast scope and overly general phrasing into usable legislation. The Duma Legislation Committee sent the authors to another round of revisions (Koposov 2010).

The new version was submitted to the Duma on 16 April 2010 and briefly stated: "Approval or denial of Nazi crimes against peace and the security of humanity as established by the verdict of the Nuremberg Tribunal shall be punishable by a fine of up to 300,000 rubles or up to three years' imprisonment" (Koposov 2010). Although it was significantly shorter, the law proposal remained obscure and continued to rely on the Nuremberg judges for clarifications.

The choice of the Nuremberg verdict may seem legitimate and difficult to argue with—indeed, Yarovaya and other sponsors of the law noted that similar laws exist in other European countries in order to gain legitimacy for its legislation.[30] Yet Koposov (2010) argues not only that the verdict serves as a cover for the law's unwritten goals—to prevent charging Russia with the responsibility for starting the war, for the war crimes of the Red Army, and for the atrocities of the Soviet occupation—but also that this choice produces various contradictions that make it very difficult to achieve these goals. First, Nuremberg did not discuss the Red Army or the Allies' actions, and so the law in fact does not protect one from claiming Russia's responsibility for crimes during World War II. Second, some historical events mentioned in the verdict have since been revealed to be different. One known example is the massacre of Polish officers in Katyn in September 1941, which was inserted to the Nuremberg verdict by the Russian prosecutor as a Nazi crime, yet was revealed to be a crime that Russia admitted to in 1990.

Additionally, the Nuremberg verdict has different categories for Nazi crimes than those used by the authors of the Russian bill, despite the recommendation of the Duma's legal department (Koposov 2010). The Nuremberg Tribunal created three categories of crimes: crimes against peace, war crimes, and crimes against humanity. The Russian law, on the other hand, mentioned crimes against the security of humanity, and it is unclear whether they are included in Nuremberg's crimes against peace or against humanity. If they are not included, it is not certain that a law that does not include crimes against humanity can pertain to Holocaust denial. Moreover, as the Russian version does not include the category of war crimes, it may leave out the denial or justification of Nazi crimes in Russia. In addition, it is unclear what would qualify as a crime: is stating that Russia is responsible for the massacre in Katyn a crime, or mentioning the crimes of Stalinism a violation of the verdict? (Koposov 2010).

Like section 4 of the "colonialism law" in France, the Russian law was drafted to protect the positive national memory of the state against the memories of groups who suffered from its violence. In both cases, those affected are not only intrastate groups but also other countries whose interpretations of the shared past are silenced. Yet while other countries have their independence and usually receive international support from fellow EU countries and monitoring human rights agencies, some of the victims of Stalinism within Russia, its historians, the liberal creative class, pro-West intellectuals, and civil society groups have no support that would allow them to speak and write freely without being prosecuted by such memory law.

With the diminishing civil society in Russia and closing of media outlets in favor of a governmental news agency, the internal public debate is very limited, and the central outlets are saved for the ideology of Putin and Medvedev (Henderson 2011; Evans 2006).[31] Social media networks host debates and calls to fire those responsible for antidemocratic legislation (Glushko 2013), yet it was not internal criticism that eventually determined the fate of this law, but the international context that shapes Russia's foreign policy. Since the height of the debate in 2009, the relationships of Russia with Poland and the United States warmed up for a period of time in 2010–2012, an atmosphere that did not accommodate an aggressive memory politics, and Putin and Medvedev distanced themselves from the law proposal. The law was put aside for a while and was not debated in the Duma. Its supporters, however, continued to propose new versions in 2012 and 2013, until a more suitable international context of hostility between Putin, Poland, and the United States in light of the Russian aggression in Ukraine enabled the rapid approval of the law just in time for the 2014 anniversary of the Allies' victory in the war.

In June 2013, Yarovaya revived the 2010 version of the negation of the Nuremberg verdict by sponsoring a law against the dissemination of "denial of the sentence passed by the international military tribunal as well as the denial of the fact that the actions of the anti-Hitler coalition were aimed at preserving the international peace and security." Yarovaya's 2013 version also criminalized the "distribution of knowingly false information about the actions of the Allied armies connected with charges of various crimes, including the artificial creation of evidence."[32] The penalty was similar to the original version. The newspaper *KM* again commended the law proposal, which it said makes it "harder for historians to falsify history" (Gortinskaya 2013). The newspaper also held an opinion survey on the question, "Should the negation of USSR victory in the Great Patriotic War be punishable?" Eighty-three percent answered yes (Gortinskaya 2013).

In addition to some historians, Russian civil society publically opposed the revived law, which it saw as a direct response to a post by the human rights blogger Leonid Guzman, who compared the Nazi SS troops and Stalin's SMERSH—the military death squads.[33] Nikolai Svanidze, a journalist and member of the Civic Chamber of the parliament—Putin's version of a civil society initiative—said that Yarovaya offers a ban of criticism against Stalin, the leadership of the Red Army, and of the Allies' armies.[34]

However, in January 2014 Yarovaya's law was pushed forward after a media-poll scandal during Russia's seventieth anniversary of the lifting of the Nazi blockade of Leningrad by the independent opposition-leaning television channel Dozhd. The poll asked if Leningrad should have been surrendered to the Nazis in order to save its residents' lives. The poll invoked outrage on mass media and social networks that prompted a renewed interest in the law—and a ban of Dozhd.[35] Yarovaya mobilized the controversy to urge the processing of her law proposal as a new article in the penal code. The law's first reading was approved unanimously on 4 April 2014 and rushed through a second and third reading to be fully approved on 23 April 2014.[36] Yarovaya told the press that the law was especially pressing is light of the political crisis in Ukraine, which according to her is launched and supported by radicals and neo-Nazis. "Ukraine is a living witness of what can be the result of such a policy, when Nazism is standing tall and manifests itself not only through propaganda but through actual crimes," she said.[37]

Indeed, like the characteristics attributed to memory laws in the French case, the Russian memory law was circumstantial and triggered by specific occurrences in the present (Wartanian 2008). It was similarly legislated by the ruling party, which reacted against contestations by opposition groups and foreign postsocialist countries. Like the Nakba law, the Russian law was pursued along with other measures, such as a reform in school curricula, to fortify a positive view of Russia's role in the Second World War, after a decade of contestations. Although the Russian law has not yet been enforced, its antidemocratic effect on public debate had already materialized during the legislation process, through the banning of a media channel that dared to ask a revisionist question regarding the war and via a very intimidating penalty that multiplies if one uses the media to express critical views on the past at issue. Both of these sanctions carry a chilling effect that may prevent civil society groups, historians, intellectuals, and media channels from publically expressing critical opinions on the past, thus damaging the freedom of speech and limiting public discourse to the official narrative.

Lessons for the Nakba Law

When compared to the Nakba Law, the French and Russian cases of memory laws raise interesting similarities regarding the role, context, and consequences of the state's reaction through legislation to calls to revise national memory. First, like section 4 of the colonialism law and the Russian Law, the Nakba Law is designed to protect the state's official memory and silence minority memories. As Wartanian (2008) argued regarding the French case, all three laws have been legislated by a dominant group with close relations to the ruling party. Assuming the foundational role assigned to memory laws—creating solidarity and strengthening the nation's stability in light of growing criticism of its past wrongs—the Nakba Law, like the other laws, has in fact created a polarizing exclusion of citizen groups and neighboring countries (or governed noncitizens in the case of Palestinians in the OPT). The debates around the Nakba Law expressed the deepening rupture in Israeli society, not only between the Left and Right about the state of the conflict and its resolution, but also between democratic liberals on the left, center, and right, and religious nationalists primarily on the right. Each of these camps has different opinion on the foundational character of contemporary Israeli society. The former see it as primarily democratic and the latter as primarily Jewish (see, for example, Kremnitzer and Fuchs 2011).

Second, the struggle between rival approaches to the national memory in the Israeli case, similar to the other cases, also support Wartanian's suggestion that memory laws are consequential—laws that respond to recent events or trends. These bring to public attention a counterinterpretation of the national past that centers on past wrongs, which the law is created to block in response.

Third, as a consequential law, the Nakba Law is a patch, a local medicine for an already growing public awareness of the contested past. This medicine is disproportional in a dual manner: On one hand, it cannot block what has already gained visibility and entered public consciousness; and on the other hand, it is often an exaggerated response to otherwise marginal groups who promote countermemory, at least in the Israeli case. The fear of the state that the national Zionist memory will be criticized was so great that it necessitated, in the eyes of the lawmakers, the extensive force of the law, which in its earlier version included three years of incarceration. The marginality of Nakba memory initiatives in a time of heightened nationalist sentiment among the majority and leadership of Israel may have been marginalized more effectively if left alone, to gain public visibility gradually or be rejected without the help of legislation. Yet the legislation paradoxically gave it the center stage, bringing it to the attention of the larger society.

I mentioned how the Israeli law, without mentioning the word *Nakba*, points to Palestinian citizens who are the group that traditionally visits their pre-1948 lands during Independence Day, a time shaped by historical circumstances that were determined by the state during the period of martial law. Owing to the different calendars, the Hebrew date for Independence Day (5 Iyar) and the Gregorian date of the official and international Nakba Day (15 May) seldom coincide, and so public commemoration on the official date of Nakba Day in Israel is actually not banned by the Nakba Law, despite repeated calls to include it in the interpretation of the law. In other words, the law does not prevent public commemoration of the Nakba—which it was created to block—but poses a specific threat to Palestinian citizens and their supporters. It does so by blocking state-sponsored institutions, including Arab Palestinian municipalities, from mentioning the Nakba in public when the majority celebrates Independence Day, in order to block a viable alternative to the hegemonic national tradition whose official events emphasize Zionist patriotism, militarism, and Jewish nationalism.

"In ten years when we have a law forbidding a Palestinian return, we'll know that we succeeded, like with the Nakba Law," said Debbie, a Zochrot activist, in a meeting on the right of return as the central redress for the Nakba in August 2014. Her quote means that the legislation of a law that forbids activist claims signals that their struggle for political change had been successful in achieving public attention, even if it is a negative one. Indeed, the Nakba Law is a bitter victory for Nakba memory over its exclusion from national memory. As we will see, the dissemination of knowledge of the contested past may have transformed Jewish Israelis' attention toward Palestinians in 1948, but it also led to misrecognition of their loss and even to justification of it in some cases. More knowledge carried a limitation of rights for Palestinian citizens, and while it may have advanced the inclusion of the Nakba in the unofficial collective memory of Jewish Israelis by turning their attention to it, exclusion and retrenchment of public debate on this issue framed this memory.

Adding a memory law that points directly to Palestinian citizens' commemoration practices is a step further from their exclusion from memorial-day laws in Israel, a more advanced stage in the state's battle against the inclusion of Palestinian citizens in the national collective memory. In addition to passively ignoring their memory and shared history in the calendar of national holidays and memorial days, the Nakba Law added an active ban on publically expressing their suffering and displacement. The ramifications of this ban, however, extend beyond state sanction of its Palestinian minority to impact the democratic public debate in Israel. Despite the fact that the Nakba Law has not yet been enforced, the threat of its enforcement limits the already shrinking boundaries of the public debate on the conflict, signaling that the Nakba is a forbidden issue that can carry sanctions. Although some of the reactions to the law were the inception of additional Nakba memorials—for example, annual Nakba memorial ceremonies on university campuses that have managed to bypass the law for now—these and other actions are increasingly condemned and threatened by an aggressive political discourse led by nongovernmental right-wing groups and coalitions of MKs who call for enforcing the law or expanding it to universities and educational institutions in particular.

The comparative perspective has shown that the state reaction to calls to revise the national memory is not unified, and the legislation of memory laws is not a linear process of constant progression. In all three cases of memory laws I examined, including the Russian case, the legislation process of memory laws included disagreements, revisions, and delays. Moreover, state legislation is a powerful measure but not one that is irreversible. In France the section that enforced the study of French colonialism as positive was canceled in a matter of months because of public disproval. In Russia, where civil society is diminishing in favor of antidemocratic advancement of nationalist ideology through progovernment media and educational system, the law was successful when the political context was right, prompting weak public criticism and serving the government in reflecting foreign policy interests. In Israel, where civil society and the media are stronger than in Russia, the Nakba Law came as part of a wave of antidemocratic legislation to exclude Palestinian citizens and their supporters and limit their participation in Israeli politics (Ozacky-Lazar and Jabareen 2016). The comparison suggests that a different political context, a higher domestic or external overseeing legal entity (like the constitutional court of France or the European Court), or changing international interests (as was the case in Russia) may bring a change regarding the Nakba Law in the future.

However, in the cases of the Russian and French memory laws, the current regime addressed the past's authoritative or colonial regime, demonstrating continuity or at least duality regarding past wrongs. In Israel, a transition from conflict with the Palestinians to peace is yet to come and the regime has not changed, so any depiction of the regime's conduct in the past carries much higher stakes for the present and future of the conflict, as it may carry responsibility and redress for future peace negotiations.

5

From Reconciliation without Truth
to Truth without Reconciliation

> The Israeli collective memory is Zionist. . . . The heavy price Arab Palestinians paid—in life, the destruction of hundreds of villages, and refugeeism—is almost without public recognition. The manipulation of constituting the collective memory also prevents the Jews from acknowledging their part of the destruction, carry the responsibility for it, and reach actual reconciliation with the Palestinians. . . . Physically marking the [Palestinian] villages and public debate—Jewish and Palestinian, apart and together—would encourage the constitution of a more moral discourse, . . . and express a true will to reconcile. (Eitan Bronstein, *Hakibutz* newspaper, 2001)

> The acknowledgement I am declaring today belongs to a glorious tradition I am proud to join. Public admission of guilt is not a weakness—quite the opposite: it expresses the human desire for reconciliation. Leaders who have ignored the suffering they have caused to other nations and human groups have come to recognize that it is impossible to seek reconciliation and true peace without acknowledging the crimes their nations have perpetrated. (Rafi Shtendel, chairperson, New KKL-JNF website, 2013)

The first text was published in the months that preceded the formation of Zochrot as an organization that would remind Jewish Israelis and mark the Palestinian life that was lost in the 1948 war. Eitan Bronstein portrayed the idea behind the organization in a 2001 article of the magazine of the kibbutzim movement. In these early days, the idea was that *airing* the Palestinian past in public (through signage that marks the destroyed villages), an act of recognition in itself, may lead Jewish Israelis to publically *acknowledge* the Palestinian displacement and destruction in 1948. Such recognition and acknowledgment could enable Jewish Israelis to take *responsibility* for their part in the Palestinian loss and by so doing, pave the way to *reconciliation*. Another outcome would be opening public debate to a "more moral discourse," thus creating a better society. Bronstein proposed that every kibbutz would post a sign marking the Palestinian villages that existed on its lands or near them before 1948.

The article received mostly negative responses from kibbutzim members, who claimed, for example, that such signs should also note the violence Palestinian residents of some of these villages inflicted on their pre-1948 Jewish neighbors, or that the signs are not a good idea as they may lead Palestinian refugees to claim their properties or a return to their lands.[1] Wakim Wakim, then the general secretary of the Association for the Defense of the Rights of the Internally Displaced (ADRID), the main organization of Palestinian refugees in Israel, was asked by the newspaper to respond to Bronstein's article. He noted that a similar idea had been raised by ADRID, yet he expressed ambivalence about it. He believed that such signposting should be agreed on by both sides, Jewish and Palestinian citizens, and receive the necessary state approval, yet he expressed concern that the state would take advantage of the signs to shape history in a manner that once again reflects its interests. He also anticipated resistance by Palestinian refugees in his association, out of fear that the signs would be seen as replacing a future return, where it would in fact be only "a nice and moving" symbolic gesture.[2] These responses to Bronstein's proposal reflected the context of the conflict in their effort to balance his one-sided gesture of marking Palestinian lands in Israeli localities.

The second quote was published online more than a decade later, in September 2013, in a statement that initiated a project that culminated in an exhibit at Zochrot's gallery in Tel Aviv from March to May 2014.[3] The initiator was again Bronstein, this time in disguise, as the fictional character of Rafi Shtendel, the chairperson of a fictional organization, the New Jewish National Fund. The name of the organization mimics the name of Israel's Land and Forest Agency, the Jewish National Fund (JNF), known in Hebrew under the abbreviation KKL. The name of the fictional chairperson also resembles the name of JNF's real chairperson at the time, Efi Stenzler. The project revolved around the story of the fictional chair's realization that his Zionist agency not only has erased the remnants of pre-1948 and pre-1967 Palestinian villages through foresting but is also continuing this erasure by excluding their history from the official signage and maps of today's national parks and forests. Shtendel's realization is transformative, and he begins to change the official JNF signs clandestinely, replacing them with new signs that include the Palestinian history of the national parks he visits.

This story of acknowledging the erasure of Palestinian history from the official signage (fixed through Shtendel's clandestine signposting, an act that Zochrot has been performing in its activist tours from its inception) and the destruction of the Palestinian villages that lay underneath the post-1948 national parks and forests are told as a new chapter in the Zionist history of the JNF. "As a leading organization in the Zionist effort to 'make the wilderness bloom,'[4] we must now lead the change and start showing everyone that lying buried underneath the green forests planted by the KKL are the remains of an entire living culture wiped out in 1948," Shtendel stated.[5] Zochrot posing as the JNF is a playful parody. Zochrot's reputation among Israeli society in 2013 was of a radically post-Zionist or even anti-Zionist organization, and thus pretending to be one of the central institutions of the Zionist settlement project in Palestine and later in the state was likely to be perceived as extremely humorous, even mocking the Zionist agency.[6] However, at the beginning there were no indications that Zochrot or Bronstein stood behind this project. According to Bronstein, the statement was supposed to bypass Jewish Israeli guards and confuse them by not revealing who really is behind it (interview 2014). Bronstein sent e-mails announcing the New KKL-JNF's website from a fictional e-mail account under the name of Shtendel. No mention to Bronstein or Zochrot appeared on the website dedicated to the fictional organization. Later on, in March 2014, Bronstein publically revealed his authorship through a statement on Zochrot's website in accordance with the related exhibit in the group's gallery. This appropriation of state rhetoric and Zionist tropes resembles the appropriation of hegemonic cultural practices that Zochrot performs in its activist tours and testimonies that was discussed in Chapter 1.

The proposal to write a new chapter in Israel's national history is, however, rooted and justified here by an international history, or "a glorious tradition" of reconciliation, as it is called in the statement above. This tradition is exemplified in the statement through apologies for state-sponsored crimes made by leaders of postconflict countries, such as Boris Tadić of Serbia, and leaders of postcolonial countries, such as Australian prime minister Kevin Rudd and British foreign secretary William Hague. Shtendel praises these leaders as "express[ing] the human desire for reconciliation" and opposes them to "leaders who have ignored the suffering they have caused to other nations and human groups." The latter are required to "recognize that it is impossible to seek *reconciliation* and true peace without *acknowledging* the crimes their nations have perpetrated."[7] The examples are brought to demonstrate the global trend of recognizing that "no morally sound future is possible so long as the crimes of the past continue to be denied." And they are followed by a declaration that "it is time we too acknowledge what is here, right underneath the surface, what is never mentioned in Israeli maps and signs: the Palestinian Nakba."[8]

The call for Jewish Israelis to one-sidedly acknowledge and take responsibility for Palestinian displacement is similar in both quotes and it has been the declared mission of Zochrot since its inception, but in the 2013 statement the mission is also linked to the globally circulating model of truth and reconciliation and the concept of historical justice that Zochrot appropriated for the Israeli-Palestinian conflict.[9] The threefold model for change that appeared in the 2001 quote is presented here as well: *knowing* through marking the prestate Palestinian life on-site, would lead to public *acknowledgment* and to taking *responsibility* for its loss. These three stages pave the way to reconciliation. Yet between the 2001 article and the 2013 parody, the ambivalence that was expressed in 2001 in the responses of primarily left-wing kibbutzim members and a Palestinian organizer has expanded to the larger society and developed in parallel with the growing dissemination of the knowledge about the Nakba in Israel. What could have been communicated directly to Kibbutzim residents of Palestinian lands in 2001 needed to be staged as a type of parody without any metacommentary in 2013. As we will see, the 2013 parody reflects and responds to the ambivalent reception, if not rejection, of the activist effort to acknowledge the Palestinian Nakba in Israel according to the transnational model of reconciliation through addressing past wrongs.

Moving from 2001 to 2013, we begin by examining how Jewish and Palestinian memory activists chose, studied, and strategically appropriated and utilized this model—an expert-based conception that is usually intended to be facilitated by the state in postconflict societies, most famously in the South African transition from Apartheid in 1995. The concepts of historical justice and a specific model of truth and reconciliation were "imported" from postconflict societies to raise a different understanding of the past and future in the prolonged Israeli-Palestinian conflict through producing and disseminating knowledge on the Nakba outside state channels. However, in this active conflict the more knowledge was disseminated and visibility given to the difficult past—Nakba memory in Israel in this case—the more ambivalence and misrecognition it encountered rather than acknowledgment. This two-directional movement, one that spreads the knowledge and grants the past visibility, the other that limits acknowledgment and inclusion of those who carry the difficult memory, reveals some of the concrete possibilities and limitations of the expert model of truth and reconciliation in the context of an ongoing conflict. It highlights some of the issues that were viewed as problematic in postconflict cases as well.

When they imported these external concepts as a new argument for reconciliation or a counterclaim regarding the origin of the conflict in the Israeli public debate, the memory activists in Israel appropriated them to fit the context of the ongoing conflict. More specifically, the groups drew on the South African model of truth and reconciliation (Campbell 2000),[10] and they appropriated it in accordance with the locally prevailing perceptions of conflict resolution and reconciliation in the Israeli-Palestinian context.

The South African model of truth and reconciliation, a mechanism developed to achieve historical justice, among other things, has three different aspects: (1) an institutional form—the truth and reconciliation state *commission*—which in itself consists of two specific forms: public hearings and a final report; (2) a *model* for conflict resolution leading from knowledge production to acknowledgment and accountability for atrocities; and (3) a transnational human rights–oriented *discourse* on the importance of coming to terms with a difficult or contested past. While the model and form have received much scholarly attention as an expert, elite, or state-based project for postconflict societies (Bickford and Sodaro 2010; Verdoolaege 2008; Payne 2008; Olick 2007; D. Levy and Sznaider 2006; Bickford 2004; Torpey 2003; Wilson 2001; Posel 2002), the discourse, which spans beyond these two aspects, has not yet been fully articulated as an object of study in its own right.[11] The traveling discourse, values, and vocabulary of truth and reconciliation can be used outside state channels, by marginalized groups, and in unintended places. Indeed, what people *do* with globally circulating ideas and models of reconciliation and peace and how they view them during an active conflict are questions that have been missing from the study of all three aspects of truth and reconciliation. The three aspects of truth and reconciliation were attractive to memory activists in Israel as a platform for intrastate struggle for political change outside state channels.

Setting the ground for a review of the activist appropriation of this model and how it was received in the Israeli public debate, I begin by contextualizing the general paradigm of historical justice in the region. This paradigm already existed when memory-activist groups began to form. It was framed, however, in a manner that did not advance peace as much as it perpetuated the conflict. Memory activists had to construct a different argument that would reframe the dominant connection between memory, history, and reconciliation in the dominant political discourse.

Historicizing Historical Justice

Historical justice is a political project that emerged in the West in a particular historical moment but has since then been widely distributed around the world. In the transnational political arena, it is seen today as a central, "universal" principle. Yet its abstract assumptions also allow much flexibility that enabled nation-states to use it not only as means for reconciliation and peace, but also to perpetuate conflict (Moses 2011; Poole 2010). Indeed, despite the normative aim of the concept of historical justice—(liberal democratic) justice as a basis for reconciliation—historical justice–oriented politics challenges and sometimes even hinders efforts to reconcile in cases of conflict.

The post-Oslo period of the Israeli-Palestinian conflict is a clear manifestation of this contradiction in terms. The shift from future to past in the political arena and the centrality of claims for historical justice have been extremely visible in the region in the second half of the 1990s and in the 2000s. As future visions for the region disappeared in the aftermath of the Oslo Peace Accords and violence and physical separation increased, each side further fortified its position through a discourse of historical rights. The past has become a central and crucial arena for political struggle.

Historical justice has been used in the region by Palestinian intellectuals from the fiftieth commemoration of the Nakba in the Occupied Territories, Israel, and the Arab world in 1998, who wished to "translate" the national Palestinian narrative to a more universalistic argument and case, using truth and reconciliation arguments about historical rights (Hill 2008). In Israel, since 2001, memory activists on the radical left have been both responding to and reproducing the

Palestinian claims and making their own claims to symbolic recognition of Palestinian suffering in 1948 for the sake of Israel's future by establishing and making public a historical and commemorative record of their suffering against widespread silence and denial (Berg and Schaefer 2009, 2). In historical justice terms, they made "commemorative claims" to remember the victims of the past and compensate them. "Transformative claims" are a different kind of claim for historical justice (Berg and Shaefer 2009, 3), claims for a profound social and political change of present society derived from the "prolonged disaster of the past" (Torpey 2001, 337). This prolonged disaster is seen as embedded in unjust structures and institutions (political, social, economic, and legal) that continue to shape present society as unjust and unequal (Berg and Shaefer 2009, 3). These claims were more marginal among the Jewish Israeli activists than among Palestinian activists at first, yet they have been increasingly discussed in the second half of the decade.

These activist claims and discussions responded to a shift in the dominant discourse between the Israeli and Palestinian leaderships in the Occupied Territories, after the failure to follow the Oslo peace negotiations to their second and third stages and bring sustainable peace. In the second half of the 1990s and the early 2000s, the "primarily interest-based discourse" that was the base for the Oslo agreement was replaced with a "justice-based" discourse (Hill 2008, 154). As reconciliation did not arrive via Oslo's political arrangements, it shifted to the discursive arena, claiming recognition of each side's historical right and historical "truth" as prerequisite for any future peace negotiations of political agreement (Hill 2008, 154). The narratives both sides established as to why Oslo failed—"two incompatible, mirror narratives," which Tom Hill laid out in the following excerpt—expressed and caused further polarization, in addition to the physical distancing that followed the building of the Separation Wall by Israel:

> Broadly, from an Israeli perspective, Palestinian public opinion is unable or unwilling to acknowledge historical truth, understood primarily in the sense of the meaning and direction of history as distinct from its particular detail—about the events of 1948 that led the refugees to flee, the nature of Palestinian history since, the Palestinians' current historical condition and/or the relevance of the Holocaust to the conflict, to name only some of the major talking points—and will be unable to reconcile themselves to Israel's existence for so long as this deficit of historical consciousness

persists. . . . From a Palestinian perspective, Israeli public opinion is unable or unwilling to acknowledge the truth, both particular and general—about largely the same issues, with the addition of the nature of the 40-year occupation of the West Bank and Gaza—and will remain unable to reconcile itself to the changes in mindset, discourse and political structures required for sustainable peace until it acknowledges such truths. (2008, 152)

The lesson of Oslo is then similar for each side: to claim from now on "the public understanding and recognition of an unpalatable and intolerable truth on the other side" as a precondition to any reconciliation (Hill 2008, 152). Although this may seem as if the language of historical justice and the jargon of truth and reconciliation already frame the public debate in the region, it reveals how elastic its use may be: here it fortifies the debate as a zero-sum game of opposite claims for historical recognition and justice. The pursuit of historical justice, therefore, can (at least in the short run) be detrimental to reconciliation and creating a peaceful and tolerant society, instead reproducing the conflict and generating chauvinistic responses.

The main problem for the Israeli memory activists that entered this context in the 2000s was how to counter the use of historical-rights discourse in the service of reproducing the rival positions; how to allow for a different framing of the conflict and its future resolution along the lines of a discourse on rights and justice before seeking any pragmatic solutions.[12] The failure of a prevalent strategy of peace activism in the Oslo period to bring peace caused a shift among Israeli and Palestinian peace activists in the early 2000s, suggesting that the solution to this failure can be found in focusing on the highly contested past of 1948. This shift is elaborated later.

To distinguish their effort from the prevalent historical-rights argument that provokes national sentiments and further fortification of the rival conflict positions, memory activists in Israel emphasized the universalistic basis of the transnational discourse of historical justice. Instead of the dominant focus on opposing national claims for each side's historical right, they tried to reframe the Israeli public debate around a postnational and "universal" sense of historical justice that would advance reconciliation. This transnational vocabulary and its normative basis also serve the activists in defining their position versus the state as well as when looking outside to other networks of activists, funders, and intellectuals around the world and in other postconflict societies. This use of postnational, "universal" vocabulary and values to reframe the dominant public debate is particularly visible in these activists' deployment of truth and reconciliation, as the next section details.

Truth and Reconciliation Outside State Channels: A Model, Discourse, and Commission

Various aspects separate the Israeli-Palestinian case of active conflict from postconflict societies. The most striking difference is, perhaps, the absence of the state from truth and reconciliation efforts during conflict. In postconflict cases, the state is the one facilitating remembrance (and forgetting) projects for its newly equal citizens. Yet the State of Israel has engaged in neither a viable peace agreement with the Palestinians in the 2000s nor in reconciliation efforts. Within Israel not all citizens are treated as equal—the 20 percent of the population who are Palestinians with Israeli citizenship, as Chapter 3 mentions, have been discriminated against in the spirit of the martial law of 1948–1966 and have been increasingly and openly alienated and marginalized over the past decade or so. In other words, in the Israeli-Palestinian case, peace is sought between two—or three, including Palestinians in Israel (see Ghanem 2005)—national communities without clear boundaries that maintain mutual connections within a territory with undefined state borders (Hill 2008).

Another fundamental difference between memory activism in Israel and truth and reconciliation in postconflict situations is of temporality: First, memory activism in active conflict publicly airs a difficult past in order to make room for discussing it in public debate, whereas postconflict societies air the difficult past in order to achieve closure and put this past behind together with the violence it may provoke. Second, in postconflict societies, truth and reconciliation is employed to make sure that an event that had ended will "never again" take place, while memory activism during conflict is an effort against the inevitability of events, and it works to correct what can still be reversed.[13]

Operating in different settings than most cases in which truth and reconciliation has been implemented, memory-activist groups in Israel came to know the 1995 South African Truth and Reconciliation Commission, as well as the model and discourse of truth and reconciliation, through transnational activist and intellectual networks. In workshops and seminars organized by their funders, primarily private international foundations,[14] the Israeli activists met their counterparts from postconflict areas such as Northern Ireland, the former Yugoslavia, South Africa, and Germany, particularly initiatives that are engaged with the commemorations of mass violence. They also visited commemorative sites and artistic projects that document past atrocities in city space, such as the Stumbling Stones project in Germany and the District 6 museum in South Africa.

Critical theory and scholarship, which most of the memory activists have encountered at the postgraduate level of their education, spurred further engagement with discourses, models, and tools used in other cases as well as an affiliation and commitment to a global ethical community that many of these share. At the same time, Israeli activists became aware of the scholarly critiques of truth and reconciliation commissions, which they have taken into account in their own efforts.[15] Yet working within a particular political context, the challenge was how to translate the transnational paradigm in a manner that reached beyond the limits of the prevalent reproduction of the conflict through a rights-based post-Oslo argumentation (Hill 2008).

A Model for Conflict Resolution

Underlying truth and reconciliation efforts around the world since the mid-1980s is a basic model of political change based on successful coming to terms with a difficult past that enables participants to ultimately leave it behind so it does not come to haunt the creation of a peaceful society in the present and future. The model was developed in truth and reconciliation commissions (TRCs) in Latin America in the 1980s but took a slightly different route in the 1990s with the South African TRC of 1995 (Hayner 2006; Verdoolaege 2008; Mamdani 2001). According to the prominent South African model of truth and reconciliation, unraveling knowledge of a violent past in an act of public witnessing leads to recognition and acknowledgment of the victims' suffering.[16] This acknowledgment is accompanied by state material and legal restitution for the victims and amnesty for many of the perpetrators who are willing to publically confess their wrongdoing. Ideally, this process enables healing, reconciliation, and political stability (albeit not always a democratic government, as the case of postconflict Rwanda demonstrated) and is believed to halt cycles of violence and revenge. At the end of this process, experts and practitioners believe, mass violence can finally be left behind, in the past, exorcized from the present and future.

This model fits the experts' perception of political reconciliation through dealing with past wrongs. While experts are divided in their views of how visible the polarizing past should be in order to assist the creation of a sustainable peace, the range of perceptions of such reconciliation view the process as (1) the end of violence, (2) a two-sided exchange of acknowledgments of past wrongs to allow (3) the resumption of equal relations between former enemies (Verdeja 2014). This expert perception of reconciliation envisions a conflict between two nation-states to be the ideal type at the basis of their assumptions, although it does not always fit the different types of conflict that exist in reality. In such ideal-type cases, reconciliation usually refers to reestablishing social, political, and economic relations between former enemies (Ackerman 1994; Bar-Siman-Tov 2004; Kwak and Nobles 2013; Verdeja 2014). Often, however, the conflict is within a nation-state, and in many cases there are no previous morally acceptable relations to return to, for example in the transition from Apartheid in South Africa (Verdeja 2014). Speaking about reconciliation as a reintegration of former peaceful mutual relations or as exchange of acknowledgments of past wrongs may be misleading in such cases, and yet this term continues to be used to deal with post-violence relations. Indeed, South Africa became a paradigmatic case for the reconciliation debate not only in academia but also in international politics that inspired other efforts to reconcile in and after conflict (including the Israeli memory activists).

As mentioned, the theoretical perceptions and model that inform efforts to achieve reconciliation through truth production and assist the transformation of a society from violent conflict to a nonviolent resolution affect not only postconflict societies but also cases of conflict. Groups claim recognition of past suffering and loss, and they look to the establishment of truth and reconciliation commissions and various modalities of transitional justice to grant symbolic or material reparations to victims (Theidon 2006).[17]

In Israel and Palestine, the model of truth and reconciliation was adopted by memory-activist groups as a strategy for conflict resolution to replace the previous strategy that failed them after Oslo. The prevalent strategy of peace activism in the Oslo period was "people-to-people" projects (or "Track II Diplomacy," as it was called in the late

1980s and early 1990s; S. Cohen 1995; Challand 2011). As mentioned briefly in the Introduction, it consisted of meetings between Jewish Israelis and Palestinians, sometimes sardonically described as "the co-existence industry," which increased in the 1990s thanks to European and American funding. These meetings were criticized by scholars and peace activists who took part in them for reproducing the power asymmetries between the two sides, bypassing any serious discussion of participants' very different perceptions of the pivotal 1948 war, and avoiding the issue of accountability, to focus instead on psychological issues such as breaking stereotypes (Tamari 2005; Challand 2011; Nashef interview 2008; Nathan interview 2008; Bronstein interview 2008).

Rejecting this strategy, new peace-activist groups on the radical left in the early 2000s concentrate on building trust not through consensus in small meetings, but rather through narratives that acknowledge conflicting histories and ideas while also promoting self-criticism of national narratives (Challand 2011). Another important shift is evident in these groups' perceptions and actions, most notably the shift in the Jewish Israeli left at the beginning of the 2000s from viewing the 1967 occupation of the West Bank and Gaza as the pivotal event in the conflict, to instead looking at the war of 1948 as the orienting moment. Rather than fighting an occupation that can be reversed, activists began examining the role of the Zionist struggle for a Jewish state in 1948 that culminated in the establishment of Israel in the ongoing conflict. Given this dramatic shift of focus and strategy, memory activists summoned the model of truth and reconciliation to guide the production of knowledge on the highly contested origins of the conflict in 1948 as a necessary step toward future resolution.

And so the model of truth and reconciliation gradually entered the Israeli "sphere of publics" (Calhoun 1997) through Israeli memory-activism groups operating in relation to other publics and discourses in the 2000s. Unlike when facilitated by the state in postconflict cases, when truth and reconciliation is used as a strategy of peace activism during conflict, it is only one argument among others. In Israel of the 2000s, the activist truth and reconciliation argument met a largely defensive battle of the state and right-wing groups against foregrounding a long-silenced past as the focal point of the conflict. The activist production of knowledge on the Palestinian displacement, that according to the transnational model was supposed to lead to public acknowledgment and accountability, did not proceed beyond the first stage in this context. The transnational model broke down. The links between knowing the other's past, to recognizing the other's suffering and loss, and to taking responsibility, were contested at every stage; starting with the facts themselves, as each side brought a different chain of facts and quarreled over what is considered legitimate evidence. A reversion to the dominant post-Oslo argumentation that puts forward acknowledgment of "our" historical truth and rights before "theirs" was almost automatic—a major obstacle the activists face in their attempted move from knowledge to acknowledgment, not to mention accountability.[18] Even if Jewish Israelis acknowledged Palestinian suffering, there was not always a will to take responsibility for it—claiming, for example, that each side had its own share of suffering during the war, or that other nation-states would have, and have in fact, acted similarly or worse. What if the situation had been reversed and Israel had lost the war? This was another popular argument for not acknowledging or taking responsibility for Palestinian suffering. As a Jewish Israeli peace activist explained: "You can say: There was the Nakba, but [you can also] . . . justify it by saying: It's either us or them. You can always go to the Holocaust [as justification, although] it is so distanced in time . . . [whereas] the security discourse is more concrete [as justification]" (Uri interview 2009). Norma Musih, Zochrot's cofounder, interprets these responses: "There was a catastrophe but I don't want to take responsibility for it" (interview 2009).

While the 1948 war is fertile ground for activist truth and reconciliation intervention efforts, even making this past publicly intelligible in Israel outside the dual-narrative construction was a high-stakes endeavor, because it can be perceived as preferring "their" rights to "ours" in line with the post-Oslo dominant argumentation. The costs of legitimizing and acknowledging this narrative were immense for the Israeli state during the current stage of the conflict, as it assigned Zionism a greater responsibility for perpetrating the conflict than the victim perception of its hegemonic national narrative. If legitimized, such responsibility could lead to the demand that Israel would redress the Palestinians in any future peace agreement. Activist models that put forward 1948 as a starting point were thus monitored and constrained.

An Institutional Form:
The Truth and Reconciliation Commission

Truth and Reconciliation Commissions (TRC) are defined by Hayner as "official, temporary bodies established to investigate a pattern of violations over a period of time that conclude with a final report and recommendations for reforms" (2006, 295). Since 1974, truth and reconciliation commissions have been established in more than thirty countries around the world, but as mentioned, the 1995 South African commission is considered today the paradigmatic case of aiding a transition from a difficult past to a more stable and peaceful future.

Modeled after colonial state commissions from the eighteenth and nineteenth centuries, this institutional form of truth and reconciliation upholds the state commission's aim of continuity and political stability for nation-building purposes through the production of a legal-scientific narrative of current or past events, all of which is rooted in a specific moral order (Stoler 2009; Posel 2002). In both forms of commission, critics have argued, the preliminary selection or constitution of categories and of the choice of a scientific-legal model of causal explanation help establish much of the findings before the questions have even been asked publicly (Stoler 2009; Frankel 2006; Posel 2002; Wilson 2001). Finally, like the colonial state commissions, the TRC is composed of two different forms of knowledge production and documentation of the past: public hearings and a final report. Each of these forms generates a different type of knowledge (Wilson 2001; Posel 2002).

Public hearings collect witness voices and detailed experiences (albeit selected, mediated, limited, and constrained in legal language, conduct, and type of information sought) to provide a bottom-up, richly textured account of "lived experience" that is perhaps best documented in vignettes. The report, on the other hand, prefers forensic, scientific-legal knowledge to produce the top-down official version (and the only one recognized) of the past through which the state asserts its authority and control. The combination of hearings and report almost guarantees that the state's voice will override, exclude, dismiss, and disqualify the voice of the witness.

Therefore, it is not at all surprising that the aim of bringing unity and peace to torn societies after violent conflicts, in which victims and perpetrators often live side by side, is very difficult to fulfill through a truth commission's version of the past, as many critics have indicated. As a mechanism that produces power through discourse (Verdoolaege 2008), TRCs have been criticized on a number of accounts: for assigning separate senses and meanings of justice to victims and perpetrators; for being centered around victims; for fixing narratives and, by so doing, silencing witnesses and war memories; for assuming an elitist perspective in their focus on the national level, for isolating individuals from their social networks; for ignoring local cleavages; and for advancing polarization among groups and increasing the threat of continued violence by revealing more details on horrific domestic events (Laplante and Theidon 2010; Payne 2008; Theidon 2006; Wilson 2001; Biko 2000).

However, despite these problems, and in addition to making visible and audible those who experienced mass violence in the hearings, a TRC embodies the official recognition of the state, which has vast significance for marginalized groups. Lacking any legal or state authority in Israel, the activist efforts draw on the commission form mainly as a history-writing agency that could provide recognition (Wilson 2001), more than a legal platform—which is almost impossible to achieve outside state channels.

For some of Baladna's counselors, an official, state-based truth commission is the only forum that could bring Palestinians recognition (for example, Hassan interview 2010), as described in the previous chapter. Yet until such a legal platform is available, they prepare a record of testimonies and other sources that can be used rhetorically and pedagogically. The link to state practices is visible in Palestinian and Jewish activists' use of the tour and survivor testimony, practices that are oriented with the state's dissemination of national ideology. The activists fused these practices with Palestinian experience and memories in a manner that can be seen as an ephemeral truth commission that appears and disappears around the country in every tour, and accumulates in online archives and information centers. Zochrot's booklet on each of the Palestinian sites the group visits can be viewed as a single "report" of such commission. The booklet is distributed to tour participants *before* the "public hearing" of refugee testimonies in the tour. This play with the forms of the TRC raises the following questions: Why isn't a history of Palestinian displacement in 1948 "commissionable"? Why hasn't it been recognized, mapped, and addressed by the state?

One of the reasons a Palestinian history of 1948 is "uncommissionable" today is that this history was for many years a "public secret" (Stoler 2009, 148)—something the public already knew but chose to ignore or hide from itself.[19] According to Stoler, state commissions are often formed to investigate such "public secrets" (2009, 148). This further complicates the link between the dissemination of knowledge on a contested past and public acknowledgment. It brings to the picture the social will to know and see the other's suffering in this and other cases, including postconflict societies. It suggests that producing polarizing and often shame-inducing knowledge on a contested past in public requires additional conditions in order to lead to public acknowledgment and responsibility. Such change cannot be rendered through a model of linear progress as the one that underlay the ideal type of the South African Truth and Reconciliation Commission.

The Truth and Reconciliation Discourse

Before 2001, contemplation of truth and reconciliation regarding the 1948 war was confined to Palestinian intellectuals, particularly around the fiftieth anniversary of the 1948 war and the Nakba in 1998, as previously mentioned (Hill 2008), but it was also buttressed by the revisionist history "new historians" and "critical sociologists" published on the war of 1948 since the late 1970s (Nets-Zehngut 2011), especially Benny Morris's 1987 book *The Birth of the Palestinian Refugee Problem*. The memory-activist efforts in Israel since 2001–2002 have echoed Palestinian arguments while advancing their own and have documented and collected information that was not publically known through special oral-history archives, as well as collections of documents, photographs, and maps, which added to the new historians' knowledge production about 1948.

The revisionist historiography of the 1948 war highlighted the Palestinian expulsion and dispossession and by 2001 and throughout the decade has served as a budding foundation of scientific knowledge for truth and reconciliation efforts (see, for example, Auron 2013). As previously mentioned in this book, the publication of revisionist academic works starting in the late 1980s has, "under the force of evidence amassed mainly by Morris" (Ram 1998, 515), disputed the previous academic accounts of the 1948 war and criticized their authors as collaborating with the state in building a historical narrative that excluded the Palestinians (Ram 1998, 2006, 2007; Pappé 1997a, 1998; Craimer 2006; Morris 1988; Shlaim 1988; Flapan 1987).

The Oslo period afforded more room to shatter national myths in light of a forthcoming peace agreement, including myths related to 1948. Yet this atmosphere radically changed in the aftermath of the Oslo Accords and especially with the eruption of the second Intifada in 2000. The body of academic literature that exposed the atrocities of the 1948 war continued to expand nonetheless throughout the turbulent decade that followed. The scholarly debate sparked a struggle over the history and representation of 1948 that extended well beyond the work of the new historians, increasingly appearing in the media and mounting with the state's reaction in 2009–2011 through the Nakba Law and other amendments, investigations, and bans.

In the academic battle between new historians and their predecessors, the struggle appears as an internal debate on historiography. More than between "old" and "new" historians, who agree on the facts but not on the intentions behind Israeli military actions during the 1948 war, the heated dispute involved, in very general terms, a dominant documents-based "objectivist" approach led by Benny Morris and Avi Shlaim versus a marginalized, interdisciplinary, "relativist" approach that included oral history narratives, championed primarily by Ilan Pappé (Ram 1998, 519–20; Craimer 2006, 4). While the former sought to produce forensic, scientific-legal truth, the latter valued narrative truth (Morris 2007; Craimer 2006, 4; Posel 2002; Pappé 1998). The inequality of sources to produce scientific-legal truth—as Chapter 3 describes, on the Palestinian side documents were destroyed, lost, and divided between different states' archives (I. Feldman 2008), which makes oral history a crucial source (Kabha interview 2009)—did not affect this hierarchy. In a sense, state documents became representative of Israeli historiography while oral history represented the Palestinian history writing, reproducing the power asymmetry of the conflict in the hierarchy of knowledge production of 1948.

Given this state of things, the Israeli memory activists used both state documents and oral history: They used documents to produce scientific-legal truth on 1948 as a legitimizing and authoritative medium, and they used testimonies as an equalizing step of history writing. Oral history also served the activist's task of interrupting any single version of the past by offering multiple, sometimes contradictory stories (interviews: Danon 2008; Bronstein 2008, 2009; Yasmin 2009; and others). The activists marked this knowledge on-site for passersby to see.

Zochrot's signposting to indicate that Palestinian life existed in various sites before the 1948 war was discussed in the opening and in previous chapters. But Autobiography of a City also marks the public space of Jaffa with fragments of its Palestinian pre-1948 past. Most of the commissioned site-specific artworks that are based on the testimonies the group collected in its online archive (see Chapter 2) left visible marks of the past on city space. The first work, by Jewish Israeli artist Ronen Edelman in 2007 marked the street grid of the Palestinian and later Jewish proletarian Manshia neighborhood onto today's Charles

Clore Park, which was built on its ruins in 1973. Another work in 2007, by the Parrhesia group of Jewish and Palestinian artists and designers assisted by young Jaffa residents, used graffiti to create a Hebrew-Arabic visual dictionary on city walls and benches of the Ajami neighborhood. The dictionary, which gave visibility to the Arabic language and culture of the city, also served as a platform for tours of the city's past guided by cofounder Sami Bukhari. Kasia Krakowiak, a Polish artist from Gdansk who collaborated with Edelman, used sound to simulate a Palestinian past and future for the city. She broadcast a clandestine program on "Free Jaffa Radio," a fictional station that occupied the airwaves in the central street of Jaffa for a few hours in April 2009.

In opposition to other peace-activism projects that try to balance two rival national narratives, Israeli and Palestinian, and that negate the incommensurability of their political claims, the memory activists' truth and reconciliation argument regarding the crucial importance of the 1948 Palestinian displacement to conflict resolution turns the transnational paradigm from an abstract moral principle to a concrete political demand in this particular conflict. It indeed marks 1948 as a no-passage point in conflict negotiations, a point that people-to-people projects tried to bypass and failed but that, once recognized as essential, also enables Jewish Israeli and Palestinian activists to start converging, despite their one-sided practices, because these practices point to the same political aim.

Discussion: Truth and/or Reconciliation

The most striking difference in the Israeli memory activists' appropriation of the globally circulating truth and reconciliation model was their emphasis on truth as crucial and urgent while moving reconciliation to the background. In the context of Israeli and Palestinian peace activism, this appropriation—*truth without/before reconciliation*—replaces the previous strategic paradigm that marked the period of the Oslo Accords and that can be termed *reconciliation without truth*. The failure to follow the Oslo Accords into their later stages brought many peace activists on both sides to view the failure as stemming from the lack of truth about the past in the accords in favor of superficial present-oriented reconciliation that ends the violence and institutionalized peaceful relationships in the present and future between the two sides. Memory activists explained that addressing 1948 and the right of return for Palestinian refugees is a crucial aspect that was missing from Oslo and that should be included in any future peace agreement (interviews: Nathan 2009; Yossi 2009; Tamer 2009). They began working on addressing the truth about this past first, while moving reconciliation to a later stage, preconditioned by one-sided truth production on Palestinian displacement and loss, acknowledgment, and responsibility.

This appropriation is apparent in the second statement in the opening of the chapter, in which the fictitious author advocates *one-sided* acknowledgement of past wrongs for the case of Palestinian displacement by Israeli forces in 1948, and likens it to other cases from around the world. Indeed, Zochrot's production of knowledge, or truth, on the silenced Palestinian past for Jewish Israeli audiences is one-sided (as are Baladna's and Autobiography of a City's, which also focus on Palestinian memories). This one-sidedness opposes both the dominant perception of reconciliation between Israelis and Palestinians in the region and the expert perceptions of political reconciliation. It offers a corresponding one-sided resolution to the prolonged conflict that views the Israeli side as largely responsible for past wrongs and thus as owing greater redress to the Palestinians than the Palestinians do to Israel.

In the region, the framing of the conflict that was manifested in the Oslo Peace Accords and in later rounds of peace talks between Israel and the Palestinian Authority was of cycles of mutual aggression and retaliation that stem from rival national interests and political claims to the same territory. The perception of the pivotal 1948 war as a zero-sum-game construction of rival national histories, Israeli and Palestinian, matches this perception of a two-sided, intractable conflict. Zochrot, on the other hand, draws on the transnational "glorious tradition" to frame the conflict and its resolution here as asymmetrical: The conflict is based primarily on the Palestinian suffering Israel caused, in 1948 and after. The corresponding future resolution thus requires Israel, as the powerful side, to acknowledge its aggression and discrimination of the Palestinian population it governs, which is the weaker side, and to account for its deeds by taking responsibility and offering redress in the form of a return of Palestinian refugees.

This one-sided perception and knowledge production are also opposed to the dominant expert perception of reconciliation as a two-sided exchange of acknowledgments to resume friendly or equal relations between former enemies, even when there are no equal relations to return to (Verdeja 2014). The three memory activism groups in Israel emphasize a move from the unjust relations of the past that continue in the present state of the conflict—these include the displacement of and discrimination against Palestinians by Israel rather than mutual aggression—to equality and redress. This requires a one-sided acknowledgment of past wrongs by the aggressor in order to reestablish equal social, political, and economic relations with the discriminated.

At the center of this one-sided activist learning and documenting is the silenced Palestinian past and more specifically marginalized perspectives within it—particularly those of women and ordinary people and of daily life. Eyal Danon, cofounder of Autobiography of a City, acknowledges the urgency of documenting Palestinian stories and lists them as the primary criterion for what the group chooses to document in its archive. They come before any concerns of a collection that is representative of all the different strata of 1948-generation Jaffans, although the archive includes a variety of testifiers. It is also an equalizing step of history writing on the part of the marginalized community (interviews 2009, 2011). Zochrot supports a one-sided learning of the Nakba among Jewish Israelis for three reasons: as a shared past that Jewish Israelis need to learn as part of their own history; as a moral duty to recognize the suffering one's state has inflicted on others and give them justice; and as a step toward coming to terms with this contested past for a better, more just, and peaceful Israeli society in the future (for example, Bronstein interview 2008).

For Palestinian memory activists in Israel, the stakes are much higher, and so is the motivation behind one-sided knowledge production. "We need to convince the Jews but I don't think this is the time. [Right now] it is more important to take care of our society, because the Jew, if he wants to, he has the chance to study on his own—I don't think it is our responsibility," said Hassan, a youth counselor from Baladna (interview 2009).

Can reconciliation begin separately and exclusively, in a one-sided framework of truth production, to balance the prevailing inequality of history writing and memory work before using it to overcome political inequality? While this is a very promising idea, especially considering critiques of depoliticization and disregard of local cleavages in postconflict TRCs, the attempted realization of the idea paradoxically sustains the inequality in the process of overcoming it.

Who tells whose story to whom in the Israeli-Palestinian case illustrates some problematic aspects of a one-sided attempt to create a shared past for the future. Zochrot recovers Palestinian memory of 1948 for Jewish Israelis with the help of a few Palestinian staff members. The assumption is that Jewish Israeli facilitation grants the knowledge greater legitimacy than it would were it transmitted by Palestinians, which is sadly the case in Israeli society. Indeed, Jewish Israeli participants in Zochrot's activities found its one-sidedness attractive: "Jewish Israeli" commemorative practices in Hebrew rather than Arabic present the past as "ours" not as "yours" (for example, David interview 2008). The boundary distinction (Fuchs Epstein 1992) between Jews and Palestinians in Israel is an existing reality, yet the activist efforts to eventually cross these boundaries are assisted by maintaining them for now. Zochrot maintains this boundary distinction as a tactic to reach a larger audience; for Baladna it is part of an effort to create national and cultural autonomy for Palestinians in Israel. But both efforts also risk a self-referential understanding of Palestinians in 1948.[20] It therefore raises the question of what the reaction would be when the boundaries are lifted.

Moreover, TRCs create victim typologies and narratives that people then use to narrate their individual experiences and claims for justice (Laplante and Theidon 2010). In Israel these typologies are first evident in individual and group truth and reconciliation narratives because they are restricted form public debate. For the memory activists, the victims are all the Palestinians, but they focus on refugees. Internal divisions are communicated more subtly in the testimonies. Defining a perpetrator's category by applying outside divisions to the Israeli political culture has been more difficult. This category is problematic in other cases as well,[21] and in Israel it is exclusively reserved for those who committed crimes against Jews because of their religion/ethnicity: first and foremost, the National Socialists of the Third Reich; and second, the Palestinian leadership(s), Arab enemy countries, and military Muslim organizations that surround Israel. In relation to the 1948 war, a category of perpetrators cannot yet be articulated owing to the impossibility of including any Jewish Israeli in it, certainly not the leaders or the soldiers whom the dominant national narrative casts as heroes and pioneers of the Zionist settlement project.

Palestinian Truth and Reconciliation in Israel

If truth is the main focus of memory activists in Israel, is the activist production of knowledge about the Palestinian experience before and during the 1948 war still conducted for the purpose of reconciliation?

While the motivation for a future reconciliation is more observable as the basis of Jewish Israeli truth production of the Palestinian experience of the 1948 war, as a trust-building step and a point of possible conversion between the dominant and discriminated sides, the way in which all-Palestinian memory activism in Israel carries the same goal seems to require further clarification. Part of it was addressed in the previous chapter. Here it is worth noting that this lack of clarity stems from the special third-party position of Palestinians who are Israeli citizens in this conflict, while truth and reconciliation appear to be capable of accommodating only two clearly defined rival sides and not more.[22]

To what extent is an all-Palestinian memory activism of the Nakba in Israel a project of reconciliation? Their in-between position in the conflict makes any comparison of Palestinian citizens to postconflict, newly equal citizens debatable and also highly contested by members of this group. Palestinian intellectuals outside of Israel claim that unlike governed noncitizen Palestinians in the Occupied Territories, Palestinian citizens of Israel have been in a unique postconflict situation since the 1948 war, or at least from the end of martial law in 1966. This is because in postconflict societies such as South Africa, the political issue at hand is enlarging the state franchise to include the discriminated and abused as equal citizens, and Palestinians in Israel were included when granted citizenship. However, Palestinian intellectuals who have citizenship disagree, stating that the constant threat to their position in Israel is more definitive of Palestinian citizens' political situation than any of their rights as second-class citizens (for example, Kanaaneh and Nusair 2010).

In any case, all-Palestinian memory activism in Israel is primarily a project of creating agency and solidarity, building an autonomous national community within a Jewish nation-state, and practicing resistance from within and outside of the state, as Chapter 3 shows. However, the need for such a project in the first place stems from the ongoing silencing of experiences and memories of 1948, which carry high stakes for the conflict's present state and for its future resolution. It also stems from Palestinian citizens' diminished hopes for equal citizenship in Israel and the establishment of new political demands for reaching an agreement that would enable peaceful and equal relations between Jewish and Palestinian citizens, recognizing the latter as both members of the Palestinian people and as citizens of Israel.

Such a political change within Israel requires that the production of knowledge of Palestinians' own past be transmitted and recognized publicly by the Jewish Israeli majority. This recognition seemed very unlikely to be willingly adopted in the nationalistic atmosphere and public debate on 1948 of the 2000s and thus required, in the eyes of some of Baladna's youth counselors, an official truth and reconciliation commission or a legal authority (Hala interview 2009; Mahmoud interview 2009; Ali interview 2009). The counselors explained that a TRC or a legal authority would "force [Jewish Israelis] to listen" and facilitate such recognition of Palestinians. Only doing so would bring justice, they maintained (Hala interview 2009; Mahmoud interview 2009; Ali interview 2009). Mahmoud told me about a meeting between Palestinian refugees and Jewish Israelis he participated in: "One of them [a Jewish Israeli] served in the army, and I asked him if he killed anyone, and he said, yes. So what do you expect? He said, 'I'm here to change myself,' but what is that worth. But go and conduct internal trials against your crime. It is not an idea; it's simply something that needs to be done; there are people here who killed people—like someone kills someone on the street. The context is less important" (interview 2009). In another interview he stated the necessity of establishing Israeli courts for the events of 1948 as the only possibility for Jewish and Palestinian reconciliation (interview 2010). These statements were made to a Jewish Israeli interviewer in a provocative tone, asking that universalistic ideas about justice and legal mechanisms will be enforced in Israel to precede any mutual reconciliation and give justice to Palestinian citizens.

Despite the activist beliefs in multiplicity of personal stories and views of 1948 and the disconnection from single truths, in this arena there can only be one version of the past to be recognized by Israel, as Mahmoud continued: "There is only one reality, no more than one reality, the reality that there were Palestinians here with them. Jews were living [here], some who also saw themselves as Palestinians, and then a Zionist—not Jewish—group came, and we see the results now. . . . I will tell the truth, that there is here a Zionist group that came and occupied the country and killed people" (interview 2009). The internal Palestinian dialogue returns here to the presentation of a Palestinian rights-based monologue to counter the dominant Zionist monologue (Goldfarb 2011, 151), reinstating the dual-narrative structure.

As mentioned, temporality is one of the basic realms of difference between truth and reconciliation in postconflict societies and in active conflict. While the former wished to eventually put the past to rest and live in the present and future, memory activism during conflict is about a lesson from the present rather than from the past, something that is most explicit in Baladna's work, as the previous chapter details.

Despite the differences, South Africa was mentioned again and again in the inner Palestinian discourse of the 2000s as a case from which to draw similarities and dissimilarities to their own situation. Tamer from Autobiography of a City, quoting Azmi Bishara, believes that Israel "is not South Africa, [or] the seriously conflicted places"; in Israel, "coexistence already exists; the question is if there is equality—in political representation, in the allocation of the budget" (interview 2009). On the other hand, Tamer's solution to the discrimination of Palestinian citizens is to let things deteriorate until the situation becomes more like the Apartheid regime in South Africa, so the world can then interfere and pressure Israel into a political transformation (Tamer interview 2009).

Palestinian citizens who are peace activists still negotiate the links between their situation and other cases of conflict and their resolution, especially the case of South Africa. The transnational discourse was thus discussed with caution, acknowledging dissimilarities as well as the possibilities opened up by other postconflict cases. In comparison, Jewish Israeli activists referred to South Africa and other cases of postconflict without hesitation, directly and explicitly to explain their strategy and reflect on Israel's current state and its future resolution (for example, Nathan interview 2008; Ariella interview 2009; Bronstein interview 2009; Musih interview 2010).

Problematic Reception

The second quote that opens the chapter by the fictitious chairperson of the make-believe institution the New JNF-KKL is a new step in Zochrot's mimicking strategy that has focused since its inception on memory practices that the state, and before it the Zionist movement, used for national education (Chapter 1). The statement mimics state rhetoric and the Zionist historical narrative in phrases such as "make the wilderness bloom," which Zochrot clearly works to prove wrong: The "wilderness" had a thriving Palestinian life that the phrase ignores. However, without knowing who stood behind this project it was very difficult to know if the project was real or not, if it identified with the Zionist narrative or mocked it.

The 2013 statement announcing the "New JNF-KKL" project was

created in a different context than the 2001 statement of Bronstein: after Zochrot's ideas about truth and reconciliation were disseminated and found to have concrete advantages and disadvantages in the Israeli public debate. The 2013 project can be seen as an attempt to institutionalize the group's early ideas, still outside state channels, by creating an alternative, non-Zionist institution to the JNF-KKL. Yet the specific sensibility of mimicking state rhetoric that the statements portrays, which stems from the group's decade-long mixed experience with Israeli public debate, might be better understood if compared to a mode of parody called Stiob, which was created in late-socialist Eastern Europe and is being used today in mainstream Western culture.

Stiob is a mode of parody that was popular in socialist public culture in Central and Eastern Europe in the 1970s and 1980s and reappeared in mainstream American public culture of the last decade (Boyer and Yurchak 2010, 180). Different from sarcasm, cynicism, or other genres of absurd comedy, Stiob is difficult to identify as critical mockery. Originally it "imitated and inhabited the formal features of authoritative discourse to such an extent" that it was difficult to determine whether it supported or ridiculed this discourse (Boyer and Yurchak 2010, 180; see also Yurchak 2006, 250). It used overidentification with state rhetoric that did not come with any metacommentary to signal its ironic purpose. These attributes fitted the overformulated authoritative discourse of late-socialism governments and the threat of sanctioning oppositional discourses. Moreover, overidentification did not require the audience to reject state ideology or to identify with recognizable political positions; it existed "outside of the familiar axes of political tensions between state and opposition, between Left and Right, aware of these axes but uninterested in them" (Boyer and Yurchak 2010, 183).

Zochrot's sensibility of mimicking state rhetoric without providing metacommentary (at first) in its 2013 project seems to resemble the mode of Stiob humor. The Stiob's external existence that is "aware of these axes [of political tensions] but uninterested in them" fits the activist perception of Zochrot (as well as Baladna; see Chapter 3) as separated from recognized political agendas and categories (for example, Musih interview 2009), particularly those agendas and categories constructed by the overpowering zero-sum game of narratives that frames the public debate on the conflict and divides Jewish Israeli and Arab Palestinians (Musih interview 2009). Zochrot never called its audiences to identify with any political party, and while trying to construct a non-Zionist historical narrative or collective memory for

Jewish Israelis, it remained open to various options and imaginations (interviews: Musih 2009; Batia 2009; Bronstein 2009). Despite its misidentification with existing categories, the group was fairly quickly categorized in the years after its inception according to the dual-narrative categories, as a radical Left, anti-Israeli organization that supports the Palestinian national narrative and thus openly betrays the Jewish majority during active conflict. This infamous reputation as radical and anti-Israeli shaped the attitudes not only of the right wing and the general public toward the group, but also of left-wing activists in the Zionist Left and in the radical Left, who distanced themselves from its activities (interviews 2008, 2010, 2011). The automatic categorization and the rejection of the truth and reconciliation model as a new argument that would reframe the dual-narrative public debate perhaps disenchanted the group regarding the possibilities of influencing it. Shifting to overidentification with existing political rhetoric and Zionist institutions as a strategic way to disseminate the truth and reconciliation argument—which is evident in the 2013 statement—could potentially maintain the group's distance from existing categories while disseminating knowledge and claims counter to the dominant ones.

In Western political culture of the last decade or so, Stiob sensibility is visible in "meta-news" TV shows like Jon Stewart's and *The Colbert Report*, and comedy shows like *South Park* that mark a "performative shift" according to which "literal criticism becomes strangely predictable and ineffective next to the parodic possibilities of inhabiting the norm" (Boyer and Yurchak 2010, 184). In both contexts, the late-socialist and the American liberal-capitalist, different as they may seem, Stiob appeared in a unified, centralized, and overformulated political public discourse, in which the content is homogeneous and repetitive, cemented in ideological consensus (Boyer and Yurchak 2010, 183). These characteristics, which fit the Israeli political discourse in the last decade or so, limit and constrain public debate and make it difficult to contest the information available in the media and disseminate alternative information and political claims (Katriel and Gutman 2015).

The "performative shift" in the United States has affected social movements and popular protest organizations around the world and the production of critical discourse outside of the United States. In Israel it can be seen, for example, in the mainstream show *Wonderful Country* on the popular channel 2. Zochrot's "New JNF-KKL" project manifests this performative shift in political culture (as well as an Israeli history of humoristic creative work). Yet more so it demonstrates the potential of appropriating and redeploying hegemonic cultural practices such as tours and testimonies to disseminate oppositional knowledge in comparison to the limitations of inserting external concepts (truth and reconciliation) as a new argument that distinguishes itself from existing categories in the limited political discourse of Israel.

After the Nakba Law was approved in 2011, there was no doubt among the activists that the public attention to the Palestinian loss and displacement has been drawn and the basic knowledge widely distributed in the media coverage of the legislative process and public debate on the bill. But when and how the next steps of the truth and reconciliation model—from knowledge to acknowledgment and to responsibility—would be reached was more difficult to foresee.

At the same time that they expressed critical skepticism about the actual weight of their contribution to the state's reaction through the Nakba Law, many of the activists also articulated a deterministic view that once the information has been released it is only a matter of time until it will be acknowledged and acted on in the desired direction. "The genie is already out; I don't believe it is possible to put it back in the box. It is a one-directional process, [Jewish Israeli] people will not stop talking about the Nakba, and the Palestinian engine [will not be stopped] once the dam has been broken," a former Zochrot activist stated to me, something that others have also articulated (Ariella interview 2009; Nathan interview 2008; Frank interview 2009). The assumption of a linear, irreversible process that this assemblage of metaphors is called to emphasize stems from placing Israel in a transnational context and comparing it to cases of nation-states that are coming to terms with their past oppression of minority groups. The transition from Apartheid in South Africa (Tamer interview 2009), acknowledging Aboriginal rights in Australia (Ariella interview 2009), thinking about citizenship in Bosnia (Musih interview 2008), making present the Jewish past in Central and Eastern Europe (Frank interview 2009), and hesitancy to acknowledge collaboration with the Nazi occupation during WWII in France (Nathan interview 2008) are but a few of the international cases the activists use to demonstrate the direction in which Israel is headed. If Israel's contested past of 1948 is heeded as the beginning of the conflict and the starting point for its resolution, it could emerge a different and better society in their minds—ceasing to continue its state of racism and inequality in favor of transitioning toward equality.

However irreversible this process is in their minds, these same activists view this progress from knowledge through recognition to responsibility and political change as a progression that cannot be timed or managed. Consequently, they are not trying "to control the change too much," as one of Zochrot's founding members put it (Frank interview 2009). Behind this stands a basic commitment to critical self-reflection and doubt rather than to any clear answer, an approach that originates from critical theory, with which many of the activists are familiar.[23]

Of course, once it is made public by the groups, the knowledge can also be used to mobilize other, sometimes opposite, goals or to produce a different change. This is acknowledged by the activists even regarding material produced specifically for educational purposes: "I don't know what's going to happen—that is part of critical theory—it can go in many directions. The fact that *we* became non-Zionists doesn't mean that it should happen to others," said a Zochrot staff member (Batia interview 2009), and Baladna's youth counselor seconds: "I don't want them [the youth] to be my army, but to be critical and know how to differentiate between propaganda and what really affects you—not what you are supposed to think as a teenager in your situation. You won't go to live in Palestine [i.e., in the Occupied Territories], you won't care for Arafat" (Yasmin interview 2009). Autobiography of a City Palestinian cofounder Sami Bukhari said that he is open to any mobilization of the knowledge in the group's archive, as long as it is not offensive to Palestinians and their history (interview 2009).

Implications for Postconflict Truth and Reconciliation

Our close look at the local appropriation of the expert discourse and model of historical justice and truth and reconciliation revealed the multiple meanings that can be attached to them in the context of active conflict. It illuminated the concrete limitations and possibilities of their strategic appropriation and deployment outside state channels for Palestinians in Israel. As we have seen, the utilization of historical justice and truth and reconciliation during conflict can take different forms and be used by both the state and activists as one of various strategies for dealing with a contested past in the context of the present state of the conflict. Competing with the dominant post-Oslo argumentation in a struggle about historical truth, legitimacy, and the status of Palestinians in the 1948 war, the activist deployment of a truth and reconciliation model was broken down by dominant justifications and ethnonational boundary distinction. However, the discourse and commission form of truth and reconciliation worked creatively using locally familiar cultural practices to mark Palestinian displacement in 1948 as a point of convergence between Israelis and Palestinians around which knowledge is produced and acknowledgment can form for future reconciliation.

The power of definitions and categories in postconflict cases and their limitations in the ongoing Israeli-Palestinian conflict is important as well. However, the inclusive ambiguity or exclusiveness of categories and typologies in both conflict and postconflict societies is indicative not only of their power to shape perceptions and policies but also of what remains unspoken and "uncommissionable." In Israel, the displacement of Palestinians in the 1948 war was a public secret for many decades. The extreme reaction of the state and society to the activist and scholarly "airing" of this secret in public opposes the assumptions of the transnational paradigms of historical justice and the model of truth and reconciliation.

First, the dissemination of knowledge on the contested past may have transformed Jewish Israelis' attention toward Palestinians in 1948, but it also led to misrecognition of their loss and even to justification of it in some cases (such as Benny Morris's; Shavit 2004). More knowledge did not lead to more power for the silenced group of Palestinian citizens in this case, and while it may have advanced the inclusion of the Nakba in the unofficial collective memory of Jewish Israelis by turning their attention to it, the exclusion of Palestinians and their supporters from public debate framed this memory.

This finding has implications for the transnational paradigm. It suggests that instead of the hoped-for progression from knowledge to acknowledgment and to accountability, acknowledgment and accountability may serve as a preliminary condition for producing knowledge on a contested past in postconflict cases. Taking for example the paradigmatic case of the South African TRC, one can argue that the public hearings and report—or the truth production on the contested and polarizing past—came as a result of the government's acknowledgment of Apartheid's wrongs and its will to take responsibility through the TRC. In other words, airing a contested past without acknowledgment and responsibility may lead to further polarization instead of advancing reconciliation both in cases of conflict and in postconflict societies.

To conclude, the Israeli case of memory activism suggests ways to expand our understanding of the globally circulating postconflict model of truth and reconciliation through some of the challenges that this case study raises. It also proposes some major revisions to the expert model of truth and reconciliation. It questions the notion of "truth" or of knowledge production as unrelated to societal wills to know or see the past. It also challenges the assumption that truth precedes reconciliation, suggesting instead that taking responsibility and acknowledging the victims may be preliminary conditions for airing a contested past in public in order to advance reconciliation and not perpetuate further polarization and violence.

Conclusion

The Future of Reimagining the Past

Despite the Nakba Law and ongoing threats and warnings, Nakba memory continued to proliferate in Israel in the first half of the second decade of the twenty-first century. In Israeli academia, from the revisionist "new historians" and "critical sociologists," the retelling of 1948 in the 1990s and 2000s expanded further in the aftermath of the Nakba Law, as manifested in conferences, research, and publications in disciplines as varied as geography, psychology, film, literature, architecture, history, sociology, and political science (Bashir and Goldberg 2015, 2014; Nehhas 2015; Jamal and Bsoul 2014; Fenster 2014; and Auron 2013, among others). Israeli and Palestinian artists and filmmakers who take part in the global interest in the conflict as well as in postcolonial identities have brought the Nakba to local and international museums and film festivals, and more mainstream best-selling authors conveyed it to their Jewish Israeli readers (among them Eshkol Nevo, Nurit Gertz, and Yoram Kanyuk). Human rights associations and activist groups have distributed the message and knowledge produced by the memory activists within the political discourse of the Left. In most fields and professional circles, however, there is still significant resistance to the idea among Jewish Israelis, and many of these events and publications were accompanied by protest. Yet "at least there is talk" about the Nakba, as an activist in Zochrot noted (Tsachi interview 2009). This quote expresses the feeling among many of the Nakba memory activists that awareness has been achieved, and the first stage of their model for change has been completed. However, the failure to proceed to the next stages of this model of truth and reconciliation, the stages of public acknowledgment and responsibility, shaped different responses and new directions of action among the different groups of memory activists.

Zochrot has experienced the greatest changes in management and focus, which may signal the completion of its initial mandate: producing and disseminating knowledge on the Nakba among Jewish Israelis. In 2011 Eitan Bronstein, the cofounder who is most identified with the group, stepped down from the director's seat he occupied from its inception and shifted to contributing through a personal blog (titled *The Decolonizer*). He also began to collect testimonies from Jewish Israeli soldiers in the 1948 war, a task that had played a marginal role in Zochrot until then (Bronstein interview 2011), as the main focus of the group concerned the long-silenced Palestinian memories. A change in emphasis from knowledge to responsibility prompted a major step in 2010–2011 after a few years of preparation: advocating the return of Palestinian refugees to their homes and preparing a concrete plan for a few localities. This area of activity, which was not part of Zochrot initially, began to develop in the second half of the previous decade together with the Palestinian Bethlehem-based NGO Badil and other Palestinian partners. A conference on "return" held in summer 2008 in Tel Aviv, and the group's participation in a similar conference in London a few months earlier, marked its conception and the active support of the group in the Palestinian right of return. Yet it was not until May 2011 that the work the group developed was made public in a special issue of its literary magazine *Sedek* (Bronstein interview 2010; Musih interview 2010).[1] While the group continued to promote knowledge through tours and refugee testimonies, the shift of focus to the right of return and Bronstein's aspiration to collect Jewish Israeli testimonies (albeit for the same purpose of learning about the Palestinian experience) are quite illustrative of the mandate that has been consumed by the entrance of the Nakba to mainstream public debate and is now seeking new direction. Thinking about different ways to realize the return of Palestinians to their pre-1948 lands was a way to move to the third and last stage of their model, that of taking responsibility, despite—or perhaps because of—the disappointment incurred after completing the second stage, that of acknowledgement of Palestinian suffering and claims among the Jewish majority.

In 2014, Bronstein left Zochrot to establish a new independent project on the Nakba. Under its new management, Zochrot took new missions and frames of reference (as with any NGO, some were shaped by available grants) and also continued to institutionalize some of the earlier ideas and actions: a course that trains tour guides who specialize in destroyed Palestinian localities; a training on testimony collecting from refugees and Jewish combatants in 1948; and a Truth Commission dedicated to the events of the Nakba in one part of the land, the Negev-Naquab in the south of Israel.[2] The commission, whose members were Jewish and Palestinian citizens of civil society organizations in the region, held a public hearing in Beer-Sheva in December 2014, in which three Jewish combatants and three Palestinians of the 1948 generation testified in front of a full hall in a local hotel. A year later the commission presented its final report and recommendations at another public event in a Bedouin site that is today unrecognized by the state.

Autobiography of a City's archive is recently offline, and new testimonies have not been added since 2006 (interviewing continued sporadically), owing to a shortage of funding and staff that has plagued the group since its inception. The founders, however, still aspire to equip the archive in the future with materials that will create a thicker web of personal stories and other documents and lectures, in order to fulfill the purpose it was designed for: to mediate life in Jaffa before, during, and after 1948 as a pedagogical tool in schools and through site-specific artworks in city space (Danon interview 2011). Its most recent commissioned art project shifts the focus from the city's past to its future, again leaping over the present state of (mis)acknowledgment of Nakba memory in Israel. The project, titled *Jaffa 2030*, was launched in September 2012, as part of the citywide events of the *Province* artistic project. It consisted of a map, guided tours of the city, and a visitor center—all pertaining to the city in the year 2030. The map depicted Jaffa as a city embedded in a different context than the present one, projecting the city's pre-1948 context as rooted in the Arab world onto its imagined future in eighteen years. The map was the basis for a pop-up visitor center in the Saraya Arabic-Hebrew Theater in Jaffa,[3] from which one could register for actual tours of the city in 2030. A quote from the project's website presents the motivation behind it: "The Visitor Center, through a 24 hours open Gallery and a human happening, will try and flame the imagination of the city as part of a vivid Arab World surrounding, illustrating how reconciling the urban space is not only a way to deal with the past, but more, a major tool for planning the future. Come visit a city we don't live in still, but we should ask ourselves how we might."[4] This is a shift to a fictional future in which Jaffa is freed from the binding borders (within and without) of the Israeli nation-state and the centrality of the Israeli-Palestinian conflict and instead reunited with cities in the Middle East and Mediterranean. This lifting of post-1948 borders connects Jaffa's prestate past, which Autobiography of a City portrays as a major urban center in the region, with its imagined future. Jaffa of 2030 is imagined to be a cosmopolitan city connected to other urban centers: from Beirut, Cairo, and Damascus to Barcelona and Marseilles. It is also presented as a city that accommodates various populations excluded from the borders of nation-states. The project explicitly proposes to reimagine Jaffa's "borderless" past as a strategy to counter the present "limiting Israeli Hegemonic historical/political points of view," which also questions the present construction of knowledge according to this national viewpoint and constrained public debate.[5] According to the mission statement, the project also aims at exposing grassroots activities that it views as opportunities to free the urban space from its national borders and create a better future for its population in the future.[6] This last aspect joins the bypassing of state acknowledgment in the present to connect knowledge of the past with accountability and redress in the future, by leaving the state out of the process of regional reconciliation and the creation of a more peaceful future.

Unlike Zochrot and Autobiography of a City, Baladna continued to connect the past with present problems of Palestinians in Israel and community-based solutions, as its operation significantly expanded. Its initial four branches of the young leadership program grew to twelve branches across Israel in which 180 young people participated regularly in 2014–2015.[7] The branches meet at the end of each year in a "Public Achievement Festival" and share their experiences and community-based projects. In the school year 2014–2015, at least four of the twelve groups organized public community projects that dealt with Palestinian history and identity in relation to the Nakba. The youth association also continued its antirecruitment advocacy as well as its meetings with Palestinians in Israel, the OPT, and abroad under the title "Together for Change." The group produced an informal educational manual and held an opinion survey among about one thousand Palestinian students in Israel in 2013.[8] Additionally, it launched programs that deal with issues of gender and intercommunity violence, including a campaign against so-called honor killings and violence against women in Palestinian society in collaboration with Kayan, a Palestinian Feminist Organization in Israel. Mariam Farah and Khaled Enbtawe, chairpersons of the board of Baladna in 2011–2015, portrayed the association's role in its annual report both in terms of addressing the concrete Palestinian struggle within and outside Israel and in more general terms of human rights education and youth empowerment and advocacy.[9] The first aspect was presented through emphasizing consciousness-raising via informal education, media, and culture; training youth as activists for change in their communities; and listing campaigns that address concrete problems such as sectarianism and recruitment to the Israeli military among Palestinians in Israel. It seemed to address competing Palestinian associations as much as, or more than, Israel-wide or international organizations. Addressing their funders, the chairpersons also connected the association more generally to education on human rights, antiviolence, racism, and gender discrimination, mentioning awards and competitions won both domestically and internationally (the United Nations Solidarity Fund competition, for example.[10] Another link between domestic and external political struggles is the popular protest in the Arab Spring, which may have raised youth participation in Baladna's activities, as Enbtawe claimed in an article on Baladna's website. "Young people are influenced by the Arab Spring and what the young people do in Egypt and in Tunisia and all we call our Spring," he said. "They were influenced by that, and also they are more aware of their identity, Palestinian identity, and their political rights."[11]

The leap of Zochrot and Autobiography of a City from the first step of the model of disseminating knowledge about the contested past to the last step of responsibility, sidestepping the failed attempt to reach public acknowledgment, marks another stage in the diffusion and the appropriation of the globally circulating, expert-based model of truth and reconciliation among memory activists in Israel. The first step, in the early 2000s, was their development of a model for reconciliation and political change that, based on the South African model of truth and reconciliation (knowledge, acknowledgment, responsibility), saw the dissemination of the contested Palestinian past as a way to understand the present state of the conflict and to project a new resolution for the future. Yet the dissemination of the knowledge did not make their claims about present problems nor their projected future resolution acceptable and legitimate in the Israeli public debate or political discourse. Quite the opposite: the Jewish Israeli majority rejected the activist claims and vision even after knowing about the displacement and dispossession of Palestinians by Israeli forces in 1948. The dissemination of knowledge did not lead to the subsequent steps required for change according to this model. In the second step, at the end of that decade and the first half of the next, the South African–inspired model was appropriated again: from knowledge to responsibility, without public acknowledgment. The activist model's temporal line was now drawn between a new understanding of past wrongs and a projected future resolution without intervening in the public debate on the present state of the conflict. This appropriated model for change carries with it risks and political consequences.

The main risk stems from leaving the state out of the processes of change and relieving it from its duties. As was previously suggested, the Palestinian Nakba is potentially a compelling point of convergence between Jewish Israeli and Arab Palestinian peace activists because it can translate the abstract discourse of truth and reconciliation into specific political demands around which a new resolution for the conflict can be debated. It replaced the framework of a two-sided acknowledgment of past wrongs as a step toward reconciliation during the Oslo years that was incommensurable: Jewish Israeli peace activists talked about 1967, and Palestinian citizens had 1948 in mind. Yet the translation to concrete demands took different forms among the three groups of memory activists in the aftermath of the Nakba Law, and all three designed resolutions and remedies that left the state free of charge. Baladna continued to focus on the daily problems of Palestinian localities and communities in Israel and to develop intercommunity solutions, with links to regional movements in the Arab world and international organizations. It had more modest expectations that the State of Israel would accept larger-scope demands that pertain to the entire conflict, such as acknowledgment and accountability for displacement and dispossession. Zochrot and Autobiography of a City, on the other hand, translated Nakba memory into these larger demands but searched for local or regional solutions that do not involve the reluctant state, at least not directly, nor require the acknowledgment of the larger Israeli society. And so, not only the public acknowledgment was left out of the model but also the accountability of the state and larger society, which now seemed unlikely to stem from the failed attempt to achieve public acknowledgment.

However, the withdrawal from viewing the state as the object of claims and from aiming to participate in its exclusive politics of legitimacy is a more complicated strategy than that. In Chapter 3 I discussed it as a strategy Palestinian memory activists used to create a free space for debate and creative cultural work outside the boundaries of this order, as Goldfarb observed regarding a different region and regime (2011, 55, 62). Yet in leaving the state out of their claims in the aftermath of the Nakba Law, a further withdrawal from the state and dominant public debate was apparent among Jewish Israeli memory activists as well. This was perhaps because, like Palestinian activists, they too now viewed collective memory and historical consciousness as the only forms of resistance that the state cannot seize, although it tried. They sought to utilize memory and history outside of state structures and institutions as the "weapon of the weak" (Scott 1985) or at least *for* the weak. Their effort to intervene in public debate and political discourse in order to change political positions regarding the Palestinian Nakba until some concessions are achieved proved frustrating and sparked a retaliatory backlash of the state and society. However, while this cultivation of memory as weapon of the weak is liberating, it is also fragile and problematic, as it lacks institutions in which to be rooted.

The second and related risk of the activists' further withdrawal from the state and formal politics while working in the realm of culture and memory is manifested in depoliticization, or the difficulty of repoliticizing after the initial process of constructing new claims outside of the constraints of a limited public debate. Depoliticization, intentionally or unintentionally, has advantages and disadvantages. The logic of appropriating and mimicking hegemonic and state-oriented cultural practices that were used for national education has been explained and demonstrated in the previous chapters, as were its results in practice in the cases of the activist tour and testimony. Depoliticization began with the activists' choice to distance themselves from political practices and from partisan politics: Instead of choosing practices that are part of the cultural repertoire of political protest—a street demonstration or a march (Tilly 2005, 313) in which participants carry signs or national flags for example—or identifying as affiliated with a formal political party, Nakba memory activists borrowed from the cultural repertoire of commemorative forms in Israel. On the one hand, inviting audiences to participate in a tour instead of a demonstration or a flag-carrying march may widen the circles of self-selected audiences, especially in a limited public debate in which any identification with far-left positions is immediately marked as illegitimate and marginalizes its holder. In principle, it is likely that only in this depoliticized manner some of the participants were able to learn about Palestinian ties and ownership of the land and to ideally also see the land differently, inclusively and not exclusively. On the other hand, in the Israeli tour in Chapter 1, this depoliticization also dislocated the experience of participants from the political and moral claim that organizers expect them to take from this experience. Participants did report that they feel transformed by the activist tour, "seeing the whole country differently," even after one tour, yet this new perspective did not entail a political claim regarding the origin of the conflict, its present state, and projected resolution. Similar to withdrawing from state institutions, depoliticization was viewed as a means to escape the boundaries of the politicized mobilization into which the 1948 war is placed in the dominant political discourse, and to open a space for new political claims regarding this past, present, and future that would eventually intervene in the dominant public debate and impact state policy. Analytically, this required a double move that begins with depoliticizing, to enable the formation of new understanding and claims outside of the constraints of the dominant public debate and political discourse, and potentially attracts new audiences and publics. Yet this depoliticization is conducted in order to repoliticize in the end. The problem was that repoliticizing did not always take place among tour participants. Moreover, in the second half of the decade, as Nakba memory became publically known among the Jewish majority in Israel and its advocates were declared illegitimate, depoliticization also became more difficult to achieve. Any activity connected to Nakba memory was immediately defined according to the positions of the dominant public debate as anti-Israeli and worthy of sanctions.

Reforming the Israeli Political Culture

Another way to look at this is from the viewpoint of political culture that comes full circle to teach us about the relationship between culture and the political—the central theoretical issue of this book. The confrontation between the dominant and activist political claims in this Israeli-Palestinian context takes place in cultural arenas: memory, art, touring, education. However, it is infused with and concerns power—not only the power to influence the political agenda and policy through the dominant public debate, but also, fundamentally, the power to reinstate or reshape the dominant political culture of this debate. Indeed, the memory war over the Nakba in Israel reveals the dynamics of the domestic sphere of publics (Calhoun 1997) and can be seen as an effort to shape its political culture (Gutman and Goldfarb 2010). The activist attempt to act outside of the dominant, Zionist-oriented political discourse, and make claims that counter the post-Oslo reproduction of the dual-narrative construction, met formal and informal resistance, including of their own audiences or peer groups, as Chapters 1 through 3 demonstrate.

To reshape the dominant political culture of this debate, memory activists have acted both from within the dominant political culture by using available means and cultural forms that are consensual, fa-miliar, authoritative, and legitimate in Israel (tours and testimonies), and outside this political culture, by disregarding the dual-narrative construction of the conflict. The dual-narrative construction constantly reappeared with and around memory work, asserting for the majority of Jewish Israelis that these memory activists prefer "their" rights over "ours," and for Palestinian citizens that they conduct ideological or partisan political work. This construction had to be refused and disre-garded by the activists again and again.

To Goldfarb, such meetings are characteristic of how political cultures are formed and reformed as culture confronts the dominant power, both through the politics of legitimacy to work from within as well as to expand the boundaries of prevailing common sense, and through disconnection from the dominant culture of power and act-ing autonomously outside of it. "The capacity to work with a cultural inheritance and the capacity to create something new presented the possibility to empower alternatives, for the reinvention of political cul-ture," he wrote (Goldfarb 2011, 135). Innovation requires liberation from the dominant political culture and available means, through discon-necting the state's narrative (its truth, or ideology) from its power, thus making available different stories about the past (Goldfarb 2011).[12] Yet acting autonomously from the common sense in order to reframe it can also lead to isolation and further marginalization of those who produce counterclaims, as is the case in Israel, where validating the Palestinian experience of the 1948 war is seen as delegitimizing the state.

In such a limited public debate, when the discursive arena tends to reflect and fortify the dominant and narrow rival positions, the non-discursive becomes crucial to the dissemination of new claims. As we have seen, a great deal of participants' reactions to the activist tour and testimony were shaped by the nondiscursive aspects of these hege-monic cultural practices: the performative, embodied, visual, and mate-rial parts of the tour of ruins, as well as digital and in situ testimonies. These cultural practices, and particularly the nondiscursive experiences they offered to participants, mediated the activist message and shaped the effectiveness of its dissemination to different audiences and pub-lics who took part in the tours or used the activist archive. Because culture is a site of many voices and meanings (Hall 1982; Sewell 1999), the utilization of cultural practices in memory activities is polysemic and involves actors in ambiguity of interpretations rather than in pre-planned, cognitive processes of decision making or persuasion. On the one hand, this complicates the link between activist movement and public: mediated by cultural practices and their nondiscursive aspects in particular, the activist message is open to alternative understandings and decided in public, yielding desired and undesired results for activists. On the other hand, this mediation provides a space in which the dominant collective memory can be fused with imagination, allowing participants to construct their own new temporal links between different pasts, presents, and futures (Gutman 2009). They can imagine alternative trajectories from the past to present problems and offer alternative visions for the future. Such a space can enable the formation of new publics engaged in a variety of interpretations and claims that would expand public debate to include a variety of voices. In so doing this process can reform political culture, opening it to some of the voices that were excluded from public debate. This is how reimagining the past can change the future and carry concrete political claims and consequences for troubled regions such as Israel-Palestine. Focusing on how memory can not only reflect and fortify but also reform political cultures and reshape mechanisms of exclusion and inclusion in different spheres of publics around the world is therefore crucial, revealing as it does the current power relations and the democratic capacity of the moment as well as potentialities and possibilities for the future.

Notes

Introduction

1. Twenty percent of Israel's population is Arab Palestinian of the Muslim or Christian faith. Israel also governs Palestinian noncitizens in the Palestinian Territories it occupied in 1967.
2. At the height of its activity, the groups counted twenty-three hundred subscribers to its newsletter, thirty volunteers, fourteen staff members, five members of the board, and two members of its oversight committee, according to its 2009 annual report.
3. The Israeli landscape was constructed to mark solely Israeli ownership on the land. See, for example, Y. Grazovsky, "Tiyul be-harim" [A journey in the mountains], and Yosef Weitz, "Herzliya," in Gondelman and Gefen 1945. For an overview, see Kadman 2008 and Shai 2007.
4. Autobiography of a City is composed of fewer than ten board members, including its two cofounders, and a consultancy board of twelve.
5. Even more marginalized fighter groups in the prestate days are today included in the dominant national memory (Lebel 2013).
6. This model had different emphases as the groups developed. For example, in Zochrot's mission statement from 2006, only knowledge and acknowledgment of the Nakba by both Jewish Israelis and Palestinians is mentioned: "mak[ing] the history of the Nakba accessible to the Israeli public so as to engage Jews and Palestinians in an open recounting of our painful common history," *nakbainhebrew.org*, accessed 1 December 2007. In the following years, however, and even more so after the knowledge on the Nakba has been circulated, more emphasis was put on acknowledgment and taking responsibility. Responsibility was imagined as the Palestinian right of return, *zochrot.org/en/content/17*, accessed 15 May 2015.
7. Most of these cultural products stirred heated public debate and criticism. Hilu was eventually forced to return the award because of claims of conflict of interest within the award committee. The play in the Cameri Theatre was even more controversial because Kanafani was not only a renowned Palestinian author but also a spokesperson for the Public Front for the Liberation of Palestine, who was assassinated in a Mossad operation in 1973 in Beirut, after the murder of Israeli athletes at the Munich Olympic Games. Although the novella has been part of the high school curriculum in Israel, right-wing organizations have protested outside the theater hall where the play was rehearsed.

1
The Activist Tour as a Political Tool

1. The excerpt is taken from the second version, published in 1953, titled "The Trip and Its Educational Value."

2. The JNF reported that during the Passover holiday alone, the week of 17 April 2011, a million and a half people visited its national parks and sites around the country (*Ha'aretz*, 25 April 2011, *www.haaretz.co.il/news/education/1.1172212*, accessed 1 December 2012). The CEO of the Nature and Parks Authority (INPA), Eli Amity, reported more than a million additional visitors, a third of them to sites that charge entrance fees (Ibid.).

3. "Knowing the land" through tours by foot complemented geography lessons at school in "homeland" classes (Lentin 2010, 67). A tour "from sea to sea" (from the Mediterranean to the Dead Sea) was a Zionist youth movement rite of passage, usually taking place in harsh conditions in order to assist in the creation of a tough "New Hebrew" person as the antithesis of the frail diaspora Jew (Y. Zerubavel 1995, 120–21; Lentin 2010, 67).

4. In June 1989 the right-wing religious settler organization Gush Emunim organized a mass "hiking operation" through the West Bank under heavy military protection. Since the second Intifada and the construction of the Separation Wall between the West Bank and Israel, left-wing organizations have been organizing tours to the Wall in order to reveal its injustices. A recent case that sparked critical debates in the media about the political mobilizations of school tours was a statement by the minister of education, Gideon Sa'ar (from the center-right Likud party), during a visit to the West Bank in February 2011. Sa'ar offered to sponsor school tours to the Patriarch Tomb (*Mearat Ha'Machpela*) in East Hebron.

5. Tour guide and retired teacher Fawzi Naser explained that the tradition of Nakba Day visits was established because the Israeli Independence Day was the only day Arab Palestinian citizens who were under martial law until the 1960s were allowed to travel around Israel and thus went to visit their former homes and village lands, where they mourned their loss and displacement with others from their village (interview 2013).

6. On sensory remembrance of the Palestinian village as "beyond the purview of western historiography," see also Shammas 1995, 7, quoted in Slyomovics 1998, xx.

7. Jewish settlers in pre-1948 Palestine draw on the native culture in various ways (see for example Benvenisti 2000, 63; Even-Zohar 1981). For more on settler's dependency on the native culture in the construction of an "authentic" national identity that has ties to the land, see Nitzan-Shiftan 2006, 2007; Hirsch 2001.

8. Tours and touring have also been analyzed by Stein as recasting military operations, such as the occupation of territories in the West Bank and Gaza in the war of 1967. For more, see Stein 2008.

9. It is worth noting that the remains in the Gilaboon that Batia mentioned are Syrian, yet for her everything may look like a Palestinian remnant after the activist tour.

10. This was the case during most of the decade since its inception, yet as Zochrot gained visibility toward the decade's end, it attracted much criticism. It was described as a national threat by right-wing groups and demonized as extreme anti-Zionist among various political circles, including in the Israeli Zionist left. Those who oppose its activity today would see the group's tours as highly ideological. In the early years, however, neither organizers nor participants knew exactly what they are going to do with the knowledge they gained about pre-1948 Palestinian life and the war and did not have fully developed agendas (interviews with Musih 2008–2009; Bronstein 2008–2009, Reich 2009, and others).

11. Memorial books are a genre of commemoration that has been prevalent among displaced groups, including, among others, East European Jewish survivors of the Holocaust and Palestinian refugees (Slyomovics 1998; Davis 2011; Horowitz 2011). Usually authored and funded by members of the displaced group, rather than by professional historians or writers (Horowitz 2011), memorial books commemorate a town, a village, or a region and document its destruction (Slyomovics 1998).

2
The Activist Archive of Survivor Testimonies

1. This is especially evident in the street names chosen for Palestinian neighborhoods in Jaffa, which portray Zionist and Jewish history. In 2009, only nine out of four hundred streets in Jaffa were named after Palestinian public figures or historical events (*www.nrg.co.il/online/54/ART1/965/929. html*, accessed 1 December 2010; see also Cohen and Kliot 1981).

2. Israeli curator and art historian Tal Ben Zvi finds that acknowledging the Nakba and retelling the history of 1948 critically or from the Palestinian point of view grants cultural capital in the fields of art and academia, although it seems very radical and contested outside of these fields in the Israeli public sphere (interview 2009). Some funding comes from the municipality's budget for culture and the arts.

3. The knowledge and connections between stories and testifiers have also been taken outside, performed in the streets as part of Autobiography's commissioned site-specific art works accompanied by tours of the city. This was an attempt to generate face-to-face interaction and discussion on 1948 within and between groups of city residents, especially Jewish Israeli and Palestinian residents.

4. In Autobiography's blog, *thejaffaproject.org/alternative-information-tours*, accessed 14 November 2013, my emphasis. The emphasis on "alternative information tours" that is evident in the blog (formed only in 2011–2012)

has developed in a 2012 artistic project by the group, titled "Jaffa 2030," that included a map and a pop-up visitors' center in the old Saraya building in Jaffa, which today houses the local Arabic Hebrew theater. In this visitors' center one could register for walking tours of the city in 2030. The project was part of the citywide *Province* artistic project. In Autobiography's 2030 map, Jaffa is a cosmopolitan city embedded in the Arab Middle Eastern world—its context before 1948. See Conclusion for more detail.

3
Similar Practices, Higher Stakes

1. Palestinians with Israeli citizenship have lived through a long history of sanctions and threats since 1948. Living under martial law in 1948–1966 (less in Jaffa), they continued to be discriminated against in the following decades and increasingly and openly in the 2000s. The decade opened with the October Events—the shooting and killing of thirteen young Palestinians by police and border police forces during demonstrations—and closed with the "Nakba Law" and "Loyalty Oath" amendment to the Law of Citizenship for non-Jewish new citizens, a battle on school and university curricula, and an investigation into human rights associations' external funding.

2. *www.haaretz.co.il/hasite/spages/1190986.html*, accessed 27 September 2010.

3. In a critical essay Yoav Peled stated: "Clearly, the impression the Arab students are supposed to imbibe from this list of terms is that the Arabs have no common historical or cultural heritage, at least since the Middle Ages, and that most definitely no such heritage exists with regard to the Palestinian Arab people." Yoav Peled, "The 100 Terms Program: A Rawlsian Critique," *Adalah's Newsletter* (2006).

4. *electronicintifada.net/content/alternative-news-briefing/2285*, accessed 2 January 2006.

5. *www.haaretz.co.il/hasite/spages/1190986.html*, accessed 27 September 2010.

6. *www.haaretz.co.il/hasite/spages/1190986.html*, accessed 27 September 2010; *www.haaretz.com/print-edition/news/top-education-official-slams-civics-curriculum-as-slanted-against-israel-1.359715*, accessed 4 May 2011.

7. *www.haaretz.co.il/hasite/spages/1185349.html*, accessed 20 August 2010.

8. Most of them remained anonymous and only one of the teachers interviewed revealed his real name. *www.haaretz.co.il/hasite/spages/1230791.html*, accessed 10 June 2011.

9. "The peace process changed the priorities of the Arab minority in Israel. . . . While for a long time priority was given to a type of Palestinian nationalism, the struggle today is focused on the civic issue," Palestinian researcher Majid Al-Haj wrote in 1998 (quoted in Rekhess 2002, 5); see also Rekhess 2002, 4–5.

10. The authors belonged to the circles of the political parties Balad and

Hadash but did not affiliate themselves with any particular political party, as Rekhess notes, 2002, 4–5.

11. While Hadash received the majority of the Palestinian votes in the 2000s elections, especially leading in urban centers, ahead of Balad and the United Arab list (leading among the Bedouins of the Negev), the national election is only one contested arena for Palestinian politics. The Islamic movement and the Ibnaa El Balad (the Sons of the Village in Arabic) movement take part only in municipal elections, and many Palestinians in Israel choose not to vote in the elections to the Israeli parliament. For more on the subject, see Brik 2005; Ghanem 2005; and Rekhess 2002, 15.

12. One example is a collection of filmed Palestinian women's testimonies by Zochrot's Raneen Jeries.

13. This distance and self-reflection among Palestinian citizens tend to be played down, when it comes to the binational front within Israel, where the fight against denial of a Palestinian memory and identity altogether makes the necessity of placing a unified counternarrative to that of the state (Yasmin interview 2009; Amr interview 2009; Amal interview 2009; Ali interview 2009; Mahmoud interview 2009).

14. The successful "encoding of the European code" by Zochrot is supported by the following quote by its cofounder Bronstein in a 2008 interview: "Mostly the donors approached us . . . from Europe, a rare situation. It shows how much what we are doing is relevant and important. Once I was grateful [to donors]; today I understand how much they need us—organizations that need to take responsibility for plights that took place partly because of European actions, particularly in Palestine, and are looking for partners that would change the situation for the best, who are essential for their existence if this is their goal." However, the government has been trying to restrict this vital source for both Jewish Israeli and Arab Palestinian organizations in Israel through a parliamentary investigation of the external funding of human rights oriented NGOs in Israel and two proposed bills (not yet approved) to expose their funders and restrict external funding.

15. Some researchers have, however, defined Israel as an "ethnocracy"—a state that "imparts constitutional exclusivity to the ethnic majority" of Jewish Israelis and thus discriminates against Arab Palestinian citizens (Rekhess 2002, 11). For the definition and scholarly debate on the issue see, for example, Yiftachel, Ghanem, and Rouhana 2000.

16. *Kull al-'Arab*, 9 February 2001, cited in Rekhess 2002, 17.

17. Kabha has been touring; interviewing; collecting documents, maps, and photos; and documenting the stories of destroyed villages for twenty years as a historian of culture and local history and as a builder (he uses the term "memory designer," *Me'atzev Zikaron*) of a national narrative from the ground up, he said (interview 2009).

4
The Shift

1.   The op-ed, by Zochrot staff member Amaya Galili, brought forth the Jewish Israeli perspective of Nakba commemoration, arguing that the Nakba is not only a Palestinian history and memory, but also an important part of Jewish Israelis' collective memory and identity that has been denied. (*zochrot.org/en/content/nakba-not-dirty-word*, accessed 29 April 2009). In 2012, a similar claim was made in an editorial in *Ha'aretz* that expressed the newspaper's position. (*www.haaretz.co.il/opinions/editorial-articles/1.1708082*, accessed 15 May 2012).

2.   *www.ynetnews.com/articles/0,7340,L-3748335,00.html*, accessed 18 July 2009.

3.   *www.jpost.com/Diplomacy-and-Politics/Nakba-law-passes-vote-in-Knesset-committee*, accessed 15 March 2011.

4.   Amendment 40 to the Budget Foundations Law (2011) was approved on 22 March 2011. Article 4 of the revised version, which fines state-supported institutions that host morning activities during Independence Day, gave it its popular name "the Nakba Law." The law also fines state-supported institutions that conduct any of the other acts described in MK Miller's first version as negating state principle: negating its existence as Jewish and democratic; calling for racism, violence, or terror; supporting the armed struggle or terror acts of an enemy country or organization; and acts of vandalism that damage the honor of the flag or state symbols.

5.   *www.haaretz.com/print-edition/opinion/silence-over-nakba-law-encourages-racism-1.351694*, accessed 25 March 2011.

6.   *www.jpost.com/Diplomacy-and-Politics/Nakba-law-passes-vote-in-Knesset-committee*, accessed 15 March 2011, my emphasis.

7.   *www.jpost.com/Diplomacy-and-Politics/Nakba-law-passes-vote-in-Knesset-committee*, accessed 15 March 2011.

8.   *www.jpost.com/Diplomacy-and-Politics/Nakba-law-passes-vote-in-Knesset-committee*, accessed 15 March 2011.

9.   *www.haaretz.com/print-edition/opinion/the-palestinian-narrative-has-won-1.351497*, accessed 24 March 2011.

10. The ruling ignores the law's chilling effect on state-supported organizations or municipalities regarding any mention of the Nakba, as Adalla and ACRI's response to the decision indicated. *www.acri.org.il/en/2012/01/05/high-court-ignores-chilling-effect-caused-by-the-nakba-law*, accessed 6 January 2012.

11. The one-state solution is opposed to the two-state solution based on the 1967 borders that was discussed in the Oslo Accords and in all the peace talks that have taken place since.

12. *www.haaretz.co.il/hasite/spages/1087791.html*, accessed 24 May 2009.

13. Surveys suggest that despite slight improvement, their marginalization

continues. For example, despite a target of 10 percent Palestinian employment in the public sector, they were only 2.7 percent of teaching staff, and
1.7 percent of administrative staff at colleges and universities in Israel in
2011, according to the Council of Higher Education, a small increase from
2010 (2.69 percent). *www.haaretz.com/news/national/arabs-make-up-only-
2-7-of-academic-teaching-staff-in-israel-1.369723*, accessed 16 June 2011.

14. In addition to the curriculum investigations and changes to high school
and university curricula, two bills to limit external funding for human
rights organizations in Israel that contributed information to the UN's
Goldstone Report on the Gaza war were proposed by Likud and Yisrael
Beitenu MKs. A controversial law by the right-wing Minister of Law,
Ayelet Shaked, requires such organizations to publically declare funding
from foreign governments. *www.haaretz.co.il/hasite/spages/1232561.html*,
accessed 26 June 2011. *www.haaretz.com/israel-news/1.730324*, accessed 13
July 2016.

15. Hilu's 2008 best seller on Jewish and Arab Palestinian relations in pre-1948
Palestine, *House of Rajani*, won the prestigious Sapir Award for Israeli
literature in 2009, but the prize was immediately withdrawn because of
allegations of a conflict of interest between the chairman of the prize
committee, former left-wing leader Yossi Sarid, and the book's editor.

16. For example, Im Tirtzu and the Legal Forum for Israel have called for
fines of Tel Aviv University for Nakba commemoration events by students
on campus in May 2012. *www.imti.org.il/Docs/Pr75/?ThisPageID=1238*,
accessed 9 June 2012.

17. Criminal laws serve to protect the fundamental values of society, what
society deems most worthy of being collectively protected. The collective
past and how it is remembered is thus considered one of the protected
interests that should be safeguarded by legal means (Fronza 2006, 610).
However, collective memory is not consensual but subject to ongoing
contestation (Halbwachs [1925] 1992; Zolberg 1998) and in some cases
society is so polarized and torn by conflict that the post-conflict state
incorporates more than one perception of the past (Dryzek 2005). This was
the case in Northern Ireland (Rolston 2010), where two rival truths about
the past are housed together in the post-conflict state, and a similar model
was proposed for the Israeli-Palestinian conflict by Israeli and Palestinian
scholars (Adwan, Bar-On, and Naveh 2012).

18. These laws include, among others, Independence Day (1949, amended in
1998 and 2004); Memorial Day for the Fallen Soldiers of Israel's Wars
(1963, amendment 2, amended again in 2004); Memorial Day for the
Holocaust and Heroism (1959, amended 1978 and 1997); Memorial to the
Holocaust and Heroism—Yad Vashem (1953); the Rabin Memorial Day
(1997); Prohibition to Open Businesses of Entertainment on the Ninth of
Av (1997); and Jerusalem Memorial Day (1998).

19. Both groups suffered when the French left. The two hundred thousand
Harkis were executed as traitors with the French withdrawal (130,000 died

as a result) or taken to France and neglected for years in remote camps (Crapanzano 2011); more than a million pied noirs fled to France, but those who stayed were massacred or disappeared. Both groups claim victim status and recognition of their efforts from France (Eldridge 2010).

20. BBC News, "Colonial Abuses Haunt France," 16 May 2005.

21. BBC News, "Chirac Plans End to Colonial Law," 4 January 2006.

22. *www.theguardian.com/world/2005/apr/15/highereducation.artsandhumanities.*

23. *www.theguardian.com/world/2005/apr/15/highereducation.artsandhumanities.*

24. *www.humanityinaction.org/knowledgebase/117-memory-laws-in-france-and-their-implications-institutionalizing-social-harmony.*

25. While Turkey continues to deny the Armenian genocide and forbid its commemoration, France and other countries in Europe that were not historically involved in the genocide have outlawed such behavior in their own territories.

26. *rt.com/politics/russian-nazi-rehabilitation-dozhd-461,* accessed 30 January 2014.

27. *www.lph-asso.fr/index.php?option=com_content&view=category&layout=blog&id=31&Itemid=78&lang=en,* accessed 22 December 2013. In her letter to Medvedev on 17 June 2009, executive director of the American Historical Association, Arnita Jones, opposed not only the Russian law proposal, but any law that determines how the past should be referred to, because of the risk of limiting the freedom of academic research (*AHA Today,* 25 June 2009).

28. *blog.historians.org/2009/06/what-were-reading-june-25-2009-edition,* accessed 20 August 2012.

29. The second version, presented in the Duma on 9 May and drafted by a group of delegates headed by Boris Gryzlov, stated: "Distortion of the Verdict of the Nuremberg Tribunal, or of the verdicts of national courts or tribunals based on the Verdict of the Nuremberg Tribunal, with the aim of fully or partially rehabilitating Nazism and Nazi criminals; declarations that actions of countries participating in the anti-Hitler coalition were criminal, and also the public approval and denial of Nazi crimes against peace and the security of humanity shall be punishable by a fine of up to 300,000 rubles, or up to three years' imprisonment" (Law project number 197582-5, in Koposov 2010). If the perpetrator of these crimes is a state official or if he or she used the media to disseminate them, the fine would be raised to 500,000 rubles and the imprisonment to up to five years (Koposov 2010).

30. See, for example, *rt.com/politics/russian-nazi-rehabilitation-dozhd-461,* accessed 30 January 2014.

31. *www.dailymail.co.uk/news/article-2520839/Vladimir-Putin-closes-news-agency-RIA-Novosti-tightens-control-Russian-media.html,* accessed 10 December 2013.

32. *rt.com/politics/jail-terms-nazism-rehabilitation-144,* accessed 15 December 2014.

33. *themoscownews.com/russia/20130624/191639432-print/Duma-to-debate-ban-on-criticism-of-wartime-Red-Army.html*, accessed 30 January 2014.

34. *www.rosbalt.ru/main/2013/06/24/1144545.html*, accessed 12 August 2014.

35. *rt.com/politics/russian-nazi-rehabilitation-dozhd-461*, accessed 30 January 2014; *rt.com/politics/leningrad-russia-siege-dozhd-284*, accessed 30 January 2014.

36. *rt.com/politics/russia-nazi-ban-prison-293*, accessed 30 April 2014.

37. *rt.com/politics/russia-nazi-ban-prison-293*, accessed 30 April 2014.

5
From Reconciliation without Truth
to Truth without Reconciliation

1. *www.kibbutz.org.il/itonut/2001/20010823_kfarShem.htm*, accessed 2 August 2011.

2. *www.kibbutz.org.il/itonut/2001/20010823_kfarShem.htm*, accessed 2 August 2011.

3. *newkklenglish.wordpress.com*, accessed 19 November 2013. See also *zochrot. org/en/content/under-forests*, accessed 22 June 2014.

4. "Make the wilderness bloom" is a Zionist trope that frames the Jewish national movements as positively reviving the biblical land that has supposedly been vacant for centuries. This frame dismisses any populations that resided in this territory when Zionist settlers first arrived to initiate the "New Jewish Settlement": primarily Palestinians and the "Old Settlement" of Sephardic Jews.

5. *newkklenglish.wordpress.com*, accessed 19 November 2013.

6. Indeed, the JNF threatened Zochrot with a lawsuit if the project is not canceled. *www.zochrot.org/en/image/jnf-kkl-legal-prosecution-threat-against-zochrot*, accessed 14 March 2014.

7. *www.zochrot.org/en/image/jnf-kkl-legal-prosecution-threat-against-zochrot*, accessed 14 March 2014.

8. *www.zochrot.org/en/image/jnf-kkl-legal-prosecution-threat-against-zochrot*, accessed 14 March 2014.

9. As mentioned in the Introduction, these specific terms were not mentioned in Zochrot's early years, but their spirit and the model for a change through coming to terms with the past was all there. Later on the terms themselves were used in the group's mission statements.

10. As will be detailed later in the chapter, this model consists of three stages: knowledge, acknowledgment, and responsibility for past wrongs (Campbell 2000).

11. But see, for example, Hill 2008.

12. Many of the activists I interviewed view the focus on pragmatic solutions and the exclusion of a discussion of rights and justice from the Oslo Accords as partially accountable for the failure of the peace agreement (for example, Tamer interview 2009; Eli interview 2009).

13. I am grateful to Nadia Abu El-Haj for this insight.

14. Among them are Oxfam Solidarity, ICCO, CCFD, Worldwide Friends, and Youth Action for Peace.

15. One example is the establishment of local agencies such as the Gacaca courts in Rwanda to avoid an alienating, top-down truth and reconciliation process. Norma Musih from Zochrot noted that she wished she could find a similar structure in Israel that is rooted in Jewish tradition, like *Tikkun* (repairing and healing society and the world in Judaism), although she was not sure if this was indeed the right equivalence for a locally rooted structure for reconciliation (interview 2010).

16. Spring 2012. For elaborated history and definition of the term, see Chapter 2.

17. The Armenian case, Israel-Palestine, and US accountability for torture during the occupation of Iraq and Afghanistan are among these conflicts. On transitional justice see, for example, Teitel 2000; on restitution, see Barkan 2000; on TRC in Israel-Palestine, see S. Cohen 1995.

18. A striking example is an interview with Benny Morris, a Jewish Israeli "new historian" who introduced the critical retelling of the 1948 war, in which he, separating his political view from his scholarship, stated that the expulsion of Palestinians in 1948 should have been completed in order to prevent the escalation of the conflict to its current state, which he places in a historical chain of Jewish suffering; Shavit 2004.

19. According to Stoler (2009, 3), what is unspoken or does not fit into any existing category either (1) is well known and needs no explicit mention, (2) is just becoming known and is not yet articulated, or (3) is not allowed to be articulated owing to the fact that its explicit mention undermines current structures and efforts.

20. Crownshaw and Hirsch expressed a general concern about the transmission of memory and perspective—or what Hirsch called postmemory's "retrospective witnessing by adoption" (2001, 10). The concern is that "seeing through another's eyes . . . remembering through another's memories" would in fact "collapse into seeing through one's own eyes and remembering one's own memories instead" (Crownshaw 2004, 215).

21. This is especially because it is often forced on a complex reality, such as Lebanon's multiple civil war parties (see McManus 2012), child soldiers (see Clarke 2009), and collaboration under threat (see Glaeser 2003).

22. This proves problematic in other cases of truth and reconciliation efforts regarding conflicts that involved more than two sides, such as the civil war in Lebanon. See, for example, McManus 2012.

23. Also, the sort of knowledge produced by the three groups deconstructs familiar categories of their audiences more than it builds alternative categories to replace them with, which might lead the audience to paralysis or encounter resistance, which stops or delays the process of change. As Batia, Zochrot's staff member who worked on the group's educational kit,

stated: "It's not just knowledge but also a process of dealing with it. The basic assumption is that the knowledge raises questions about who we are, our identity, and challenges [our] fundamental assumptions. . . . I advise teachers to raise questions and give tools, but I don't have any answers; we should all ask these questions" (interview 2009).

Conclusion

1. The project followed several seminar meetings that brought architects and urban planners together with refugees and Jewish residents to plan local sites for the return of specific villagers to their lands as a case study.
2. I have been following the commission since its first call for volunteers. I participated in the tour-guide course in 2013 and in 2014 as a guest lecturer on the history of touring in the Zionist and Palestinian cultures.
3. The Jaffa Theater—the Arab-Hebrew Theatre Center—is the first binational theater in Israel. Since its inception in 1998, it has focused on Middle Eastern culture and the Israeli-Palestinian conflict. In 2000 it produced the play *The Truth and Reconciliation Commission*, directed by Yigal Azrati, which included real testimonies on Palestinian life under Israel's occupation of the West Bank and Gaza since 1967.
4. *thejaffaproject.com/visitor-center-event-program*, accessed 12 September 2012.
5. *thejaffaproject.com/jaffa-visitor-center*, accessed 12 September 2012.
6. *thejaffaproject.com/jaffa-visitor-center*, accessed 12 September 2012.
7. According to Baladna annual report, 2014–2015.
8. Baladna biannual report, 2011–2013, 7.
9. Baladna annual reports, 2013–2014, 2014–2015.
10. Baladna biannual report, 2011–2013, 9.
11. *www.momken.org/?mod=articles&ID=5693*, accessed 20 August 2013.
12. To what extent there can be autonomy from the prevailing political culture is an important question here, of course.

References

Abu-Lughod, Ibrahim. 1971. *The Transformation of Palestine: Essays on the Origin and Development of the Arab-Israeli Conflict*. Evanston, IL: Northwestern University Press.

Abu-Lughod, Lila. 2007. "Return to Half-Ruins: Memory, Postmemory, and Living History in Palestine." In *Nakba: Palestine, 1948, and the Claims of Memory*, edited by Ahmad H. Sa'di and Lila Abu-Lughod, 77–106. New York: Columbia University Press.

Abu-Sitta, Salman H. 2001. *From Refugees to Citizens at Home: The End of the Palestinian-Israeli Conflict*. London: Palestine Land Society and the Palestinian Return Centre.

———. 2004. *Atlas of Palestine 1948*. London: Palestine Land Society.

Ackerman, Alice. 1994. "Reconciliation as a Peace-Building Process in Postwar Europe: The Franco-German Case." *Peace and Change* 19 (3): 229–50.

Adwan, Sami, Dan Bar-On, and Eyal Naveh, eds. 2012. *Side by Side: Parallel Histories of Israel-Palestine*. New York: The New Press.

Al-Haj, Majid. 1997. "Identity and Orientation among the Arabs in Israel: A Situation of 'Double Peripherality.'" *State, Government and International Relations* 41-42 (Summer): 103–22. Hebrew.

———. 1998. "Education toward Multi-culturalism in Light of the Peace Process." In *Multi-culturalism in a Democratic and Jewish State*, edited by Menachem Mautner, Avi Sagi, and Ronen Shamir, 703–13. Tel Aviv: Tel Aviv University Press. Hebrew.

———. 2002. "Multiculturalism in Deeply Divided Societies: The Israeli Case." *International Journal of Intercultural Relations* 26:169–83.

Allan, Diana K. 2007. "The Politics of Witness: Remembering and Forgetting 1948 in Shatila Camp." In *Nakba: Palestine, 1948, and the Claims of Memory*, edited by Ahmad H. Sa'di and Lila Abu-Lughod, 253–84. New York: Columbia University Press.

Anderson, Benedict. 1991. *Imagined Communities: Reflections on the Origin and Spread of Nationalism*. 2nd ed. London: Verso.

Andrieu, Kora. 2011. "An Unfinished Business: Transitional Justice and Democratization in Post-Soviet Russia." *International Journal of Transitional Justice* 5 (2): 198–220.

Arendt, Hannah. 1958. *The Human Condition*. Chicago: University of Chicago Press.

Arora, Vibha. 2010. "Resistance and Activism in Place and Cyberspace." Paper presented at the RC7 Future Moves session, International Congress of Sociology, Gothenburg, Sweden.

Assmann, Jan. 1997. *Moses the Egyptian: The Memory of Egypt in Western Monotheism*. Cambridge, MA: Harvard University Press.

Auron, Yair. 2013. *The Holocaust, the Rebirth and the Nakba*. Tel Aviv: Resling. Hebrew.

Badinter, Robert. 2012. "Is This the End for the Historical Memory Laws?" Liberté pour l'histoire website, 4 December. *www.lph-asso.fr/index. php?option=com_content&view=article&id=182%3A-intervention-de-robert-badinter-a-lassemblee-generale-de-liberte-pour-lhistoire-2-juin-2012*, accessed 4 January 2013.

Barel, Zvi. 2011. "Who Is a Traitor." *Ha'aretz*, 3 April. Hebrew. *www.haaretz. co.il/opinions/1.1169765*, accessed 5 April 2011.

Barkan, Elazar. 2000. *The Guilt of Nations: Restitution and Negotiating Historical Injustices*. New York: Norton.

———. 2013. "Justifying Atrocities: Contested Victims." Keynote lecture, "Legal Frames of Memory: Transitional Justice in Central and Eastern Europe." Conference of the European Network Remembrance and Solidarity. University of Warsaw, Poland, 27 November.

Bar-Siman-Tov, Yaacov. 2004. "Introduction: Why Reconciliation?" In *From Conflict Resolution to Reconciliation*, edited by Yaacov Bar-Siman-Tov, 3–10. New York: Oxford University Press.

Bar-Tal, Daniel. 2000. "From Intractable Conflict Through Conflict Resolution to Reconciliation: Psychological Analysis." *Political Psychology* 21 (2): 351–65.

Bashir, Bashir. 2014. "Deliberating the Holocaust and the Nakba: Disruptive Empathy and Binationalism in Israel/Palestine." *Journal of Genocide Research* 16 (1): 77–99.

Bashir, Bashir, and Amos Goldberg. 2015. *The Holocaust and the Nakba: Memory, National Identity and Jewish-Arab Partnership*. Jerusalem: Van Leer Jerusalem Institute and Hakibbutz Hameuchad.

Ben-Amos, Avner, and Tammy Hoffman. 2011. "'We Came to Liberate Majdanek': The Israeli Defense Forces Delegations to Poland and the Military Usage of Holocaust Memory." *Israeli Sociology* 12 (2): 331–54.

Ben-David, Orit. 1997. "Tiyul (Hike) as an Act of Consecration of Space." In *Grasping Land: Space and Place in Contemporary Israeli Discourse and Experience*, edited by Eyal Ben-Ari and Yoram Bilu, 129–45. Albany: State University of New York Press.

Benford, Robert D., and David Snow. 2000. "Framing Processes and Social Movements: An Overview and Assessment." *Annual Review of Sociology* 26:611–39.

Benjamin, Walter. (1982) 2002. *The Arcades Project*. New York: Belknap Press of Harvard University Press.

Benn Michaels, Walter. 2006. *The Trouble with Diversity: How We Learned to Love Identity and Ignore Inequality*. New York: Metropolitan Books.

Benvenisti, Meron. 1998. *The Sling and the Club: Territories, Jews and Arabs.* Jerusalem: Keter. Hebrew.

————. 2000. *Sacred Landscape: The Buried History of the Holy Land since 1948.* Berkeley: University of California Press.

Ben-Yehuda, Nachman. 2002. *Sacrificing Truth: Archeology and the Myth of Masada.* Amherst, NY: Prometheus Books/Humanity Press.

Ben-Ze'ev, Efrat. 2004. "The Politics of Taste and Smell: Palestinian Rites of Return." In *The Politics of Food,* edited by Marianne Lien and Brigitte Nerlich, 141–59. Oxford: Berg.

Ben Zvi, Tal, and Hanna Farah-Kufer Bir'im. 2009. *Men in the Sun.* Herzliya: Herzliya Museum of Contemporary Art.

Berg, M., and B. Schaefer, eds. 2009. *Historical Justice in International Perspective: How Societies Are Trying to Right the Wrongs of the Past.* Cambridge: Cambridge University Press.

Berkhofer, Robert F. 2008. *Fashioning History: Current Practices and Principles.* New York: Palgrave Macmillan.

Bernhard, Michael, and Jan Kubik, eds. 2014. *Twenty Years after Communism: The Politics of Memory and Commemoration.* New York: Oxford University Press.

Bickford, Louis. 2004. "Transitional Justice." *Macmillan Encyclopedia of Genocide.* *www.ictj.org/static/TJApproaches/WhatisTJ/macmillan.TJ.eng.pdf,* accessed 5 April 2010.

Bickford, Louis, and Amy Sodaro. 2010. "Remembering Yesterday to Protect Tomorrow: The Internationalization of a New Commemorative Paradigm." In *Memory and the Future: Transnational Politics, Ethics, and Society,* edited by Yifat Gutman, Adam Brown, and Amy Sodaro, 66–86. Basingstoke, England: Palgrave Macmillan.

Biko, Nkosinathi. 2000. "Amnesty and Denial." In *Looking Back, Reaching Forward: Reflections on the Truth and Reconciliation Commission of South Africa,* edited by C. Villa-Vicencio and W. Verwoerd, 193–98. Cape Town: University of Cape Town Press.

Bishara, Azmi. 1995. "Between Nationality and Nation: Thoughts on Nationalism." *Theory and Criticism* 6:19–43.

————. 1996. "The Israeli Arab: Scrutinizing a Cloven Political Discourse." In *Zionism: Contemporary Debate,* edited by G. Penhas and B. Avi, 312–39. Sade Boker, Israel: Center for Ben-Gurion Legacy.

————. 1999. "The Process of Sovereignty Has Not Been Completed Yet." *Panim* 9:113–15. Hebrew.

Bourdieu, Pierre. 1991. *Language and Symbolic Power.* Cambridge, MA: Harvard University Press.

Boyer, Dominic, and Alexei Yurchak. 2010. "American Stiob; or, What Late-Socialist Aesthetics of Parody Reveal about Contemporary Political Culture in the West." *Cultural Anthropology* 25 (2): 179–221.

Bresheeth, Haim. 2007. "The Continuity of Trauma and Struggle: Recent Cinematic Representations of the Nakba." In *Nakba: Palestine, 1948, and the*

Claims of Memory, edited by Ahmad H. Sa'di and Lila Abu-Lughod, 161–87. New York: Columbia University Press.

Brik, Salim. 2005. "The Arab Political System: Unification, Separation, and Participation." Paper presented at the symposium "Arab Politics in Israel toward the Next Election" at the Moshe Dayan Center, Tel Aviv University, 15 December. Hebrew.

Calhoun, Craig, ed. 1993. *Habermas and the Public Sphere*. Cambridge, MA: MIT Press.

———. 1997. "Nationalism and the Public Sphere." In *Public and Private in Thought and Practice: Perspectives on a Grand Dichotomy*, edited by Jeff Weintraub and Krishan Kumar, 75–102. Chicago: University of Chicago Press.

Campbell, Patricia J. 2000. "The Truth and Reconciliation Commission (TRC): Human Rights and State Transitions—the South Africa Model." *African Studies Quarterly* 4 (3): 41–63.

Challand, Benoit. 2011. "Coming Too Late?" In *The European Union, Civil Society and Conflict*, edited by Nathalie Tocci, 96–125. New York: Routledge.

Clarke, Kamari Maxine. 2009. *Fictions of Justice*. Cambridge: Cambridge University Press.

Cohen, Chanan. 2014. "Israeli Public Opinion on Reducing Funding to Organizations that Mark Independence Day as the 'Nakba.'" Israel Democracy Institute website. *en.idi.org.il/analysis/articles/public-opinion-on-reducing-funding-to-organizations-that-mark-independence-day-as-the-nakba*, accessed 10 May 2014.

Cohen, Saul B., and N. Kliot. 1981. "Israel's Place Names as Reflection of Continuity and Change in Nation Building." *Names* 29 (3): 227–46.

———. 1992. "Place-Names in Israel's Ideological Struggle over the Administered Territories." *Annals of the Association of American Geographers* 82 (4): 653–80.

Cohen, Stanley. 1995. "Justice in Transition." *Middle East Report* 194/195 (May–August): 2–5.

Confino, Alon. 2005. "Remembering the Second World War 1945–1965: Narratives of Victimhood and Genocide." *Cultural Analysis* 4:47–65.

Copti, Scandar, and Rabia Buchari. 2003. *Truth*. Video, 15 min.

Coy, Patrick G., Lynne M. Woehrle, and Gregory M. Maney. 2008. "A Typology of Oppositional Knowledge: Democracy and the U.S. Peace Movement." *Sociological Research Online* 13 (4): 3. *www.socresonline.org.uk/13/4/3.html*, accessed 31 July 2008.

Craimer, Aliza. 2006. "Do the 'New Historians' Practice What They Preach? Objectivity and Neutrality in the Israeli Historiographical Debate about 1948." Paper presented at the Twenty-Second Annual Meeting of the Association for Israel Studies, Banff, Canada (May).

Crownshaw, Richard. 2004. "Reconsidering Postmemory in W. G. Sebald's *Austerlitz*." *Mosaic* 37 (4): 215–36.

Curran, Vivian Grosswald. 2015. "Evolving French Memory Laws in Light of Greece's 2014 Anti-Racism Law," *CritCom: A Forum for Research and Commentary on Europe*, 20 February. *councilforeuropeanstudies.org/critcom/ evolving-french-memory-laws-in-light-of-greeces-2014-anti-racism-law*.

Dana, Tariq. 2015. "The Structural Transformation of Palestinian Civil Society: Key Paradigm Shifts." *Middle East Critique* 24 (2): 191–210.

Davis, Rochelle. 2007. "Return to Half-Ruins: Memory, Postmemory, and Living History in Palestine." In *Nakba: Palestine, 1948, and the Claims of Memory*, edited by Ahmad H. Sa'di and Lila Abu-Lughod, 53–75. New York: Columbia University Press.

———. 2011. *Palestinian Villages Histories: Geographies of the Displaced*. Stanford, CA: Stanford University Press.

Dawes, James. 2007. *That the World May Know: Bearing Witness to Atrocity*. Cambridge, MA: President and Fellows of Harvard University.

Dayan, Daniel. 2005. "Mothers, Midwives and Abortionists: Genealogy and Obstetrics of Audiences and Publics." In *Audiences and Publics*, edited by Sonia Livingstone, 43–76. Bristol: Intellect Press.

de Groot, Jerome. 2011. "Affect and Empathy: Re-enactment and Performance as/in History." *Rethinking History: The Journal of Theory and Practice* 15 (4): 587–99.

Derrida, Jacques. 1998. *Archive Fever: A Freudian Impression*. Chicago: University of Chicago Press.

Dryzek, John. 2005. "Deliberative Democracy in Divided Societies: Alternatives to Agonism and Analgesia." *Political Theory* 33 (2): 218–42.

Durkheim, Emile. (1912) 1995. *The Elementary Forms of the Religious Life*. New York: Free Press.

Echevarría, Roberto González. 1990. *Myth and Archive: A Theory of Latin American Narrative*. Cambridge: Cambridge University Press.

Eisenstadt, S. E. 2000. "Multiple Modernities." *Daedalus* 129 (1): 1–29.

Eldridge, Claire. 2010. "Blurring the Boundaries between Perpetrators and Victims: Pied-noir Memories and the Harki Community." *Memory Studies* 3 (2): 123–36.

Epstein, Cynthia Fuchs. 1992. "Tinker-Bells and Pinups." In *Cultivating Differences: Symbolic Boundaries and the Making of Inequality*, edited by M. Lamont and M. Fournier, 232–56. Chicago: University of Chicago Press.

Esber, Rosemary M. 2008. *Under the Cover of War: The Zionist Expulsion of the Palestinians*. Alexandria, VA: Arabicus Books and Media.

Evans, Alfred B. 2006. "Civil Society in the Soviet Union?" In *Russian Civil Society: A Critical Assessment*, edited by A. B. Evans Jr., L. A. Henry, L. M. Sundstrom, 28–54. Armonk, NY: M. E. Sharpe.

Even-Zohar, Itamar. 1981. "The Emergence of a Native Hebrew Culture in Palestine 1882–1948." *Studies in Zionism* 4:167–84.

Feldman, Ilana. 2008. *Governing Gaza: Bureaucracy, Authority and the Work of Rule (1917–67)*. Durham, NC: Duke University Press.

Feldman, Jackie. 2008. *Above the Death Pits, Beneath the Flag: Youth Voyages to Poland and the Performance of Israeli National Identity*. New York: Berghahn Books.

Felman, Shoshana, and Dori Laub, M.D. 1992. *Testimony: Crises of Witnessing in Literature Psychoanalysis, and History*. New York: Routledge, Chapman, and Hall.

Fenster, Tovi. 2014. "Do Palestinians Live across the Road? Address and the Micropolitics of Home in Israeli Contested Urban Spaces." *Environment and Planning A* 46:2435–51.

Flapan, Simha. 1987. *The Birth of Israel: Myths and Realities*. New York: Pantheon Books.

Foucault, Michel. 1984. "Truth and Power." In *The Foucault Reader*, edited by Paul Rabinow, 51–75. New York: Pantheon Books.

Frankel, Oz. 2006. *States of Inquiry*. Baltimore: Johns Hopkins University Press.

Fraser, Nancy. 1993. "Rethinking the Public Sphere: A Contribution to Critique of Actually Existing Democracy." In *Habermas and the Public Sphere*, edited by Craig Calhoun, 108–42. Cambridge, MA: MIT Press.

———. 2005. "Transnationalizing the Public Sphere." In *Globalizing Critical Theory*, edited by Max Pensky, 37–48. Lanham, MD: Rowman and Littlefield.

Fridman, Orli. 2015. "Alternative Calendars and Memory Work in Serbia: Anti-war Activism after Milošević." *Memory Studies* 8 (2): 212–26.

Fronza, Emanuela. 2006. "The Punishment of Negationism: The Difficult Dialogue between Law and Memory," *Vermont Law Review* 30:609–26.

Funkenstein, Amos. 1993. *Perceptions of Jewish History*. Berkeley: University of California Press.

Garami, Bosmat. 2016. "The 1948 Palestine War: A Comparative Analysis of Its Representation in Two Israeli Television Series." *Israel Studies* 21 (1): 27–53.

Garton Ash, Timothy. 2008. "The Freedom of Historical Debate Is Under Attack by the Memory Police." *Guardian*, 16 October.

Gellner, Ernest. 1983. *Nations and Nationalism*. Ithaca, NY: Cornell University Press.

Gertz, Nurit, and Gal Hermoni. 2008. "Ethics and National Revival: The Memory of 1948 in Israeli Cinema." Paper presented at the Seventh Tel Aviv International Colloquium on Cinema Studies, Tel Aviv University (June 3–6).

Ghanāyim, Mahmud. 2008. *The Quest for a Lost Identity: Palestinian Fiction in Israel*. Wiesbaden: Harrassowitz.

Ghanem, As'ad. 1997. "The Palestinians in Israel Are Part of the Problem and Not of the Solution: The Question of Their Status in an Era of Peace." *State, Government and International Relations* 41–42 (Summer): 154–123. Hebrew.

———. 2005. "The Leadership Crisis and Possible Alternatives." Paper presented at the symposium "Arab Politics in Israel toward the Next Election" at the Moshe Dayan Center, Tel Aviv University. Hebrew.

Ghanem, As'ad, and Sarah Ozacky-Lazar. 2001. "Intifadat Al-Aksa among the Palestinian Citizens in Israel: Motives and Results." *Surveys on the Arabs in Israel* 27 (January): 18–19. Hebrew.

Glaeser, Andreas. 2003. "Power Knowledge Failure." *Social Analysis* 47 (1): 10–26

Gluck, Carol. Forthcoming. *Past Obsessions: War and Memory in the Twentieth-Century*. New York: Columbia University Press.

Glushko, Elena. 2013. *Hope for Justice: The Dream of Lustrations in Present-Day Russian Society*. Paper presentation at the Legal Frames of Memory Conference. University of Warsaw, Poland, 15 November.

Goldfarb, Jeffrey C. 2006. *The Politics of Small Things: The Power of the Powerless in Dark Times*. Chicago: University of Chicago Press.

———. 2009. "Resistance and Creativity in Social Interaction: For and Against Memory in Poland, Israel–Palestine, and the United States." *International Journal of Politics, Culture, and Society* 22 (2): 143–8.

———. 2011. *Reinventing Political Culture: The Power of Culture versus the Culture of Power*. New York: Polity.

Gondelman, A., and Y. Gefen, eds. 1945. *From Dan to Beer Sheva to the Fourth and Fifth Grades*. Tel Aviv: Am Oved.

Goodwin, Jeff, James M. Jasper, and Francesca Polletta, eds. 2001. *Passionate Politics: Emotions and Social Movements*. Chicago: University of Chicago Press.

Gortinskaya, Ulyana. 2013. "Bill Proposal That Bans Slandering Our Army during WWII: What Is It About?" *Odnako* online. *www.odnako.org/blogs/zakonoproekt-zapreshchayushchiy-klevetat-na-nashu-armiyu-vo-vtoroy-mirovoy-o-chyom-on*, accessed 20 August 2014.

Gutman, Yifat. 2009. "Where Do We Go from Here: The Pasts, Presents and Futures of Ground Zero." *Memory Studies* 2 (1): 55–70.

———. 2015. "Looking Backward to the Future: Counter-Memory as Oppositional Knowledge Production in the Israeli-Palestinian Conflict." *Current Sociology* published online before print, doi:10.1177/0011392115584644.

Gutman, Yifat, and Jeffrey C. Goldfarb. 2010. "The Cultural Constitution of Publics." In *The Handbook of Cultural Sociology*, edited by John Hall, Laura Grindstaff, and Ming-Cheng Lo, 494–503. London: Routledge.

Ha'aretz. 2012. "Haaretz Editorial: Nakba Is Part of Israel's History." *Ha'aretz*, May 15. *www.haaretz.com/opinion/nakba-is-part-of-israel-s-history-1.430501*, accessed 15 May 2012.

Habermas, Jurgen. 1989. *The Structural Transformation of the Public Sphere*. Translated by Thomas Burger. Cambridge, MA: MIT Press.

Haidar, Aziz. 1997. *The Palestinians in Israel in the Shadow of the Oslo Agreements*. Beirut: Institute for Palestine Studies. Arabic.

Halbwachs, Maurice. (1925) 1992. *On Collective Memory*. Chicago: University of Chicago Press.

Hall, Stuart. 1982. "The Rediscovery of 'Ideology': Return of the Repressed in Media Studies." In *Culture, Society and the Media*, edited by Michael Gurevitch, Tony Bennett, James Curran, and Janet Woollacott, 56–90. New York: Methuen.

Halpern, Orit. 2005. "Dreams for Our Perceptual Future: Temporality, Storage, and Interactivity in Cybernetics." *Configurations* 13 (2): 283–319.

Handelman, Don. 2004. *Nationalism and the Israeli State: Bureaucratic Logic in Public Events.* Oxford: Berg.

Hasan, Manar, and Ami Ayalon. 2011. "Arabs and Jews, Leisure and Gender, in Haifa's Public Spaces." In *Haifa before and after 1948: Narratives of a Mixed City Part 2*, edited by Mahmoud Yazbak and Yfaat Weiss, 69–99. Durdrecht, The Netherlands: Institute for Historical Justice and Reconciliation.

Hayner, Priscilla B. 2006. "Truth Commissions: A Schematic Overview." *International Review of the Red Cross* 88 (862): 295–310.

Henderson, Sarah L. 2011. *Civil Society in Russia: State Society Relations in the Post-Yeltsin Era.* University of Washington: National Council for Eurasian and East European Research.

Henley, Jon. 2005. "French Angry at Law to Teach Glory of Colonialism." *Guardian*, 15 April. *www.theguardian.com/world/2005/apr/15/highereducation. artsandhumanities*, accessed 1 December 2012.

Hermann, Tamar. 2009. *The Israeli Peace Movement: A Shattered Dream.* Cambridge: Cambridge University Press.

Herzog, Hanna. 2011. "NGOization of the Israeli Feminist Movement." In *The Contradictions of Israeli Citizenship: Land, Religion and State*, edited by Guy Ben-Porat and Bryan S. Turner, 158–79. London: Routledge.

Hill, Tom. 2005. "Historicity and the *Nakba* Commemorations of 1998." EUI Working Papers No. 2005/33. Florence, Italy: Robert Schuman Centre for Advanced Studies, EUI.

———. 2008. "1948 after Oslo: Truth and Reconciliation in Palestinian Discourse." *Mediterranean Politics* 13 (2): 151–70.

Hirsch, Marianne. 2001. "Surviving Images: Holocaust Photographs and the Work of Postmemory." *Yale Journal of Criticism* 12 (1): 5–37.

Horowitz, Rosemary, ed. 2011. *Memorial Books of Eastern European Jewry: Essays on the History and Meanings of Yizker Volumes.* Jefferson, NC: McFarland.

Horwitz, Tony. 1999. *Confederates in the Attic.* New York: Vintage.

Irwin-Zarecka, Iwona. 1994. *Frames of Remembrance: The Dynamic of Collective Memory.* New Brunswick, NJ: Transaction.

Jabareen, Hassan. 2014. "The Nakba, the Law and the Loyalty: The Hobbesian Moment of the Palestinians." *Theory and Criticism* 42:19–34.

Jamal, Amal. 2007. "Nationalizing States and the Constitution of 'Hollow Citizenship': Israel and Its Palestinian Citizens." *Ethnopolitics* 6 (4): 471–93.

Jamal, Amal, and Samah Bsoul. 2014. *The Palestinian Nakba in the Israeli Public Sphere: Formations of Denial and Responsibility.* Nazareth, Israel: I'LAM-Media Center for Arab Palestinians in Israel. Hebrew.

Jansen, Robert S. 2007. "Resurrection and Appropriation: Reputational Trajectories, Memory Work, and the Political Use of Historical Figures." *American Journal of Sociology* 112 (4): 953–1007.

Jelin, Elizabeth. 2007. "Public Memorialization in Perspective: Truth, Justice and Memory of Past Repression in the Southern Cone of South America." *International Journal of Transitional Justice* 1:138–56.

Kadman, Noga. 2008. *Erased from Space and Consciousness.* Jerusalem: November Books. Hebrew.

Kanaaneh, Rhoda Ann, and Isis Nusair. 2010. *Displaced at Home: Ethnicity and Gender among Palestinians in Israel.* Albany, NY: SUNY Press.

Katriel, Tamar. 1991. *Communal Webs: Communication and Culture in Contemporary Israel.* Albany: State University of New York Press.

———. 1996. "Touring the Land: Trips and Hiking as Secular Pilgrimages in Israeli Culture." *Jewish Folklore and Ethnology Review* 17 (1/2): 6–13.

———. 1997. *Performing the Past: A Study of Israeli Settlement Museums.* Mahwah, NJ: Lawrence Erlbaum.

———. 2009. "Inscribing Narratives of Occupation in Israeli Popular Memory." In *War Memory and Popular Culture*, edited by M. Keren and H. Herwig, 150–65. Jefferson, NC: McFarland.

Katriel, Tamar, and Yifat Gutman. 2015. "The Wall Must Fall: Memory Activism, Documentary Filmmaking, and the Second Intifada." In *Cultural Memories of Nonviolent Struggles*, edited by Anna Reading and Tamar Katriel, 205–25. Basingstoke, Hampshire: Palgrave Macmillan.

Katriel, Tamar, and Aliza Shenhar. 1990. "Tower and Stockade: Dialogic Narration in Israeli Settlement Ethos." *Quarterly Journal of Speech* 76:359–80.

Katz, Shaul. 1985. "The Israeli Teacher-Guide: The Emergence and Perpetuation of a Role." *Annals of Tourism Research* 12:49–72.

Khalidi, Walid. 1988. "Plan Dalet: Master Plan for the Conquest of Palestine." In "Palestine 1948," special issue of *Journal of Palestine Studies* 18 (1): 4–33.

———. 1992. *All That Remains: The Palestinian Villages Occupied and Depopulated by Israel in 1948.* Washington, DC: Institute for Palestine Studies.

King-Irani, Laurie. 2005. "To Reconcile, or to Be Reconciled? Agency, Accountability, and Law in Middle Eastern Conflicts." *Hastings International and Comparative Law Review* 28:369–86.

Kletter, Raz. 2006. *Just Past?* London: Equinox.

Koposov, Nikolay. 2005. "Historical Memory Laws in Russia and Eastern Europe." Speech delivered at the Liberté pour l'histoire general assembly in Paris, France, 21 May.

———. 2009. "The Debate in Russia over the 'History' Law." Liberté pour l'histoire website, 5 July. *www.lph-asso.fr/index.php?option=com_content&view=article&id=73%3Ale-debat-russe-sur-les-lois-memorielles*, accessed 30 November 2013.

———. 2010. "Does Russia Need a Memory Law?" *Democracy in Action*, 16 June.

———. 2011. "'The Armored Train of Memory': The Politics of History in Post-Soviet Russia." *Perspective on History: The Newsmagazine of the American Historical Association*, January.

Kremnitzer, Mordechai, and Roy Konfino. 2009. "Implications of the 'Nakba Law' on Israeli Democracy." Israel Democracy Institute website, 22 June.

en.idi.org.il/analysis/articles/implications-of-the-nakba-law-on-israeli-democracy, accessed 22 June 2009.

Kremnitzer, Mordechai, and Amir Fuchs. 2011. "The Nakba Bill: A Test of the Democratic Nature of the Jewish and Democratic State." *Ynet*, 13 March 2011. *en.idi.org.il/analysis/articles/the-nakba-bill-a-test-of-the-democratic-nature-of-the-jewish-and-democratic-state*, accessed 13 August 2014.

Kritz, N., ed. 1995. *Transitional Justice: How Emerging Democracies Reckon with Former Regimes.* Washington, DC: United States Institute of Peace Press.

Kwak, Jun-Hyeok, and Melissa Nobles, eds. 2013. *Inherited Responsibility and Historical Reconciliation in East Asia.* New York: Routledge.

Landsberg, Alison. 2004. *Prosthetic Memory: The Transformation of American Remembrance in the Age of Mass Culture.* New York: Columbia University Press.

Laplante, Lisa. J., and Kimberly Theidon. 2010. "Commissioning Truth, Constructing Silences: The Peruvian TRC and the Other Truths of 'Terrorists.'" In *Mirrors of Justice*, edited by Kamari Maxine Clarke and Goodale Mark, 291–315. Cambridge: Cambridge University Press.

Lentin, Ronit. 2010. *Co-memory and Melancholia: Israelis Memorialising the Palestinian Nakba.* Manchester, UK: Manchester University Press.

Levy, André. 2004. "Homecoming to the Diaspora: Nation and State in Visits of Israelis to Morocco. In *Homecomings: Unsettling Paths of Return*, edited by Fran Markowitz and Anders Stefansson, 92–108. Lanham, MD: Lexington.

Levy, Daniel. 2010. "Changing Temporalities and the Internationalization of Memory Cultures." In *Memory and the Future: Transnational Politics, Ethics and Society*, edited by Yifat Gutman, Adam Brown, and Amy Sodaro, 15–30. Basingstoke, England: Palgrave Macmillan.

Levy, Daniel, and Natan Sznaider. 2006. "Sovereignty Transformed: A Sociology of Human Rights." *British Journal of Sociology* 57 (4): 657–76.

Linell, Per, and Ragnar Rommetveit. 1998. "The Many Facets of Morality in Dialogue." *Research on Language and Social Interaction* 31 (3/4): 465–73.

Lobba, Paolo. 2014. "A European Halt to Laws against Genocide Denial? In Perinçek v. Switzerland, the European Court of Human Rights Finds That a Conviction for Denial of Armenian 'Genocide' Violates Freedom of Expression." *European Criminal Law Review* 4 (1): 59–77.

Lofland, John. 1993. "Theory-Bashing and Answer-Improving in the Study of Social Movements." *American Sociologist* 24:37–58.

Löytömäki, Stiina. 2013. "The Law and Collective Memory of Colonialism: France and the Case of 'Belated' Transitional Justice." *International Journal of Transitional Justice* 7 (2): 205–23.

Lubin, Orly. 2007. "How to Photograph What's Not There." *Ha'aretz*, 18 September. *www.haaretz.co.il/literature/study/1.1442642*, accessed 1 December 2007. Hebrew.

Lustick, Ian S. 2007. "Leaving the Middle East: Israel and '*HaBotz HaMizrach-Tichoni*' ('The Middle Eastern Mud')." Paper presented at the

Twenty-Third Annual Meeting of the Association for Israel Studies, Open University, Israel (June).

MacLagan, M. 2006. "Introduction: Making Human Rights Claims Public." In "Technologies of Witnessing: The Visual Culture of Human Rights," special issue of *American Anthropologist* 108 (1): 191–95.

Mamdani, Mahmood. 2001. "A Diminished Truth." In *After the TRC: Reflections on Truth and Reconciliation in South Africa*, edited by James Wilmot and Linda van de Vijver, 58–61. Athens: Ohio University Press.

Manna, Adel. 1995. "Identity in Crisis: The Arabs in Israel vis-à-vis the Israel-PLO Agreement." In *Arab Politics in Israel at a Crossroad*, edited by Elie Rekhess and Tamar Yegnes, 81–86. Tel Aviv: Open University Press. Hebrew.

Masalha, Nur. 1992. "The Palestinians inside the Green Line." *al-Sinara*, 3 January. Arabic.

Matynia, Elzbieta. 2009. *Performative Democracy*. Yale Cultural Sociology Series. Boulder, CO: Paradigm.

McAdams, James A., ed. 1997. *Transitional Justice and the Rule of Law in New Democracies*. Notre Dame, IN: University of Notre Dame Press.

McManus, Shea. 2012. "Constituting Transitions: Truth, Justice, and Reconciliation in Postwar Lebanon." PhD diss., City University of New York.

Melamed, Laliv. 2013. "Close to Home: Privatization and Personalization of Militarized Death in Israeli Home Videos." *New Cinemas: Journal of Contemporary Film* 11 (2-3): 127–42.

Michlic, Joanna B., and John-Paul Himka, eds. Forthcoming. *Bringing the Dark to Light: The Reception of the Holocaust in Postcommunist Europe*. Lincoln: University of Nebraska Press.

Morris, Benny. 1987. *The Birth of the Palestinian Refugee Problem, 1947–1949*. Cambridge: Cambridge University Press.

———. 1988. "The New Historiography: Israel Confronts its Past." *Tikkun* 3 (6): 19–23, 99–102.

———. 1990. "The Eel and History: A Reply to Shabtai Teveth." *Tikkun* 5 (1): 19–22, 79–86.

———. 2004. *The Birth of the Palestinian Refugee Problem Revisited*. Cambridge: Cambridge University Press.

———. 2007. "The New Historiography." In *Making Israel*, edited by Benny Morris, 11–28. Ann Arbor: University of Michigan Press.

Moses, Dirk. 2011. "Genocide and the Terror of History." *Parallax* 17 (4): 90–108.

Moyn, Samuel. 2011. "Bearing Witness: Theological Roots of a New Secular Morality." In *The Holocaust and Historical Methodology*, edited by Dan Stone, 159–86. New York: Berghahn Books.

Nadim, Nashef. 2003. "Both of Us Together or Each of Us Separately: On the Association for Arab Youth and Youngsters (Baladna)." *Society* 6. Hebrew. *www.yesod.net/hevra/6/6–4.htm*, accessed 4 June 2011.

Naor, M., ed. 1989. *The Youth Movements 1920–1960: Idan 13*. Jerusalem: Yad Ben Zvi. Hebrew.

Nehhas, Eman. 2015. "Telling the Memory." In *The Nakba in the National Memory of Israel*, edited by A. Jamal and E. Lavie. Tel Aviv: Tel Aviv University Press. Hebrew.

Nets-Zehngut, Rafi. 2011. "Origins of the Palestinian Refugee Problem: Changes in the Historical Hemory of Israelis/Jews 1949–2004." *Peace Review: A Journal of Social Justice* 24 (2): 187–94.

Nitzan-Shiftan, Alona. 2006. "To Nationalize and Conceal: Grasping Place in Jerusalem." *Alpaim* 30:134–70. Hebrew.

———. 2007. Seizing Locality in Jerusalem. In *Reapproaching Borders: New Perspectives on the Study of Israel-Palestine*, edited by Sandra Sufian and Mark LeVine, 223–42. Lanham, MD: Rowman and Littlefield.

Nora, Pierre. 1989. "Between Memory and History: Les Lieux de Mémoire." *Representations* 26 (Spring): 7–24.

———. 1996. "The Era of Commemoration." In *Realms of Memory: The Construction of the French Past*. Vol. 3, *Symbols*, edited by P. Nora and L. D. Kritzman, 609–37. New York: Columbia University Press.

———. 2008. "Historical Identity in Trouble." In *Liberté pour l'histoire*. Paris: CNRS Editions. *www.lph-asso.fr/index.php?option=com_content&view=articl e&id=152&Itemid=182&lang=en*.

Noy, Chaim, and Eric Cohen. 2005. *Israeli Backpackers and Their Society: A View from Afar*. Albany: State University of New York Press.

Ofer, Dalia. 2000. "The Strength of Remembrance: Commemorating the Holocaust during the First Decade of Israel." *Jewish Social Studies* 6 (2): 24–55.

Olick, Jeffrey K. 2007. *The Politics of Regret: On Collective Memory and Historical Responsibility*. London: Routledge.

Olick, Jeffrey K., and Brenda Coughlin. 2003. "The Politics of Regret: Analytical Frames." In *Politics and the Past: On Repairing Historical Injustices*, edited by John Torpey, 37–62. Lanham, MD: Rowman and Littlefield.

Olick, Jeffrey K., and Joice Robbins. 1998. "Social Memory Studies: From Collective Memory to the Historical Sociology of Mnemonic Practices." *Annual Review of Sociology* 24:105–40.

Osiel, Mark. 1997. *Mass Atrocity, Collective Identity, and the Law*. New Brunswick, NJ: Transaction.

Ozacky-Lazar, Sarah, and As'ad Ghanem. 1990. "Autonomy for the Arabs in Israel—a Preliminary Discussion." *Survey on the Arabs in Israel*, 257–58. Givat Haviva, Israel: Institute for Peace Research. Hebrew.

Ozacky-Lazar, Sarah, and Yousef Jabareen. 2016. *Conditional Citizenship: On Citizenship, Equality and Offensive Legislation*. Haifa, Israel: University of Haifa Press, Van Leer Jerusalem Institute, and Pardes Publishing. Hebrew.

Papailias, Penelope. 2005. *Genres of Recollection: Archival Poetics and Modern Greece*. New York: Palgrave Macmillan.

———. 2006. "Writing Home in the Archive: 'Refugee Memory' and the Ethnography of Documentation." In *Archives, Documentation, and Institutions of Social Memory: Essays from the Sawyer Seminar*, edited by Francis X. Blouin Jr. and William G. Rosenberg, 402–16. Ann Arbor: University of Michigan Press.

Pappé, Ilan. 1997a. "Post-Zionist Critique on Israel and the Palestinians: Part I: The Academic Debate." *Journal of Palestine Studies* 26 (2): 29–41.

———. 1997b. "Post-Zionist Critique on Israel and the Palestinians: Part III: Popular Culture." *Journal of Palestine Studies* 26 (4): 60–69.

———. 1998. "Fifty Years through the Eyes of 'New Historians' in Israel." *Middle East Report* 207 (Summer): 14–23.

Payes, Shany. 2003. "Palestinian NGOs in Israel: A Campaign for Civil Equality in a Non-Civic State." *Israel Studies* 8:60–90.

Payne, Leigh A. 2008. *Unsettling Accounts: Neither Truth nor Reconciliation in Confessions of State Violence.* Durham, NC: Duke University Press.

Peled, Yoav. 2006. "The 100 Terms Program: A Rawlsian Critique." *Adalah's Newsletter* 27. *www.adalah.org/newsletter/eng/jul-aug06/ar1.pdf*, accessed 10 June 2011.

Perks, Robert, and Alistair Thomson. 2006. *The Oral History Reader.* 2nd ed. London: Routledge.

Plate, Liedeke. 2006. "Walking in Virginia Woolf's Footsteps: Performing Cultural Memory." *European Journal of Cultural Studies* 9:101–20.

Podeh, Eli. 2000. "History and Memory in the Israeli Educational System: The Portrayal of the Arab-Israeli Conflict in History Textbooks (1948–2000)." *History and Memory* 12:65–100.

———. 2002. *The Arab-Israeli Conflict in Israeli History Textbooks, 1948–2000.* Westport, CT: Bergin and Garvey.

Poole, Ross. 2008. "Memory, History and the Claims of the Past." *Memory Studies* 1 (2): 149–66.

———. 2010. "Misremembering the Holocaust." In *Memory and the Future: Transnational Politics, Ethics and Society,* edited by Yifat Gutman, Adam Brown, and Amy Socdaro, 31–49. Basingstoke, England: Palgrave Macmillan.

Posel, Deborah. 2002. "The TRC Report: What Kind of History? What Kind of Truth?" In *Commissioning the Past: Understanding South Africa's Truth and Reconciliation Commission,* edited by Deborah Posel and Graeme Simpson, 147–72. Johannesburg: Witwatersrand University Press.

Rabinowitz, Dan. 1993. "Oriental Nostalgia: How the Palestinians Became 'Israel's Arabs.'" *Teorya Uvikoret* 4:141–52. Hebrew.

———. 2001a. "End of Conflict or Recycled Violence?" In *Real-Time: The Al-Aqsa Intifada and the Israeli Left,* edited by Adi Ofir, 33–45. Jerusalem: Keter. Hebrew.

———. 2001b. "The Palestinian Citizens of Israel, the Concept of Trapped Minority and the Discourse of Transnationalism in Anthropology." *Ethnic and Racial Studies* 24 (1): 64–85.

Rabinowitz, Dan, and Khawla Abu-Baker. 2002. *The Stand-Tall Generation.* Jerusalem: Keter. Hebrew.

Ram, Uri. 1998. "Postnational Pasts: The Case of Israel." *Social Science History* 22 (4): 513–45.

———. 2006. *The Time of the Post.* Tel Aviv: Resling. Hebrew.

———. 2007. "The Future of the Past in Israel: A Sociology of Knowledge

Approach." In *Making Israel*, edited by Benny Morris, 202–30. Ann Arbor: University of Michigan Press.

Rekhess, Elie, ed. 1998. *The Arabs in Israeli Politics: Dilemmas of Identity*. Tel Aviv: Dayan Center, Tel Aviv University. Hebrew.

———. 2002. "The Arabs of Israel after Oslo: Localization of the National Struggle." *Israel Studies* 7 (3): 1–44.

Rolston, Bill. 2010. "'Trying to Reach the Future through the Past': Murals and Memory in Northern Ireland." *Crime Media Culture* 6 (3): 285–307.

Rorty, Richard. 1993. "Human Rights, Rationality and Sentimentality." In *On Human Rights*, edited by S. Shute and S. Hurley, 111–34. New York: Basic Books.

Rothberg, Michael. 2009. *Multidirectional Memory: Remembering the Holocaust in the Age of Decolonization*. Stanford, CA: Stanford University Press.

Rothberg, Michael, and Jared Stark. 2003. "After the Witness—A Report from the Twentieth Anniversary Conference of the Fortunoff Video Archive for Holocaust Testimonies at Yale." *History and Memory* 15 (1): 85–96.

Rothberg, Michael, and Yasemin Yildiz. 2011. "Memory Citizenship: Migrant Archives of Holocaust Remembrance in Contemporary Germany." *Parallax* 17 (4): 32–48.

Rouhana, Nadim. 1990. "The Intifada and the Palestinians of Israel: Resurrecting the Green Line." *Journal of Palestine Studies* 19 (3): 58–75.

Sarkar, Bhaskar, and Janet Walker, eds. 2009. *Documentary Testimonies: Global Archives of Suffering*. New York: Routledge.

Sassen, Saskia. 2009. "The Diversity of Digital Cultures of Use." Paper presented at the 104th American Sociological Association Annual Meeting, San Francisco (August 8–11).

Sasson-Levy, Orna, Yagil Levy, and Edna Lonsky-Feder. 2011. "Women Breaking the Silence: Military Service, Gender, and Antiwar Protest." *Gender and Society* 25 (6): 740–63.

Sasson-Levy, Orna, and Tamar Rapoport. 2003. "Body, Gender, and Knowledge in Protest Movements: The Israeli Case." *Gender and Society* 17 (3): 379–403.

Savelsberg, Joachim J., and Ryan D. King. 2011. *American Memories: Atrocities and the Law*. New York: Russell Sage Foundation.

Schudson, Michael. 1992. *Watergate in American Memory: How We Remember, Forget, and Reconstruct the Past*. New York: Basic Books.

Schwartz, Barry. 1982. "The Social Context of Commemoration: A Study in Collective Memory." *Social Forces* 61 (2): 374–402.

Scott, James C. 1985. *Weapons of the Weak: Everyday Forms of Peasant Resistance*. New Haven, CT: Yale University Press.

Seed, Patricia. 1992. "Taking Possession and Reading Texts: Establishing the Authority of Overseas Empires." *William and Mary Quarterly*, 3rd ser., 49 (2): 183–209.

Sewell, William H., Jr. 1999. "The Concept(s) of Culture." In *Beyond the Cultural Turn: New Directions in the Study of Society and Culture*, edited by Victoria E. Bonnell and Lynn Hunt, 35–61. Berkeley: University of California Press.

Shai, Aron. 2007. "The Fate of Abandoned Arab Villages in Israel 1965–1969." *History and Memory* 18 (2): 86–106.

Shammas, Anton. 1995. "Autocartography." *Threepenny Review* 63:7–9.

Shavit, Ari. 2004. "Waiting for the Barbarians." *Ha'aretz Weekend Supplement*, 6 January, 14–17.

Shehadeh, Raja. 2008. *Palestinian Walks: Notes on a Vanishing Landscape.* London: Profile Books.

Sheizaf, Noam. 2010. "Endgame." *Ha'aretz*, 15 July. *www.haaretz.com/israel-news/endgame-1.302128*, accessed 15 July 2010.

Shenhav, Yehouda. 2010. *The Time of the Green Line: A Jewish Political Essay.* Tel Aviv: Hakibbutz Hameuchad. Hebrew.

Shenker, Noah. 2010. "Embodied Memory: The Institutional Mediation of Survivor Testimony in the United States Holocaust Memorial Museum." In *Documentary Testimonies: Global Archives of Suffering*, edited by Bhaskar Sarka and Janet Walker, 35–58. New York: Routledge.

Shlaim, A. 1988. *Collusion across the Jordan: King Abdullah, the Zionist Movement, and the Partition of Palestine.* New York: Columbia University Press.

———. 1995. "The Debate about 1948." *International Journal of Middle East Studies* 27:287–304.

Slyomovics, Susan. 1998. *The Object of Memory: Arab and Jew Narrate the Palestinian Village.* Philadelphia: University of Pennsylvania Press.

Snow, David A., Louis A. Zurcher, Jr., and Sheldon Ekland-Olson. 1980. "Social Networks and Social Movements: A Microstructural Approach to Differential Recruitment." *American Sociological Review* 45 (5): 787–801.

Sodaro, Amy. 2011. "Exhibiting Atrocity: Presentation of the Past in Memorial Museums." PhD diss., New School for Social Research.

Spring, Kimberly. 2012. "Challenging the (Moral) Order: Military Service Members as Public Witnesses to War." PhD diss., New School for Social Research.

Staggenborg, Suzanne. 1998. "Social Movement Communities and Cycles of Protest: The Emergence and Maintenance of a Local Women's Movement." *Social Problems* 45 (2): 180–205.

Stahl, Avraham. 1985. *Changes in the Jews' Attitudes toward Nature and Trips.* Tel Aviv: Society for the Protection of Nature. Hebrew.

Stein, Rebecca L. 2008. "Souvenirs of Conquest: Israeli Occupation as Tourist Events." *International Journal of Middle East Studies* 40:647–69.

Steinberg, Marc W. 1999. "The Talk and Back Talk of Collective Action: A Dialogic Analysis of Repertoires of Discourse among Nineteenth-Century English Cotton Spinners." *American Journal of Sociology* 105 (3): 736–80.

Stoler, Ann Laura. 2009. *Along the Archival Grain: Epistemic Anxieties and Colonial Common Sense.* Princeton, NJ: Princeton University Press.

Swedenburg, Ted. 1990. "The Palestinian Peasant as National Signifier." *Anthropological Quarterly* 63 (1): 18–30.

Tamari, Salim. 2003. "Bourgeois Nostalgia and the Abandoned City." *Comparative Studies of South Asia, Africa and the Middle East* 23 (1 and 2): 172–81.

———. 2005. "Kissing Cousins: A Note on a Romantic Encounter." *Palestine-Israel Journal* 12/13 (4/1): 16–18.

Tarrow. Sidney. 2001. "Transnational Political Contention and Institutions in International Politics." *American Review of Political Science* 4:1–20.

Teachout, Peter R. 2006. "Making 'Holocaust Denial' a Crime: Reflections on European Anti-negationalist Laws from the Perspective of U.S. Constitutional Experience." *Vermont Law Review* 30:655–92.

Teitel, Ruti. 2000. *Transitional Justice*. New York: Oxford University Press.

Theidon, Kimberley. 2006. "Justice in Transition: The Micropolitics of Reconciliation in Post-War Peru." *Journal of Conflict Resolution* 50 (3): 433–57.

Tilly, Charles. 2005. "Introduction to Part II: Invention, Diffusion, and Transformation of the Social Movement Repertoire." *European Review of History: Revue européenne d'histoire* 12 (2): 307–20.

Torpey, John. 2001. "'Making Whole What Has Been Smashed': Reflections on Reparations." *Journal of Modern History* 73 (2): 333–58.

———. 2003. "Introduction." In *Politics and the Past: On Repairing Historical Injustices*, edited by J. Torpey, 1–34. Lanham, MD: Rowman and Littlefield.

Turner, V. 1969. *The Ritual Process: Structure and Anti-structure*. Chicago: Aldine.

———. 1973. "The Center Out There: Pilgrim's Goal." *History of Religions* 12 (3): 191–230.

———. 1974. *Dramas, Fields, and Metaphors: Symbolic Action in Human Society*. Ithaca, NY: Cornell University Press.

Turner V., and E. Turner. 1978. *Image and Pilgrimage in Christian Culture*. New York: Oxford University Press.

van Gennep, A. (1909) 1960. *The Rites of Passage*. London: Routledge.

Verdeja, Ernesto. 2014. "What Is Political Reconciliation." *Mobilizing Ideas*, 3 February. *mobilizingideas.wordpress.com/2014/02/03/what-is-political-reconciliation*, accessed 26 March 2014.

Verdoolaege, Annelies. 2008. *Reconciliation Discourse: The Case of the Truth and Reconciliation Commission*. Amsterdam: John Benjamins.

Vilna'i, Zeev. 1953. *The Trip and Its Educational Value*. Jerusalem: Youth Department of the Zionist Agency. Hebrew.

Vinitzky-Seroussi, Vered. 2001. "Commemorating Narratives of Violence: The Yitzhak Rabin Memorial Day in Israeli Schools." *Qualitative Sociology* 24 (2): 245–68.

———. 2009. *Forget-Me-Not: Yitzhak Rabin's Assassination and the Dilemmas of Memory*. Albany: State University of New York Press.

Wagner-Pacifici, Robin. 2010. "Theorizing the Restlessness of Events." *American Journal of Sociology* 115 (5): 1351–86.

Wagner-Pacifici, Robin, and Barry Schwartz. 1991. "The Vietnam Veterans Memorial: Commemorating a Difficult Past." *American Journal of Sociology* 97 (2): 376–420.

Wapner, Paul. 1996. *Environmental Activism and World Civic Politics*. Albany: State University of New York Press.

Warner, Michael. 1993. "The Mass Public and Mass Subject." In *Habermas and the Public Sphere*, edited by Craig Calhoun, 377–401. Cambridge, MA: MIT Press.

———. 2005. *Publics and Counterpublics*. New York: Zone Books.

Wartanian, Raffi. 2008. "Memory Laws in France and Their Implications: Institutionalizing Social Harmony." *Humanity in Action*, June. *www. humanityinaction.org/knowledgebase/117-memory-laws-in-france-and-their-implications-institutionalizing-social-harmony*, accessed 25 May 2012.

Wieviorka, Annette. 2006. *The Era of the Witness*, translated by Jared Stark. Ithaca, NY: Cornell University Press.

Wilson, Richard A. 2001. *The Politics of Truth and Reconciliation in South Africa*. Cambridge: Cambridge University Press.

Winter, Jay. 1999. "Remembrance and Redemption: A Social Interpretation of War Memorials." *Harvard Design Magazine* 9:1–6.

———. 2001. "Film and the Matrix of Memory." *American Historical Review* 66 (3): 857–64.

———. 2011. "From War Talk to Rights Talk: Exile Politics, Human Rights, and the Two World Wars." In *European Identity and the Second World War*, edited by Menno Spiering and Michael Wintle, 55–74. New York: Palgrave Macmillan.

Wüstenberg, Jenny. 2009. "Vom alternativen Laden zum Dienstleistungsbetrieb: The *Berliner Geschichtswerkstatt*; A Case Study in Activist Memory Politics." *German Studies Review* 32 (3): 590–618.

———. 2011. "Transforming Berlin's Memory: Non-state Actors and GDR Memorial Politics Today." In *Remembering the German Democratic Republic: Divided Memory in a United Germany*, edited by David Clarke and Ute Wölfel. 65–76. Basingstoke: Palgrave Macmillan.

Yablonka, Hanna. 2003. "The Development of Holocaust Consciousness in Israel: The Nuremberg, Kapos, Kastner, and Eichmann Trials." *Israel Studies* 8 (3): 1–24.

Yiftachel, Oren, As'ad Ghanem, and Nadim Rouhana. 2000. "Is an 'Ethnic Democracy' Possible? Jews, Arabs and the Israeli System of Government." *Jama'a* 6:58–78. Hebrew.

Young, James E. 1993. *The Texture of Memory: Holocaust Memorials and Meaning*. New Haven, CT: Yale University Press.

Zelizer, Barbie. 1995. "Reading the Past against the Grain: The Shape of Memory Studies." *Critical Studies in Mass Communication* 12:204–39.

Zerubavel, Eviatar. 2003. *Time Maps: Collective Memory and the Social Shape of the Past*. Chicago: University of Chicago Press.

Zerubavel, Yael. 1995. *Recovered Roots: Collective Memory and the Making of Israeli National Tradition*. Chicago: University of Chicago Press.

Zolberg, Vera. 1998. "Contested Remembrance: The Hiroshima Exhibit Controversy." *Theory and Society* 27 (4): 565–90.

Index

www.ingramcontent.com/pod-product-compliance
Lightning Source LLC
Chambersburg PA
CBHW031134270326
41929CB00011B/1626